ance # ANNE LINE

ANNE LINE

Shakespeare's Tragic Muse

Martin Dodwell

Book Guild Publishing
Sussex, England

First published in Great Britain in 2013 by
The Book Guild Ltd
The Werks
45 Church Road
Brighton, BN3 2BE

Copyright © Martin Dodwell 2013

The right of Martin Dodwell to be identified as the author of
this work has been asserted by him in accordance with the
Copyright, Designs and Patents Act 1988.

All rights reserved. No part of this publication may be reproduced, transmitted, or stored in a retrieval system, in any form or by any means, without permission in writing from the publisher, nor be otherwise circulated in any form of binding or cover other than that in which it is published and without a similar condition being imposed on the subsequent purchaser.

Typesetting in Garamond by
YHT Ltd, London

Printed and bound in Great Britain by
CPI Group (UK) Ltd, Croydon, CR0 4YY

A catalogue record for this book is available from
The British Library.

ISBN 978 1 84624 931 0

Contents

Foreword by Clare Asquith		vii
Introduction Shakespeare's Muse		xi

Part One   Alice

1	Places	3
2	Single Nature's Double Name	10
3	Unwholesome Fens	16
4	The Case of John Payne	23
5	The Guldeford Connection	31

Part Two   Anne

6	The Bells of St Clements	41
7	To the Counter in Wood Street	54
8	The Babington Plot	61
9	Separation	67
10	The Bells of Shoreditch	82

Part Three   Martha

11	Relieved by the Jesuits	87
12	Mrs Martha	91
13	Fetter Lane	97
14	A Gentlewoman Hanged	107
15	Memoria	115

Epilogue The Symbol-Line Allegory	128
Acknowledgments	178
Bibliography	179
Index	189

Foreword

One reason why the historical background to early modern literature in England often feels inadequate is the rarity of scholars as single-minded and dedicated as Martin Dodwell. In his introduction Dodwell compares his work to that of an archaeologist. Many historians could say the same, but in the traditionally marginalised field of Catholic recusant studies, the parallel is particularly apt. Given the pariah status of dissidents like Anne Line, the level of primary material is inevitably thin, and usually overlaid by a strata of anti-Catholic propaganda. Next comes a scattering of unreliable hagiography, written by indignant exiles abroad or by chaplains retained in grand Catholic households in England. Finally there are drifts of largely neglected works by Jesuit historians and other occasional revisionists, recorded piecemeal down the centuries in obscure articles, journals and family papers. All this material has to be sifted and analysed by the historian, who may well find that beneath all the layers, his subject remains as shadowy as ever. Not surprisingly, the Forty Martyrs of England and Wales have few serious biographers.

Nonetheless, two aspects of this book establish a genuine advance in our understanding of Anne Line. The first is the wealth of historical detail Martin Dodwell has uncovered about her family and its connections, illuminating the little we know of Anne Line's life and establishing at least one surprisingly close link with the known career of William Shakespeare. In this he has been assisted by the new accessibility of family and local records, which are beginning to transform our view of the extent to which England remained conflicted about Catholicism up to the end of Elizabeth's reign and beyond. The second is a controversial thesis, persuasively argued, that Anne Line's memory was perpetuated not in the histories but, more safely and deniably, in the literature of the day. Chief exhibits in this argument are Shakespeare's elegiac poem, *The Phoenix and the Turtle*, and his late plays, *Cymbeline* and *The Tempest*.

For a twenty-first century reader, this hypothesis might at first sight seem at the very least improbable. Anne came from a respectable but undistinguished family, and those who do look for contemporary allusions in Shakespeare's plays on the whole look for figures of national importance, familiar to his high-level courtly audience. Dodwell however builds on the recent researches of Finnis and Martin among others to expand a new picture of a wide-reaching, underground political network answerable to the central figure of the Earl of Worcester, which was clearly considered by many in the court to be of paramount national importance, affecting as it did the succession, and the key question of the nature of religious toleration after Elizabeth's death. This book demonstrates that Anne Line was an integral part of this network.

But she was more than that. By the late 1590s, the choice was stark for those uncompromising English Catholics who could not accept the double-life of a 'church papist'. Either they could make the perilous trip into exile, where they might hope for the assistance of a Spanish pension, but where many starved or led lives of great hardship; or they could remain at home, supporting the secret mission of new priests from Douai and Rheims who advocated quiet resistance rather than compromise. By the turn of the century, under the immense pressures imposed by the government, rifts were appearing between those Catholics who had chosen exile and those who remained in England, and indeed between angrily warring factions on both sides of the Channel. It so happened that the divided lives of Anne and her husband Roger embodied precisely the predicament of the divided body of English Catholicism at this crucial moment, and provided an iconic example of how to react to it – not with recrimination, but with heroic fidelity. To those who know something of the recusant records of the time, Roger and Anne's story will be familiar. Both were disinherited by their families for professing the old faith. Shortly after their marriage, Roger was imprisoned for his religion and finally driven into exile, where not long after, he died, having kept in continual contact with Anne, to whom he sent half his Spanish pension. In his absence, Anne dedicated her life to supporting the underground mission with such courage that she was considered a living saint by leading figures including Henry Garnet and John Gerard, to whom we owe the most reliable records of her later life. She was finally arrested and executed as a traitor for harbouring priests. Dodwell brings to light another sad detail – Anne bore a son in the short time the couple had together, who was either sent or taken away to be brought up by Roger's alienated parents. One can see how the image of a marriage which survived on a transcendental level across the Channel divide might provide an inspiring symbol of heroism and unity to the riven and wilting English Catholic community at the turn of the century.

FOREWORD

It is something of a step to move from the overlooked contemporary significance of Roger and Anne Line, to detecting their presence in Shakespeare's work. But a moment's reflection might remind one of a consistent theme in his work which becomes more insistent over the years – the theme of the exiled and the lost, and more graphic still, the trials of those left behind. Add to this a deep understanding of the Catholic dilemma which many now detect in his work, and it may not be so remarkable to find him using figures like Edmund Campion and Anne Line as symbols of certain standpoints in a complex political conundrum with profound national implications. Dodwell traces a web of potential contemporary allusion, and highlights the sacramental dimension in which Shakespeare characteristically sets this divided unity by recalling the transcendental language of division and oneness of *The Phoenix and the Turtle*, and the sublime, specifically Catholic, farewell of the newly-weds parted by exile at the beginning of *Cymbeline*.

Not just a patient archaeologist, Dodwell is also a bold pioneer, advancing a theory which might just cast the sharpest of all lights on a character whose importance to her time would otherwise be lost.

Clare Asquith

Introduction: Shakespeare's Muse

'My life hath in this line some interest'
(Shakespeare, Sonnet 74)

This book is a biography, but of an unusual kind. It concerns an almost-forgotten woman, hidden, chameleon-like, in the work of our most remembered writer. In 2003, the *Times Literary Supplement* ran an article by John Finnis and Patrick Martin claiming that Shakespeare's cryptic poem 'The Phoenix and the Turtle' was a tribute to this shadowy figure from Essex, Anne Line – aka Anna Lina, Mistris Lyne, Mrs Martha, Alice Higham – who worked closely with the hated Jesuits and who was hanged for assisting a priest. This idea was not new. It had first been suggested in the 1930s, when G.K. Chesterton described the relevant analysis as 'the only serious and convincing note on ["The Phoenix and the Turtle"] I happen to have read'.[1] Since then, significant new material has come to light and Anne Line has been canonised by the Roman Catholic Church, but surprisingly little has been written about her life. Perhaps both Catholics and non-Catholics alike have been too ready to place her in the box marked 'Roman Catholic Saint', and to assume that her story reads, 'She prayed, she suffered, she died' and move swiftly on. However, new research is not only confirming the Anne Line connection to 'The Phoenix and the Turtle', but suggesting a wider and deeper understanding of her significance for William Shakespeare than has been guessed at before.

The implication is that England's favourite son, the cultural garland it has waved proudly before the world for four hundred years, was viscerally opposed to the religio-political establishment of his day. All those subversive hints of 'art tongue-tied by authority', 'standing alone, hugely politic', 'outrageous fortune', an obsession with power usurped or wielded with cynical corruption, and prayers at the grave of 'Truth and Beauty', begin to sound like the music of the man himself. Suddenly it becomes clearer why he

---

[1] Quoted in Collins, *Chesterton on Shakespeare*, 137.

comes across as the outsider on the inside. The *TLS* article seemed convincing enough, but so do many claims made by clever people. It was impossible to evaluate without a serious investigation into what we know about Anne Line from contemporary sources, and this book is the fruit of just such an investigation. It has clarified the difficult issues of her identity and precisely where she came from, and this has opened up an exciting new interpretation of Shakespeare's *Cymbeline*. The discovery that her mother's first cousin was the Puritan Giles Alleyne, whose long dispute with the Burbages led to the building of the Globe Theatre, show us how the circumstances of her marriage and conversion could have come to the attention of William Shakespeare fifteen years before her eventual arrest and execution. Other details, such as that her great-uncle had been Sir John Alleyne, the Lord Mayor of London, have fewer implications, but they still help us to place her in context.

Painstaking efforts have been put into the research for this biography, but inevitably lots of gaps remain as the documentary evidence we have to go on is very scant. Perhaps 'The File on Anne Line' might be a better description for the present work than 'biography' because it is more a collection of evidence and possible leads than a vivid portrait of a character. Anne Line herself remains elusive. Her story, in brief, is that she was born sometime between *c.*1555 and 1565 in the mists of Essex and was brought up as a Protestant in a family of minor landed gentry. In 1583 she married a young man called Roger Line of Ringwood of similar background and circumstance, but when it became apparent that both husband and wife had converted to Catholicism they were cast off and disinherited by their respective families. Subsequently, Roger Line was arrested for attending the banned Catholic Mass, and later went into exile, where he died. Anne Line then dedicated herself to working for the so-called English Mission and was closely associated with Henry Garnet, the Jesuit superior, and his fellow Jesuit, John Gerard, not the least of whose claims to fame is that he is one of the very few men ever to have escaped from the Tower of London.

The story of Anne and Roger must have had a particular poignancy for English Catholics as it demonstrated that Catholicism remained a vibrant force capable of attracting idealistic young converts, but at the same time their story exemplified the air of tragedy haunting the English Catholic community. In an insecure and grasping age, Anne and Roger Line had been a golden young couple with a future amply provided for, who suffered both public disgrace and the loss of all their worldly goods for the sake of their Catholic faith. The consequence of their moral courage was that they were parted from their families, their money, and then each other. It is a story of conflict, arrests, aliases and hiding places, of fines, imprisonment, exile and death, but also of faith and of a love that survives every calamity. Their co-religionists could identify all too well with the tribulations, but more than that, the treatment of this couple highlighted the most fundamental hurt of the community that they chose to join, because it seemed that England had turned on virtue itself as it pursued a ruthless persecution of the Catholic faith that had been its very soul for 800 years. From this perspective, Anne and Roger Line were like the pearls cast before swine that turned and trampled them underfoot. Every individual aspect of their tale can be found repeated many times in the lives of their contemporaries, and yet as a whole their story remains both ordinary and extraordinary. For Anne Line, the path up the aisle became the path to Tyburn and a grave in the road.

So what became of this narrative? The history books, it is said, are written by the winners, and from the winner's point of view, Anne Line was merely among the support cast of the losers. It is no surprise, then, that she receives the briefest of mentions in Stow's *Chronicle* for 1601 (written that year) and none at all in the official history of the reign of Queen Elizabeth written by another contemporary, William Camden, and first published in 1615. Material from Catholic sources did exist but initially it was hidden in private letters and manuscripts and only emerged to public view in a piecemeal way over the next four hundred years. Indeed, the most extensive contemporary account of Anne Line's execution remained unpublished until the 1970s, when the first transcription appeared in a little-known journal. Despite this scholarly neglect – and partly because of it – there is clearly a possibility that Anne Line's story had greater currency among her contemporaries than historians have hitherto realised. Of course, in the years immediately following Anne Line's death, her connection to the Jesuits made her a dangerous subject to write about, and these circumstances raise another possibility – namely, that her contemporaries did make reference to her, but in hidden ways, in a nursery rhyme, a song, a cryptic poem, or a play. Thus, you will find here both historical fact and an investigation of some intriguing possibilities. For example, did Anne Line's execution give rise to the children's game 'Oranges and Lemons'? There can be no certainty that it did, but I challenge anyone to identify a set of historical circumstances that fit more accurately. This investigation of what *might be* extends to the more conventional biographical material. Can I prove that Anne Line's father was involved in a famous series of Essex witch trials? No, I cannot, but I can point to the documentary evidence that a man with the same name as Anne Line's father accused a woman of witchcraft in a village called Hatfield Peverell, which is no more than six miles from where Anne Line's father lived, and is the village where her mother's family owned land. Evidence that is ambiguous is still evidence and we should assess it as best we may. If we wish to pick up historical allusions in Shakespeare's writing, we need to be as aware as we can be of the historical context, including what the historical context *might have been*. The important thing is to be clear about what we know with certainty, what is likely, given the documentary evidence, and what may be no more than an interesting possibility.[2] I hope I have succeeded in that much.

With regard to Shakespeare and specifically the disputed question of Shakespeare's religious sympathies, first, I start from the supposition that Shakespeare was at the very least a writer whose work provided ammunition to Catholic propagandists, and I do so for a very good reason: the earliest source we have on the subject, a remark by the Protestant John Speed in 1611, indicates quite clearly that this was the case. As far as I am concerned, it follows that this should be the working assumption until someone comes up with some convincing evidence that Speed was wrong. Second, I am not setting out to prove that Shakespeare was himself a Catholic – others have written extensively on that subject – but I do believe that evidence presented here strongly supports that view. I have combined historical writing with what may be termed 'literary archaeology'. I have been digging into texts and into contemporary events, and endeavouring to reveal artefacts and interpret the finds – sometimes speculating as an archaeologist would, but doing so strictly within the bounds set by the evidence. Such theorising is necessarily provisional and to some extent conjecture. The question is whether or not it is convincing, and that is something that the reader must decide for himself or herself.

To those who find it irritating when Roman Catholics are referred to simply as Catholics, I apologise in advance as this is the practice I have followed in this book for reasons of convenience rather than theology. The same applies to 'Anne Line' versus 'Saint Anne Line'. With regard to certain aspects of the symbolism, particularly relating to 'The Phoenix and the Turtle' poem, for reasons of space I have stated my hypothesis without going into the detailed argument for it, but this will be dealt with in a separate volume.

Turning back to the issue of how a little-known Catholic martyr relates to

---

[1] Key elements of my own historical research into Anne Line concerning her origins and the chronology of her life up to the time her husband went into exile have been written up in a journal article to which I refer readers who are interested in the more detailed argumentation. See Dodwell, 'Revisiting Anne Line: Who was she and where did she come from?', *Recusant History*, Vol 31, No 3, May 2013.

the master of English letters, could it be that Anne Line was to Shakespeare something like Beatrice was to Dante? I believe so, but this brings with it a problem for the biographer, because it is not easy to write about an elusive paragon of virtue in an age when we prefer our heroes both to be flawed and to reveal plenty of trivia about their lives. The Jesuit John Gerard tells us that Anne Line 'was full of kindness, very discreet and possessed her soul in great peace', but no one tells us what she looked like or what she had for breakfast. As I approached the end of my study I was very aware of this problem and the limits of my ability to bring my subject to life and to evoke what it was like to meet her. I had plenty of interesting facts, but they were like fine detail in the background of a portrait in which the face had almost faded out. Strictly speaking that remains the case, but there is a tantalising possibility that Shakespeare has sketched in some of those missing features. My initial study had been of 'The Phoenix and the Turtle', and I had devoted considerable effort to researching the development of the phoenix myth, but for some reason I had neglected to look closely at Shakespeare's use of it in the play *Cymbeline*. I had read somewhere that Coleridge believed there was a connection between these two works but had died before he explained what he thought it was. Probably it related to symbolism and numerology, but whatever mysterious idea distilled itself in the opium-fuelled limbeck of Coleridge's brain, it is clear that there are parallels between the two pieces of writing. It is, of course, the heroine Imogen who is the phoenix of *Cymbeline* and it is my strong suspicion that in this delightful character we have the face to add to our portrait. In other words, Imogen is based, at least in part, on Anne Line.

I say 'in part' because of a certain pattern in renaissance poetry. Both Dante's Beatrice and Petrarch's Laura were poetic symbols based on real women. They are both historical and allegorical as they inhabit the world of walking, talking, living metaphors. Simply put, these women become symbols used by the poets to stand for some broader reality or concept. The poets were fated to admire the real women from a distance as they were married to other men. In fact Dante claimed that he only met Beatrice twice, once when she was eight and he was nine, and then again precisely nine years later when she greeted him in the street. But there were other occasions when they were in close proximity in their home town of Florence, such as the one depicted famously in Henry Holiday's painting *Dante and Beatrice*, when Beatrice passed by without acknowledging Dante's presence as he stood gazing at her from a bridge over the Arno. In the poems, whatever else they are, Beatrice and Laura are symbols of virtue, and when they die, their deaths have spiritual import for the poets. It is Beatrice who appears in the *Divine Comedy* to guide the soul of Dante from the regions of purgatory to heaven. My contention is that Anne Line is to Shakespeare something like Beatrice is to Dante, but because of the highly conflicted religious situation in England, Shakespeare had to conceal the identity of his symbolic muse. This is of course a big claim to make, but the evidence I submit is compelling. It has affected the writing of this book in the following ways. First, at various points in the biography that are clearly identified, I have used the character of Imogen to add colour to my portrait of Anne Line. Or rather, I have invited the reader to note the parallels between the fictional Imogen and the factual Anne and draw their own conclusions. Second, in an extended epilogue to the biography I have argued the case for Anne Line indeed being the vital missing source that unlocks the deeper meaning of *Cymbeline*.

Anne Line Family Tree

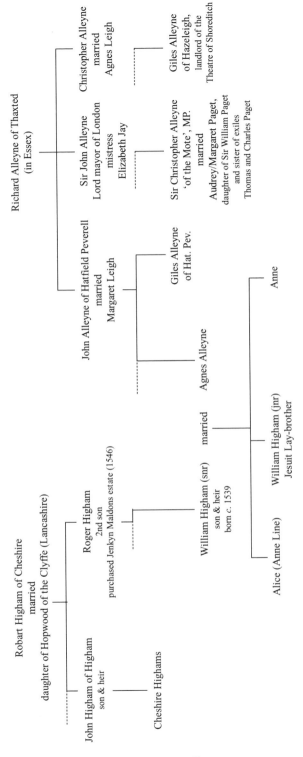

Alternate spellings of names include:
Higham, Heigham;
Line, Lyne;
Alleyne, Aleyne, Aleyn, Allen.

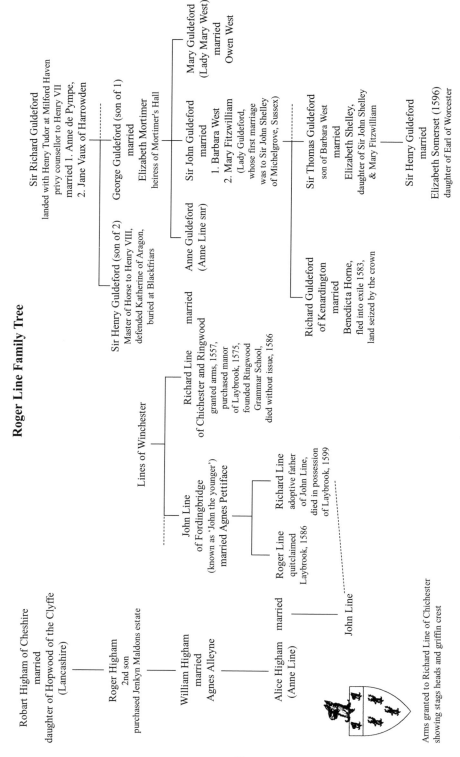

Part One
Alice

'Here the Antheme doth commence'

1

Places

For Anne Line, the beginning of the timeline is lost, as neither the date nor place of her birth are recorded. No priest or minister's hand marked her christening on the page of a ledger, at least none that has been found. The most likely explanation for this absence being that she was baptised in a rural parish which, unlike Shakespeare's bustling home-town of Stratford, has not left us a register of baptisms that goes back quite far enough to satisfy our thirst to identify a particular day in a particular year. As we shall see, there is a prime candidate for the parish in question, and one that unlocks a series of connections between Anne Line and her future husband, between the respective families of Anne Line's father and mother, and between Anne Line's family and Burbage's theatre in Shoreditch – one-time professional home of William Shakespeare.

Ironically perhaps, given the fog that has long settled over the question of Anne Line's origins, the name of that parish is Hazeleigh, the baptism register for which begins in the year 1590, and it has to be admitted that great uncertainties remain. Indeed, popular history has it that she came from the town of Dunmow, twenty miles to the north west, where she is celebrated in the dedication of the local Catholic parish to 'Our Lady and St Anne Line', and it has been customary to inform visitors that she lived in a Tudor dwelling known as 'The Clock House' that sits on the route heading north through the town. This house owes its impressive aspect to a grand brick frontage that was added sometime after the mid-1580s, and this would be after Anne Line had been kicked out of the family nest. It is quite possible that Anne Line's parents owned property in both Dunmow and Hazeleigh, but until we teach beams to speak we must be content with silence as to whether she was born in the older part of the Clock House. There is in fact no documentary evidence of a connection to this building and little enough to the town, though Anne Line's father William is described as 'of Dunmowe' in an entry in the herald's visitation records, and it could be that the local tradition about the Clock House preserves a 400-year-old memory.[1]

---

[1] *Visitations of Essex* (1612), 218.

Curiously enough, there is some indication, however tenuous, that Anne Line and Dunmow were linked in Shakespeare's mind. His poem 'The Phoenix and the Turtle', that is said to be a tribute to Anne Line, is also a tribute to fidelity and ideal married love, and Dunmow, more than any other town in England, is associated with just these same themes through local folk tradition. The seventh stanza of the poem reads as follows:

> So they lov'd, as love in twain
> Had the essence but in one;
> Two distincts, division none:
> Number there in love was slain.[2]

There is a paradox running through 'The Phoenix and the Turtle' that Shakespeare uses as a riddle of love. It is the paradox of two-things-becoming-one-thing-without-loss-of-identity, and the existence of this theme is one of the few points of general agreement about a poem which is a riddle from start to finish – so much so that the brightest of minds have been at a loss to fully decipher it. It is as though we had been left a crossword puzzle that no one had been able to do – for hundreds of years. But, as a tiny example of what happens when we introduce Anne Line into the puzzle, consider the following. A line consists of the joining of two distinct points, does it not? The two points remain two points but the line between them is a single thing. A[nne] Line both embodies in her name the central paradox of the poem and, together with her husband, resolves the riddle of the seventh stanza. If Shakespeare knew that Anne Line came from Dunmow, a town associated with the sacrament of marriage whereby two become one, we should not be surprised by a poem which brings these associations together. We expect the poet to make connections of this kind.

Dunmow itself, for what it is worth, has a twofold identity, consisting of the market town of Great Dunmow and the village of Little Dunmow two miles to the east in which there was an Augustinian priory. There was a period in the twelfth century when the Lord of the Manor was called Reginald Fitzwalter, and a year and a day after his wedding, so the story goes, Fitzwalter and his wife dressed as commoners and knocked on the door of the priory to ask for a blessing on their marriage. The prior, impressed by their devotion, gave them a flitch of bacon – that is to say, a whole side of a pig that has been cut in twain. The prior's generosity reaped a rich harvest because Reginald Fitzwalter would later bestow land on the priory with the

---

[2] 'The Phoenix and the Turtle', stanza 7.

condition that a flitch of bacon should be given every year to a couple who had remained faithful to each other without quarrelling for a twelvemonth and a day after their wedding. Soon the tradition became widely known, and couples travelled from all over the country to compete in 'The Trial of the Dunmow Flitch' – the most devoted couple being feted in procession to the market square, and getting to take home the bacon. By the fourteenth century the custom had so entered the cultural imagination that we find casual reference to it in *Piers Plowman* (1362) – 'He may fetch a flitch of bacon from Dunmow' – and in Chaucer's prologue to the *Wife's Tale* (1386).[3] It is also referred to in the seventeenth century, indicating that the tradition continued after the suppression of the priory of Little Dunmow by that marital enthusiast Henry VIII.

Where Anne Line herself was born we may never know for certain, but her grandparents on her mother's side came from the pretty village of Thaxted that lies on the river Chelmer about six miles north of Great Dunmow.[4] Her mother's maiden name was Agnes Alleyne and her father was called William Higham. Both parents were from families of landed gentry – a cut above the Shakespeare's of Stratford, but not enormously wealthy. Gentry status implied both the right to bear arms (as in weapons) and to the heraldic symbols that make up a coat of arms. Such rights were jealously guarded and spasmodically checked during visitations of the counties of England by the heralds, the original records of whom have proved of great value to historians but must be treated with caution as the information they contain is always limited and not always accurate. Thus, 'of Dunmowe', as applied to William Higham, probably indicates that he had a house in that town, but may mean that he owned land in the Hundred of Dunmow, a division of the county that extended for many miles and included Thaxted; it could even be a mistake by a hurried or lazy scribe confusing details of the Highams with those of the Alleynes due to their intermarriage, a factor that may explain the two families being ascribed the same crest: a raised arm holding a broken sword. But if visitation records must be treated with caution, legal documents and parish records are more reliable, and we have enough of them to say with some confidence that at least one of Anne Line's homes as a child was a property with the curious name of Jenkyn Maldons.

---

[3] Langland *P. Pl.* ix. 5515 (Wright) I. 169; Chaucer *W. of Bath's Prol.* I.217. See *Oxford Dictionary of English Proverbs*, 269.
[4] *Visitations of Essex* (1612), 133.

Jenkyn Maldons

The river Chelmer flows more or less south from Thaxted to Dunmow and on through pleasant farmland another ten miles or so to Chelmsford, the county town of Essex, from whence it meanders east nine miles to meet the Blackwater estuary at the port of Maldon. Good arable land lies north of the river, but on the Dengie peninsula to the south farmers have battled with poor drainage and the encroachment of the salt marshes. Their efforts did not go unrewarded, and the area supported significant numbers of livestock, as is clear from Camden's *Britannia* published in 1586:

> Betweene these Creekes lieth Dengey Hundred, in ancient times Dauncing plentifull in grasse and rich in cattaile, but sheepe especially, where all their doing is in making of cheese, and their shall yee have men take the womens office in hand and milke ewes, whence those huge thicke cheeses are made that are vented [distributed] and sould [sold] not only into all parts of England, but into forraine nations also, for the rusticall people, labourers, and handicraftes men to fill their bellies and feed upon.[5]

Maldon's historical claim to fame derives from a sharper conflict than the struggle with boggy ground, and is recorded in one of the rare surviving poems in Anglo-Saxon, *The Battle of Maldon*, which tells of the defiant Essex chieftain Bryhtnoth who challenged an invading force of Vikings in AD 991 and was slain in the resulting clash. The poet relates the brave words of the mortally injured Bryhtnoth to those who stood by him while others fled: 'The bolder be each heart, each spirit stronger, courage greater, as our company is less.'[6] One wonders if these words were taught to the young Anne Line, who was raised about two miles from the battle site.

By the mid-sixteenth century Maldon was hosting foreign visitors of a different kind as its access to the North Sea enabled a tidy trade to develop with continental neighbours that included the fiercely Calvinist Dutch, and this was no doubt a factor in the growing influence of Puritanism in the region. Maldon in particular became a noted venue for evangelical preachers, but the Protestant fervour that permeated much of Essex had a shadow side

---

[5] *Britannia* was first published in Latin. This quote is from Philemon Holland's translation published in 1607 (para. 10, 'Description of Essex').
[6] Lines 312, 313, my translation. Cf. 'Battle of Maldon' in Cook and Tinker, *Select Translations from Old English Poetry*.

tinged with paranoia over witchcraft and papistry, twin vices of the godless in the minds of the Calvinists. Not for them Shakespeare's nostalgia over the 'bare ruined choirs' of the old religious houses.[7] It was one of these medieval foundations, the Hospital of St Giles at Maldon, that had owned an estate comprising various holdings to the south and west known as Jenkyn Maldons, the income from which had supported a community of brothers tasked with caring for 'the lepers of the town'.[8] At the dissolution of the monasteries in 1538, Henry VIII seized the property and granted it to a layman, but with an annuity attached to it of one hundred marks to be paid yearly to his delightful new queen, Jane Seymour, 'in consideration of the true and undoubted marriage between us and her solemnised'.[9] On 15 November 1546 the property, comprising about 90 acres, was acquired by Anne Line's grandfather, Roger Higham, and when he bequeathed it to his nineteen-year-old son William in 1558 it was held 'by the 20th part of a knight's fee, and yearly rent of 54s, 3d', and there was no mention of Jane Seymour.[10]

Shoreditch

Anne Line's father, William Higham, was a Puritan of firm conviction. The manor house of Jenkyn Maldons was situated in the parish of Hazeleigh, and the woman he married, Agnes Alleyne, was the cousin (or sister) of a neighbouring landowner, Giles Alleyne, described in the register of St Nicholas church on his death in 1608 as 'Lord & patron of this parish'.[11] This man, related to Anne Line through the Alleynes of Thaxted, was also a Puritan. We know of his religious affiliation because about two years before the publication of 'The Phoenix and the Turtle', Giles Alleyne had a run-in with people intimately connected to William Shakespeare. Back in 1576, when James Burbage constructed the first purpose-built theatre in Britain (at least since the time of the Romans), he built it on land rented on a twenty-one-year lease from Giles Alleyne. The site in Shoreditch, a little way out of

---

[7] Sonnet 73.
[8] *VCH Essex*, vol 2, 189–190.
[9] SP, *Letters & Papers Hen VIII*, vol 13 Part I (1538), entry num 1529, p. 572.
[10] Morant, *The History and Antiquities of Essex*, vol 1, part 2, 330.
[11] ERO, D/P 123/1/1, image 31. William Higham and Giles Alleyne lived in the only two manor houses in the parish of Hazeleigh, which were about a mile or so apart. Agnes Alleyne was a first cousin of Giles Alleyne from the village of Hatfield Peverell, about six miles from Hazeleigh. They were both grandchildren of Richard Alleyne of Thaxted, and nephew and niece respectively of Sir John Alleyne, Lord Mayor of London (Morant, vol. I, 343f; Alleyne mural monument, Gresley Parish Church).

the city of London from the Bishopsgate entrance, had belonged to the nuns of Holywell Priory before the dissolution. By the time the lease was up for renewal in 1597, 'The Theatre', as it was called, had become a huge success, not least because it was the professional home of William Shakespeare, the greatest 'Shake-scene in a countrie'.[12] It could have been no surprise that Giles Alleyne wanted an increase in his rent, but as a Puritan he also felt the need to insist that within five years the property should be put to a more worthy use than for the performance of plays. This awkward man knew he was in a strong position, and negotiations dragged on for many months before drastic action was taken. One night when Alleyne was away in the country, Burbage and fifteen other men dismantled the wooden theatre, and in an heroic act of scene-shifting, transported the timbers through snow-covered streets to a warehouse by the river at Blackfriars. From there, a few months later, the wood would be conveyed across the water to Southwark, where it would be used in the construction of the renowned Globe Theatre.[13] Such travails were part of the ongoing conflict over the public theatres that bothered thespian Londoners like an in-growing toenail during the decade in which Shakespeare made his name. To be sure there were worse problems, but for those directly affected it was still a source of anxiety and annoyance. Puritans exploited both fears of the spread of plague and offence provoked by satirical and seditious scripts to demand the closure of the playhouses. The issue of the lease was therefore another problem to contend with in an already fraught atmosphere. The darker reality lurking in the background was that bickering over the playhouses was merely the surface excrescence of a division that cleft the country to the depths. Puritans reviled the old faith with its nuns and friars, priories and devotions; Shakespeare, most certainly, did not. It has long been recognised that the Shoreditch site owned by Alleyne is identified in *The Comedy of Errors*:

> By this, I think, the dial points at five:
> Anon, I'm sure, the duke himself in person
> Comes this way to the melancholy vale,
> The place of death and sorry execution,
> Behind the ditches of the abbey here (V.i.118–122).[14]

---

[12] Robert Greene, *Groats-worth of Wit* (1592), originally meant ironically. Quoted in Munro, *The Shakespeare Allusion Book*, 2.
[13] Wilson, *Shakespeare: the evidence*, 71f, 237, 250. Shapiro, *Shakespeare: 1599*, 4, 7.
[14] The identification of the abbey in *Comedy of Errors* with the Holywell site of the theatre was first made by T.W. Baldwin in *Shakespeare Adapts a Hanging* (1931). For the Catholic subtext of the play as a whole, see Asquith, *Shadowplay*, 55–61.

To the east the site was bounded with a ditch, and beyond that lay Finsbury Fields where, from time to time, a gallows was set up.[15] Some among the audience who saw *The Comedy of Errors* performed at Shoreditch would have witnessed the execution of a Catholic priest called William Hartley that took place '[b]ehind the ditches of the abbey here' in 1588. The Catholic reference, possibly signalled by the number five, is confirmed by the phrase 'melancholy vale', which evokes in Catholic ears the 'vale of tears' of the popular prayer 'Hail Holy Queen', sung daily as the *Salve Regina* of Evening Prayer.[16] To the south of the site, on the other side of Holywell Lane, was the 'Prioresses Pasture', and in this area a second theatre, the Curtain, was built. When we encounter in Shakespeare's play a priory with a wonderful prioress, the audience could be in little doubt that the play's setting in the pagan Classical world was a very thin cover for a story that was much closer to home. And, of course, there was little room for doubt either that the sympathies of the players were diametrically opposed to those of Puritans such as Giles Alleyne. *The Comedy of Errors* is a meditation on doubleness featuring two sets of twins, two realities in Ephesus and Syracuse, and the incomprehension that arises from two sets of people apparently seeing the same thing but telling radically different stories about it. We encounter themes of painful relevance to Catholics such as banishment, the threat of execution and false accusation, as well as the hope for reunion with the severed past, represented by the Abbess. If Anne Line saw this play, one hopes it brought a smile to her face and made her see beyond the melancholy vale.

---

[15] For information on the Shoreditch site, see Chambers, *Elizabethan Stage*, Vol. II, 383–400.
[16] Asquith (*Shadowplay*, 292) suggests five as a Catholic marker derived from the banner of the five wounds adopted by the Pilgrimage of Grace.

2

Single Nature's Double Name

Anne Line had a brother who was named William, like her father. She also had a younger sister about whom we know virtually nothing except her name, but this is enough to infer that she may have died young, for her name was Anne too. This curious fact is one of a series of minor riddles that confront the investigator. The visitation records list three siblings; William, Alice and Anne, and suffice it to say at this point that there are various other documents indicating that the woman known to history as Anne Line was known to her family as Alice. In fact she continued to be known by this name, and not only was she married under it, but when her mother-in-law wrote in her will more than a decade later that she wished to bequeath her a red petticoat and 'a kirtle of silk', she referred to her as Alice. The explanation for this one woman having two names appears to lie in the defining decision of Alice/Anne Line's life – namely, her conversion as a young woman to the Catholic faith. The younger sister, Anne, died in childhood, and the elder sister, Alice, adopted the name on her conversion.[1] Subsequently, Catholics knew her as Anne, while officially, and as far as her Protestant relatives were concerned, she was Alice.

Garnet

Henry Garnet was a modest man who wore his apparent ordinariness like a cloak of invisibility. Born in 1555, he had served as an apprentice at Tottel's the printers in Fleet Street, where he set the type and made corrections. It was Mr Tottel's custom to invite miscellaneous clients visiting the premises

---

[1] Thus, Kelly, 'Line, Anne [St Anne Line] (d. 1601)', ODNB. It is by no means certain that Anne Line's sister called Anne died young, as there are contemporary examples of siblings having the same name, including Anne Line's maternal grandfather and great uncle, both called John. Nothing is known of the younger Anne Higham beyond the listing of her name as a daughter of William Higham in the visitation records.

to share his table, and here Garnet met a lawyer called John Popham, whom Aubrey would later describe as 'a huge, heavy ugly man' who 'lived like a hog'.[2] As Garnet recalled, 'I dined often with him and told him I was beginning the law.'[3] More than thirty years later, as Lord Chief Justice, it would be Popham who would condemn Anne Line to death, prompting Henry Garnet, a few days after the hanging, to write a letter that is both a priceless source of information about her life and a shining encomium. Five years after Anne Line died, Garnet himself faced Popham across the courtroom table and received equally merciless judgment.

Perpetua and Felicity

Anne Line grew up in a place where the barely faded past was inscribed in the landscape, and stories of epic battles were about places she could walk to on a summer afternoon. Long before the Danes came, the Romans had been in the area, and Maldon had been the chief city of a great tribe of ancient Britons known as the Trinovantes who combined with Boudica's Iceni to fight the Roman occupiers. According to Camden, the ninth legion had been destroyed there in a rare British victory, and visible remains of a Roman camp lay to the west of the town. No doubt William Higham was proud to relate that the Romans had been vanquished at Maldon, perhaps even on his own land. If his daughter ever asked him about the old hospital for the lepers, sad that it was gone, he could have pointed to the bare old walls of a ruined choir that had once been the chapel of the religious foundation and was now being used as a barn. He could explain to his daughter that times change and the old must give way to the new. According to the *Topographical Dictionary of Essex* of 1831, the surviving remnants of the leper hospital, still being used at that time as a farm building, 'exhibit in their structure a mixture of stone and of bricks and tiles, which appear to have been of Roman origin' – thus one ruin had become another in the rise and fall of the ages.

At some point, perhaps around the time of Anne Line's death, an extremely rare Roman coin was found at Jenkyn Maldons, another tangible

---

[2] Aubrey, *Lives*, 245.
[3] Caraman, *Garnet*, 8.

link to a far-off time.⁴ An eighteenth-century antiquarian writes of it excitedly, 'This I have seen; it is Gold, about the Breadth of a milled Six-pence, on one Edge thicker than a Shilling, on the other thinner; with the Heads of *Nero* and *Agrippina* on one Side.'⁵ In 2011 I was given the opportunity to inspect this coin at close quarters in an office at Maldon Town Council. There are some signs of wear from distant usage, but the gold still glowed in my hand as it must have done anciently on many a palm. It is kept with a battered base-metal coin of Vespasian in a special tiny box. Every year the coins are brought out of the Town Council safe and presented ceremonially to the Mayor along with the more usual regalia, but no one in the town seems to know why. It is simply a tradition. Camden's argument that Maldon was once the Roman town of Camulodunum and before that the seat of King Cymbeline has long since been dismissed and forgotten. The discovery of such coins is no longer taken to imply that this unassuming provincial town was once the capital of the ancient Britons and thus had an antique seniority to London.

Agrippina was Nero's mother and a notoriously ruthless figure according to the classical sources which relate that she poisoned her husband, the Emperor Claudius, with a dish of mushrooms. She resorted to this extremity in order to secure the throne for Nero, who was her son from a previous marriage. Despite this touching example of maternal predilection, the relationship between Nero and Agrippina became somewhat strained and Nero made a series of increasingly bizarre attempts to have her murdered discreetly. These included having a lead ceiling designed to crash down on her bed – she was saved by the arm of a sofa – and planning a trip for her in a self-sinking boat – she swam to shore. In the end he took to the more direct expedient of hiring assassins with knives, resulting in his mother's defiant command, as the classical historians tell it, that she be stabbed first in the womb that bore her such a son.

For Christians, of course, Nero would always be remembered for the martyrs he made. Many centuries later, when a divided Europe was making new martyrs in the aftermath of the Reformation, both sides saw themselves

---

⁴ The find is first mentioned in print in Gibson's additions to his edition of Camden's *Britannia*, published in 1695; however, it may have turned up much earlier. Gibson writes: 'In a garden at *Maldon*, was found a piece of gold, almost as large as a Guinea. It has on one side *Nero*, and on the reverse *Agrippina*, and is very exactly done' (258). Gibson has obviously received his information at second hand because had he seen the coin he would have realised that Nero and Agrippina are featured on the same side, with the quadriga of elephants on the reverse. According to the latest edition of Spink's *Roman Imperial Coinage* (1984), there are no more than ten specimens of this coin listed in the major collections around the world. The British Museum has two of them.
⁵ Salmon, *A New Survey*, 134. The coin is 19 millimetres in diameter.

as being in direct continuity with the heroes of the Roman persecutions. This was the tenor of Fox's great tome *Acts and Monuments* that detailed the burnings of Protestants under Mary Tudor, and it soon found its equivalent in books and pamphlets distributed throughout Europe that detailed the barbarous cruelty being inflicted on Catholics in the England of her sister Elizabeth. Anne Line was brought up hearing the echoes of all this, and decades later, Rome itself would hear another echo in the weeks that followed Anne Line's death:

> There still remains for me to relate more beautiful subject matter: of a wife who has already taken the path to become an enviable saint, as those saints the devout Roman Matrons, and all five devout of the female sex. She was in London (but already is in heaven) … This lady is called Anna Lina.[6]

It was with these words that Henry Garnet, head of the Jesuit mission in England, conveyed to Rome the name of a woman he had known for perhaps ten years. Garnet was writing one of his reports on various matters concerning the English mission that he sent intermittently and secretly back to his Superior General. Written in his distinctive Italian, Garnet's account of the 'bella materia' of Anne Line is found among the twenty-two pages of a letter of 11 March 1601. Anne Line had been hanged at Tyburn two weeks prior to this date for the felony of assisting a priest. Her body, cut down and stripped, was cast without ceremony into a common grave that was dug not in consecrated ground but in the highway, an act that symbolised contempt and utter rejection. She drew such ire not so much for her personal qualities, of which the Judge knew little, but for what she stood for – the hated and feared Jesuit mission. In Garnet's eyes, Anne Line was a paragon of virtue to be praised literally to the heavens; for her accusers, even her death was not enough – her lifeless body itself was to be cast out and trampled underfoot by men. Anne Line's story takes us to the heart of the division that afflicted the schizophrenic England of Queen Elizabeth I.

When Henry Garnet compared his London friend to the 'Roman Matrons' he was apparently referring to the martyrs Perpetua and Felicity, whose story he would have pondered a few days before as he read his breviary on their feast day of 7 March. They are described as matrons because, unlike other notable female martyrs of the early Church, they were married women, as Anne Line herself had been. Garnet's 'five devout of the

---

[6] Garnet, Letter, 11/3/1601, f.179v.

female sex' probably refers to the five other women who are listed together with Perpetua and Felicity among the 'holy apostles and martyrs' in the prayers of the Catholic Mass.[7] Behind the obvious implication that Garnet believed Anne Line to be a saint worthy of extraordinarily high honour, there are certain parallels between the life of Anne Line and those of Perpetua and Felicity that he may be hinting at but does not spell out. For example, a poignant feature of Perpetua's story is her distress at being parted from her nursing baby after her arrest. It has only recently been realised that Anne Line also had a child who was taken from her, probably when very young – a son called John, who was brought up by her husband's estranged family. In Perpetua's case, the authorities relented and allowed her to nurse her baby in jail, whereupon she wrote, '... immediately I grew strong and was relieved from distress and anxiety about my infant; and the dungeon became to me as it were a palace'.[8] Anne Line seems to have been completely cut off from her only child, who would have been thirteen or fourteen when she died.

Perpetua and her servant Felicity were executed in North Africa in AD 203 during the rule of the Emperor Septimius Severus (a North African who, in addition to persecuting Christians, campaigned against the Scots, basing his court for several years at York, where he died in 211). Both the Roman matron Perpetua and the English gentlewoman Anne Line had a social status that clearly added to the pathos of their public executions, and of course their gender added further horror to the spectacle. Details in the accounts evoke their femininity. When Perpetua was flung in the air by a wild cow in the Carthaginian Circus, she landed heavily in the dust and was seen to draw her dress across a tear exposing her thigh and then to pin up her dishevelled hair. Anne Line, in like manner, was observed carefully 'binding her garments beneath about her knees' in an attempt to preserve her modesty in the minutes before she was hanged (the scaffold was between twelve and eighteen feet high and it was a windy day). There are other parallels. Perpetua was a visionary who had prophetic dreams; Anne Line saw a mysterious light and heard music that she took as a sign from God. Perpetua prayed for a brother who had died as a child; Anne Line had a sister who had died young. Perpetua's pregnant servant Felicity feared that she would die in childbirth, depriving her of the honour of dying as a martyr alongside her fellow prisoners. Anne Line feared that she would die of a fever before she had the honour of dying a martyr's death. And finally, both Perpetua and Anne were

---

[7] Roman Canon, Eucharistic Prayer 1.
[8] *The Passion of the Holy Martyrs Perpetua and Felicity*, 1.2.

in conflict with fathers who urged them vehemently to conform. Perpetua writes:

> ... my father was liked to vex me with his words and continually strove to hurt my faith because of his love: Father, said I, Do you see (for examples) this vessel lying, a pitcher or whatsoever it may be? And he said, I see it. And I said to him, Can it be called by any other name than that which it is? And he answered, No. So can I call myself nought other than that which I am, a Christian.
>
> Then my father angry with this word came upon me to tear out my eyes; but he only vexed me, and he departed vanquished, he and the arguments of the devil.[9]

To the Christian, martyrs die for their faith in Christ; yes certainly. But martyrs arrive at this point by virtue of their refusal to live a lie. They die for their courage in simply being who they really are. Shakespeare, who disguised himself in so many ways, and went 'a motley [fool] to the view', respected that profoundly.

Sonnet 110

Alas, 'tis true I have gone here and there
And made myself a motley to the view,
Gored mine own thoughts, sold cheap what is most dear,
Made old offences of affections new;
Most true it is that I have look'd on truth
Askance and strangely: but, by all above,
These blenches gave my heart another youth,
And worse essays proved thee my best of love.
Now all is done, have what shall have no end:
Mine appetite I never more will grind
On newer proof, to try an older friend,
A god in love, to whom I am confined.
Then give me welcome, next my heaven the best,
Even to thy pure and most loving breast.

---

[9] *The Passion of the Holy Martyrs Perpetua and Felicity*, 1.2.

3

Unwholesome Fens

Henry Garnet tells us that Anne Line was chronically ill for the last fourteen years of her life.[1] Anthony Champney, another Elizabethan priest, is the source for the description of Anne Line's 'infirm constitution of body, troubled with almost continual headaches, and withall inclined to dropsy', found in Challoner.[2] Every year, it seems, particularly in the winter and spring, she was subject to episodic bouts of 'extreme illness' that could be so severe that Garnet writes, 'More than once I myself have seen her completely exhausted and apparently dead.'[3] Quite possibly the same affliction had carried off her younger sister, because the symptoms are consistent with a disease that was strongly associated with the brackish marshes of the coastal parts of Essex. It is referred to in the literature of the day as 'the ague'. It was this disease, endemic in England at this period, that was to finally carry off the ageing Oliver Cromwell in 1658. We know it as malaria, a name derived from the Italian *mal aria*, meaning bad air. The role of the mosquito in the transmission of this scourge was not understood until the nineteenth century, and in Shakespeare's day it was assumed that it was the air itself, the 'reek a' th' rotten fens', that bore the infectious agent.[4] Shakespeare's Caliban, ever the charmer, curses Prospero with the following words: 'All the infections that the sun sucks up / From bogs, fens, flats, on

---

[1] Garnet, Letter, 11/3/1601, f.180v.
[2] Challoner, 257. Challoner relies on the manuscript history of the reign of Queen Elizabeth known as Champney's *Annales,* written in Latin and dated 1618. This is held at the Westminster Diocesan Archive in London, and remains unpublished (material relevant to Anne Line is on pages 1009–1013). The author, Anthony Champney was a Catholic priest who ministered in Yorkshire until his imprisonment from 1599 to 1603 (in Marshalsea in London, and then in Wisbech, Norfolk) when he was banished. He probably knew Anne Line by repute even if he did not meet her in person, and he no doubt remembered her husband Roger, as they had both been students at the English college at Rhiems in 1592. 'Dropsy' refers to water-retention and the associated swelling this causes. However, by the time of Anne Line's execution, it is clear from Garnet's account that she was very thin, suggesting that Champney's information may refer to her condition some years earlier.
[3] Caraman, *Garnet*, 278, from 11 March letter.
[4] Coriolanus: 'You common cry of curs, whose breath I hate / As reek a' th' rotten fens, whose loves I prize / As the dead carcasses of unburied men / That do corrupt my air – I banish you!' *Coriolanus* III.iii.120–123.

Prosper fall and make him / By inch-meal a disease!'[5] Closer to home, in Chester's *Loves Martyr* (1601), the phoenix complains: 'O what a misty Damp breaks from the ground, / Able it self to infect the noisome Air' (spelling modernised).[6] Aubrey provides an anecdote that illustrates the reputation that Essex was to gain in this respect:

> Gilbert Sheldon, Lord Bishop of Lundon, gave Dr. Pell the scurvy Parsonage of Lanedon cum Basseldon in the infamous and unhealthy (aguesh) Hundreds of Essex (they call it Kill-priest sarcastically) and King Charles the second gave him the Parsonage of Fobing, 4 miles distant.
>
> At Fobbing, seven curates dyed within the first ten years; in sixteen yeares, six of those who had been his Curates at Laindon are dead; besides those that went away from both places; and the death of his wife, servants, and grandchildren.
>
> … and complaining one day to his Grace at Lambith of the unhealthiness of his Benefice as abovesayd, sayd my Lord, I doe not intend that you shall live there. No sayd Pell, but your Grace does intend that I shall die there.[7]

The 'quartan ague' referred to a strain of malaria that causes a fever which then recurs on the fourth day, after two days of respite. Tertiary ague is another variant in which the fever returns on the third day. This periodicity is not noted in the case of Anne Line, but it may be that she suffered from a third variant in which fever was continuous for several days. Both weight loss and hallucinations can occur with malaria, and both elements feature in the accounts of Anne Line's last fever-racked week.[8]

The first effective treatment for malaria in Europe was introduced from South America by the Jesuits, who had learned from indigenous people the curative properties of the bark of the cinchona tree. The active ingredient of this natural remedy is quinine, which remained the principal treatment up to the mid-twentieth century. Initially, however, it was known as *Jesuit's-powder*, and treated with such suspicion by Protestants that it was not widely used in

---

[5] *The Tempest* II.ii.1–3.
[6] *Loves Martyr*, 28. See also 'The noisome air is growne infectious', *Loves Martyr*, 30; [Caliban: 'As wicked dew as e'er my mother brush'd / With raven's feather from unwholesome fen / Drop on you both!], *Tempest* I.ii.321–323; [With rotten damps ravish the morning air; / Let their exhal'd unwholesome breaths make sick / The life of purity, the supreme fair.], *Lucrece* 778–780.
[7] Aubrey, *Brief Lives*, 231.
[8] Cf. 'that same ague that hath made you lean', *Julius Caesar* (II.ii.113). See page 170.

England. There were also doubts about how this putative cure should be applied and in what dosage. These obstacles were to be overcome by the celebrated Robert Talbor with his 'English Remedy', and it turns out that Essex was central to his breakthrough, for the medical historians tell us that 'the effective use [of quinine] ... for malaria therapy was first developed in tests with ague patients living in the salt marshes of Essex'.[9] Talbor himself would write: 'I planted myself in Essex near the sea side, in a place where agues are the epidemic diseases, where you will find but few persons but either are, or have been afflicted with a tedious quartan.'[10]

The title of one of Talbor's publications on his discoveries is worthy of note. He called it *Pyretologia: a Rational Account of the Cause and Cures of Agues* (1672).[11] Pyretology is the study of fevers, taking its name from the 'burning' and 'heating of the blood' that afflicts the sufferer. It seems highly likely that Anne Line burned with malarial fever, which, if it does not kill and is not cured, can remain in the body for many years, to re-emerge again and again with increasingly debilitating consequences. At this time there was no cure. When the paroxysm occurs at the height of the fever it may seem that the victim has succumbed and died, only to be revived – as a poet might see it – like a phoenix rising from the flames. When Anne Line was in prison she apparently suffered a particularly severe bout of illness, during which, we are informed, she 'was revived from death to life about [twenty] times in that one night, as divers that watched with her can witness'.[12]

Jenkyn Maldons, Anne Line's childhood home, was on the landward side of the Dengie peninsula, which had some particularly notorious marshlands. The Dengie bogs were noted by Daniel Defoe, of *Robinson Crusoe* fame, who travelled to the area in the 1690s and observed 'a strange decay of the [female] sex here'. In view of Anne Line's chronic illness, and the premature death of her sister, his account is striking, even allowing for an element of exaggeration. He writes:

> it was very frequent to meet with men that had had from five to six, to fourteen or fifteen wives ... the reason ... was this; that they [the men] being bred in the marshes themselves, and seasoned to the place, did pretty well with it; but that they always went into the hilly country ... for a wife: that when they took the young lasses out of the wholesome

---

[9] Reiter, 'From Shakespeare to Defoe: Malaria in England in the Little Ice Age', 6.
[10] Talbor, *The English Remedy: Talbor's Wonderful Secret for Curing of Agues and Feavers* (1682), quoted in Reiter, 7.
[11] See Reiter, 6.
[12] Brudenell MS, 2.117.

and fresh air, they were healthy, fresh and clear, and well; but when they came out of their native aire into the marshes ... they presently changed their complexion, got an ague or two, and seldom held it above half a year, or a year at most; and then ... [the men] would go to the uplands again, and fetch another; so that marrying of wives was reckoned a kind of good farm to them.[13]

We can only guess at the effect that all this arbitrary suffering and death had on the collective psyche, but it is not entirely surprising to learn that in the latter half of the sixteenth century, Essex was acquiring a reputation for witchcraft.

Of Witches and Old Higham

The future Anne Line was brought up in a corner of the world where the atmosphere could prove fatal in more ways than one, where religious fears and superstitions swirled and threatened. Perhaps she observed the irony that both female suspected witches and male Catholic priests were being condemned on the flimsiest of evidence by people who raged against 'superstition' and were the self-proclaimed champions of 'conscience' and 'law'. If she had the intelligence to see this, it would help to explain how she became alienated from the family and places from whence she came. Barbara Rosen, editor of *Witchcraft in England, 1558–1618*, assures us that '[b]y 1580, Essex had already become notorious for witches and Protestant zeal', but Essex covers a wide area, and it is rather striking that the witchcraft obsession was often linked specifically to places *within* Essex frequented by the Highams, such as Maldon and, as we shall see, Chelmsford and Hatfield Peverell. It is all the more so when we learn that the notorious series of Essex witch trials began in 1566, and it may have been Anne Line's father who brought one of the first cases.

What the records tell us is that a man called William Higham had some livestock near Hatfield Peverell, a village a few miles to the north-west of Maldon, and during the winter of 1565 a number of his animals died.[14]

---

[13] Defoe, *A Tour through the Whole Island of Great Britain*, quoted in Reiter, 8.
[14] I consider William Higham of Jenkyn Maldons is very likely to be the same man recorded as William Higham of Hatfield Peverell, both because of the proximity – the two locations are about six miles apart – and because his in-laws were closely associated with Hatfield Peverell. The Alleyne family had owned land in this village since a double marriage with the Leigh family that had been granted the priory of Hatfield Peverell by Henry VIII. One of these marriages was between Anne Line's maternal grandparents, John Alleyne (of Thaxted and Hatfield Peverell) and Margaret Leigh. See *Visitations of Essex*, 133, 333.

Harbouring dark suspicions, Higham accused a certain Lora Wynchester of bewitchment. The case was heard at the Assizes held at Chelmsford on 26 July 1566, and the indictment is as follows:

> Lora Wynchester of Hatfield Peverel, wife of 'Jeromie' (occupation not given) there, being a common witch, by the use of diabolical sorcery bewitched and killed a cow worth 20s., six sheep worth 20d. each, and four pigs worth 20d. each, belonging to William Higham. Pleads not guilty.[15]

There was a spate of such claims in the area. From the same Assizes there is another indictment, reading:

> Agnes Waterhowse of Hatfield Peverel widow, being a common witch, by diabolical arts, bewitched William Fynee there, so that he languished from 1 October until 1 November, when he died. Jurors say she murdered him. Confesses to the felony and murder.[16]

And a third:

> Elizabeth Fraunces of Hatfield Peverel, spinster, wife of Christopher Fraunces, being a common witch, by diabolical arts bewitched John an infant belonging to William Auger of Hatfield, so that it became decrepit. Confesses to the indictment. Judgement, that she be imprisoned for one whole year.[17]

The Hatfield Peverell cases became the subject of a pamphlet entitled *The examination and confession of certaine Wytches at Chensforde in the Countie of Essex before the Quenes majesties Judges, the XXVI daye of July Anno 1566*. According to Rosen, this is 'the earliest published account of a trial', but more to the point, Rosen notes that it betrays an anti-Catholic bias that can be seen in numerous accounts of witchcraft in England in the sixteenth and seventeenth centuries. Indeed, it is clear that in many cases paranoia about witchcraft was linked to paranoia about Catholicism. Agnes Waterhouse told the court that she attended church and said her prayers, but when

---

[15] ERO T/A 418/10/6, ASS 35/8/4/6.
[16] ERO T/A 418/10/22, ASS 35/8/4/22.
[17] ERO T/A 418/10/21, ASS 35/8/4/21. See also *The examination and confession of certaine Wytches at Chensforde* ... Extract, Rosen, *Witchcraft in England*, 73–82.

questioned further, her response immediately raised suspicions: 'And when she was demanded what prayer she said (at church) she answered, "The Lord's Prayer, the Ave Maria, and the Belief [the Creed]". And then they demanded whether in Latin or in English and she said "In Latin".'[18] No doubt Agnes Waterhouse had been taught these prayers as a child and had said them ever since, but as Rosen comments, 'The old prayers are already becoming weapons of the Enemy, in the public view, not a superseded good but a positive evil.'[19]

Agnes Waterhouse was hanged on 29 July 1566, but despite the efforts of William Higham, Lora Wynchester was found not guilty. Elizabeth Fraunces faced further charges in 1572 that resulted in her being pilloried and then imprisoned for another year; then, in 1578, the stakes were raised as she was accused of bewitching a certain Alice Pole who 'languished in all her body from the above date until 1 November next following, when she died at the same; and the jurors say that the said Elizabeth killed and murdered the said Alice by malice aforethought.'[20] For the latter crime, Fraunces was hanged. We can only guess at the extent to which the young Anne Line was aware of these events, but by 1579, when she was probably about fifteen, Essex witches were becoming national news and she could have read of the case of Elizabeth Fraunces in a lurid tract published in London that year that mentioned her own father. The tract was entitled *A Detection of damnable driftes, practised by three Witches arraigned at Chelmisforde in Essex, at the laste Assises there holden, whiche were executed in Aprill, 1579 etc.*

In this publication we are told that Elizabeth Fraunces had accused another woman of being a witch, alleging that she had caused the death of *a servant of 'old Higham'* by 'a piece of an apple cake which she gave her, upon the eating whereof she presently sickened and not long after died' [my italics].[21] One suspects that 'Old Higham' may have been feeling slightly intimidated by this time – first his livestock under diabolical attack, now a servant. What next?

Another of the alleged witches was from Maldon and was accused by her own son, who claimed:

his mother did keep three spirits, whereof the one called by her great Dick, was enclosed in a wicker bottle, the second, named Little Dick,

---

[18] *The examination ... etc.*, Rosen, 82.
[19] Rosen, 72.
[20] ERO Q/SR 69/47.
[21] *A Detection of damnable driftes etc.*, Rosen, 94 (modernised spelling etc.). Old Higham is identified as William Higham in the Assizes Records (*Calendar of Assize Records: Essex Indictments, Elizabeth 1*, 264, p. 46 [m.6]).

was put into a leather bottle, and the third, termed Willet, she kept in a wool-pack; and thereupon the house was commanded to be searched. The bottles and pack were found, but the spirits were vanished away.[22]

And there is much more in similar vein: 'they did see a rat run up the chimney, and presently it did fall down again in the likeness of a toad'.[23] Essex had more than its fair share of such goings-on, and the Chelmsford Assizes of 1582 heard the notorious case pursued by a young Justice of the Peace called Mr Darcy, which became known as the St Osyth witch trial.[24] Fourteen women were accused and five confessed to being witches, of whom two, Ursula Kempe and Elizabeth Bennett, were hanged. In 1921 the skeletons of two females, believed to be these two women, were discovered in a garden in St Osyth with iron staples driven through the elbows and knees, apparently in an effort to stop them rising from their graves.

From 1582, Maldon had a well-known non-conformist preacher called George Gifford who considered himself an authority on witches – he has left us two books on the subject: *A Discourse of the subtill Practises of Devilles by Witches and Sorcerers* (1587), and a more popular work intended for less-educated folk, *A Dialogue concerning Witches and Witchcrafts* (1593). Incidentally, the best-known book on the subject from this period, Reginald Scot's *The Discovery of Witchcraft*, which takes a sceptical viewpoint, is thought to have been prompted by the 1582 witch trial at Chelmsford.[25] These dramatic events were the talk of the country, and must have been followed avidly by people living near enough to go and see for themselves the accused and their accusers. The Highams lived less than ten miles away from Chelmsford, and the previous family brushes with bewitchment doubtless gave them a particular interest in the outcome. But for all the excitement generated by Mr Darcy's pursuit of Elizabeth Bennett et al., it may have been another trial held at the same sessions that played the decisive role in setting Anne Line on the path to Tyburn, for it was at these same Chelmsford Assizes that a priest called John Payne was convicted of treason, and it is not unlikely that John Payne played a key role in her conversion.

---

[22] *A Detection of damnable driftes etc.,* Rosen, 95 (modernised spelling etc.).
[23] *A Detection of damnable driftes etc.,* Rosen, 95 (modernised spelling etc.).
[24] See Barbara Rosen, *Witchcraft in England 1558–1618*, 103–157.
[25] Hence, Rosen, 171. Scot was famously sceptical of such trials and doubted the guilt of many of those who were condemned by them, but despite this he did not doubt the existence of supernatural powers. He also shared in the bias that tended to equate witchcraft with the 'hocus-pocus' of Catholicism.

4

The Case of John Payne

By now it will be obvious that there is a great deal that we do not know about Anne Line. Even the simplest questions about her conversion to Catholicism remain unanswered. Who or what was it that influenced her to take such a daunting step? Where exactly did it happen and in what year? We can be reasonably certain that it took place at some point between the spring of 1583 and the summer of 1585, in which case the priest John Payne could not have been the man who reconciled Anne Line to the Catholic Church, as he was executed in 1582. However, conversion rarely occurs with road-to-Damascus suddenness. It is more usually a process that takes time to mature and it usually involves contact with the community of existing believers. It is therefore quite likely that Anne Line had either met John Payne in person or knew people who knew him. Furthermore, it could even be that it was the circumstance of his public execution in Chelmsford that triggered in Anne Line a determination to take the path that would eventually lead to her own death. If so, this would fit a pattern that would become increasingly familiar. The execution of the Jesuit Edmund Campion in 1581 is known to have had a profound effect on the young Henry Walpole, who later joined the Jesuits and was executed at York in 1595, and on Philip Howard, Earl of Arundel, who died in the Tower of London during that same year after a long imprisonment following his conversion to the Catholic faith. Whatever the uncertainties about the extent to which their paths crossed, John Payne's story can help us to understand the context of Anne Line's, and it is in this spirit that I recount it here.

John Payne was one of the new breed known as 'seminary priests'. In fact, he was one of the first of two such priests to arrive in England from the Continent, making landfall on the south coast in 1576 in the company of Cuthbert Mayne, the first of the seminary priests to be martyred. The seminarists were the product of the new institutions for training priests introduced by the Council of Trent as part of the drive of the Catholic Church to reform itself in response to the crisis of the Reformation. Circumstances in Protestant England, which had essentially outlawed the

Catholic priesthood, forced Catholic students for the priesthood to study abroad, and created a particular urgency to the situation. This resulted in the foundation of the English College in Douay in the Spanish Netherlands in 1568, which was the first seminary anywhere in the world to receive papal approval following the Council of Trent. Other English seminaries followed, in Rome in 1579, and then in Valladolid and Seville in Spain in 1589 and 1592, respectively. The seminaries in Rome and Valladolid remain in use to this day. To contemporaries, the term 'seminary priest' denoted a new kind of priest, just as the Jesuits also represented a new breed, born of the Catholic response to the Reformation. Whether they represented a threat or a promise obviously depended on one's point of view.

John Payne stayed briefly with the Roper family in Beckenham, Kent, where he blended into the background as a household servant. He was in distinguished company, for the Ropers were related to the martyred Thomas More (the poet John Donne was another relative), but it was at the Ropers' house that John Payne became acquainted with the soon-to-be-notorious George Eliot, the man who would betray him. Both Payne and Eliot moved on to Essex, to the Catholic household of the dowager Lady Petre, who lived at Ingatestone, between Chelmsford and London.[1] Eliot was employed as a regular servant, and Payne was able to use the house as a base from which to conduct his missionary work both in Essex and on journeys further afield. More than ten years after Payne's death Anne Line was to be found in the company of two sisters from the Roper family, and the networks of people associated with her and with this particular priest intersect at several points. Lady Petre's son, Sir John Petre, lived near to Ingatestone and was an important patron of the Catholic musician William Byrd, who was in turn a friend of the Jesuit Henry Garnet. Sir John was a friend of the Earl of Worcester, who was another patron of Byrd and the most senior Catholic nobleman to retain a position at Court (Queen Elizabeth is reported to have said of Worcester that he 'reconciled what she thought inconsistent, a stiff papist, to a good subject').[2] Anne Line is linked to Worcester through a 1593 report to Lord Burghley stating that Mass was being said in Worcester's London house attended by 'Mrs Lyne and her acquaintance Mr. Shelly and others' (Mr Shelley was a cousin).[3] One wonders if she sang William Byrd's motets in the choir at Mass and whether she was led by the great composer

---

[1] Payne witnessed the will of Lady Ann Petre in June 1578 (Anstruther, *Seminary Priests*, 266) and he had been listed as a recusant in Lady Petre's household in the previous year.
[2] Lloyd, *State Worthies*, 469.
[3] *CSP Addenda 1580–1624*, 32.64.

himself. It is not unlikely – he is recorded as having rooms at the Earl of Worcester's house in the Strand a few years later – and the friendship between Byrd, Worcester and Petre remained strong. From 1594, Byrd's country house was at Stondon Massey in Essex, within convenient visiting distance of Sir John Petre's residence where all three men had been present during the Christmas season of 1589, and a few years after this a son of the Earl of Worcester would marry a daughter of Sir John Petre.

The priest John Payne is first recorded at the house of Lady Petre in a recusant list dating from 1577, but the hunt for his whereabouts did not begin to hot up until after the Jesuit mission to England had begun with the arrival of Edmund Campion and his companions in 1580, an event that raised the political temperature considerably. This gave Payne several years in which to go about his work as a priest in Essex in relative quiet, and it appears that he was widely known to the Catholics of the county. Meanwhile, it has been alleged that George Eliot was nursing a grudge:

> [Eliot] had a personal quarrel with Payne about some gentlewoman of Mr. Roper's household with whom he had eloped to London, in hopes that the priest would marry him to her, and on this being refused, had resolved on revenge.[4]

After George Eliot had moved on to the service of Lady Petre, he was accused of embezzling money from his new mistress and then imprisoned on more serious charges of rape and murder. At some point, probably to escape the penalty for his crimes, he began writing to the Earl of Leicester with information about Catholic fugitives.[5] He was soon released and on the trail of his former colleague. John Payne was arrested in Shakespeare's home county of Warwickshire, and committed to the Tower of London on 14 July 1581. But John Payne was relatively unknown and George Eliot was to become famous for his discovery three days later of the most wanted priest in England, the Jesuit Edmund Campion, hiding in a loft at the farmhouse of Lyford Grange.[6] For his betrayal of Campion, Catholics would refer to

---

[4] Simpson, 309, citing an allegation made by 'early Catholic biographers of Campion'. Eliot may have been responsible for introducing Fr Payne to the Petre household. It is generally assumed that Eliot was employed to track down Fr Payne, whom he knew well, but happened on Campion by chance. Questier, *Catholicism and Community in Early Modern England*, 196.
[5] *Lansdowne MSS*, 33, f.145–149.
[6] The July arrest of Edmund Campion is alluded to by the nurse in *Romeo and Juliet* (I.iii.). See Asquith, *Shadowplay*, 75f.

Eliot as 'Judas', and the trial of John Payne in the following year would provide a chance for him to reprise the role.

On 14 August and again on 31 October 1581, the Privy Council authorised that John Payne be interrogated under torture, implying that he was racked, and then in March 1582 he was suddenly hurried back to Essex so that his trial could be held at the Chelmsford Assizes.[7] The contemporary account of his case was written by William Allen, the priest who founded the seminary at Douay. It was a busy session; Allen reports, 'On Thursday at night his name was recited with about 13 witches, other murderers and theeves.'[8] Payne was arraigned on the Friday and accused of High Treason on the evidence of a statement from his old acquaintance Mr George Eliot. A witness with less credibility would have been hard to find, and yet the omens were bleak for the accused. Eliot claimed that in a private conversation, Fr Payne had commended a plan to change the religion of the country. According to this, '50 men well appointed with privy coats and daggers, should espy some opportunity when the Queen was in her progress, and slay the Queen's Majesty, the *E[arl] of Leicester*, and *Mr. Walsingham*, and then to proclaim the Queen of Scots Q[ueen].'[9] His source of information was alleged to be three well-known Catholic exiles, the 'Earl of *Westmoreland*, Dr. *Allen*, and Dr. *Bristow*'. Moreover, Eliot alleged that Payne had told him 'that it should be no greater an offence to kill the Queen, than to despatch a brute beast'.[10] These accusations played precisely to the fears of the ruling elite and to English Protestants generally. Catholic resistance to Protestant rule, combined with the presence of the Catholic Mary Queen of Scots, had led to the rebellion of the Northern Earls in 1569, the most serious challenge to the regime to date.[11] The earl who got away, the Earl of Westmoreland, was said to be plotting further insurrection from his base in Flanders.

Answering the indictment, Fr Payne replied:

---

[7] Anstruther, 266.

[8] Allen, 131. The witch case became known as the St Osyth witch trial. A connection between anti-Catholic feeling and paranoia about witchcraft in England in the sixteenth and seventeenth centuries has been noted many times, some, such as Barbara Rosen, in her discussion of the St Osyth case, suspects a more specific link, suggesting that 'the government was really looking for a Catholic plot'. The implication is that the government was hoping either that John Payne's case would be overshadowed by the witch trial, or somehow associated with it in the minds of the public. Similar motives may have been in play in 1601, when Anne Line was executed just three days after the Earl of Essex and during the period when a series of trials and executions of his followers was taking place.

[9] Allen, 132 (italics [*sic*] and ff)

[10] Allen, 132.

[11] For Shakespeare's view, Asquith suggests a close reading of *Henry IV Part 1*; see *Shadowplay*, 122f.

he always in mind and word honoured the Queen's Majesty above any woman in the world, that he would gladly always have spent his life for her pleasure in any lawful service; that he prayed for her as for his own soul: that he never invented or compassed any treason against her Majesty, or any of the nobility of England.[12]

Fr Payne's conscience may have been as pure as the driven snow but he was not going to be believed. He had trained at the seminary at Douay established by the Dr Allen referred to by Eliot. It was Dr Allen who had persuaded the Jesuits to embark on the mission to England and there is little doubt that Allen was also engaged, along with the Jesuit exile Persons, in political efforts to promote what we would now call 'regime change' in England, repeatedly urging the Spanish to invade and restore the old faith.[13] John Payne, who had met Allen at Douay, could only respond to the implication of treachery by claiming 'that Dr. *Allen* and Dr *Bristow* never talked to his knowledge of any such things'.[14]

Fr Payne was on more solid ground when he spoke of his accuser:

> He refelled *Eliot's* deposition, first, taking God to witness on his soul that he never had such speech with him. Secondly, he brought two places of scripture, and a statute to prove that without two sufficient witnesses no man should be condemned. Thirdly, he proved *Eliot* insufficient to be a witness, for [having been guilty of] oppression of poor men, even to death, for a Rape, and other manifest lewd acts with women, for breach of contract, for cozening the L[ady] *Petre*, [widow of Sir *William Petre*,] of Money, for changing oft his religion, for malice against himself, for being attached of murder, and such like acts. [A]fter he made a long discourse of Eliot's dissembling.[15]

It was to no avail: the jury, 'on friday, after dinner, brought evidence [gave their verdict] that he was guilty'.[16] Plainly, the lack of a trustworthy witness

---

[12] Allen, 132.
[13] During the following year, 1583, Allen was apparently involved with the Duke of Guise in the Throckmorton Plot to replace Queen Elizabeth with Mary Queen of Scots. Throckmorton was Allen's brother-in-law. See Bossy 'The Heart of Robert Persons', in McCoog (ed.), *The Reckoned Expense: Edmund Campion and the Early English Jesuits*, 150. Allen was made 'Prefect of the English Mission' by Pope Gregory XVI in 1591 (McCoog, *English and Welsh Jesuits*, 11).
[14] Allen, 133. It has been suggested that William Allen may have been the Allen paid by alderman John Shakespeare to teach children in Stratford in 1564–5 (Milward, *Shakespeare's Religious Background*, 41).
[15] Allen, 133.
[16] Allen, 133f.

or anything more than hearsay evidence was not going to prevent the authorities from getting the convictions that they wanted.

It was clear that Fr Payne did not relish the prospect of his martyrdom scheduled for the following Monday morning. He protested: 'it was against the law of God and man that he should be condemned for one man's witness notoriously infamous', and that the jury were 'not at all understanding what treason is'. He concluded, 'all was but treachery in seeking of his blood'.[17] Later he was subject to the usual blandishments to evangelical conversion that, to Catholics, proved that they were being persecuted for their religion. Allen records:

> All Sunday till [five] of the clock, one Dr. *Withers* and Dr. *Sone* were with him, persuading him earnestly to change his religion, the which (said they), if you will alter, we doubt not to procure mercy for you. This Mr. *Payne* told me himself, saying, 'that the ministers, by their foolish babbling, did much vex and trouble him.[18]

On Monday, 2 April 1582, John Payne again protested his innocence, this time from the gallows, engaging in an exchange with the Puritan Lord Rich, who called on him to admit the charge of treachery. Fr Payne responded by requesting the Lord Rich to be a witness to his death, saying, as Allen records, 'Sweet my Lord certify her Majesty thereof, that she suffer not hereafter innocent blood to be cast away seeing it is no small matter.'[19] This clash of worlds at the Chelmsford gallows was observed by a crowd of onlookers, among whom the young Anne Line and her brother William may have found a place. Stephen Alford, biographer of William Cecil, Lord Burghley, summarises the conflict thus:

> Were Burghley and his colleagues atheist persecutors [as Allen alleged] who sought the blood of innocent priests?[20] Or were they merely dutiful public servants who were doing their best to protect the realm against rebel insurgents? The answers to these questions were anything but clear, and they depended (and depend still, perhaps) very much on one's point of view. But one fact is beyond any doubt. This was the great ideological battle of Elizabeth's reign – conscience set against the

---

[17] Allen, 134.
[18] Allen, 134f.
[19] Allen, 136.
[20] Atheist in the sense of 'One who practically denies the existence of a God by disregard of moral obligation to Him; a godless man' (OED).

state, treason against martyrdom – and Burghley was right at the heart of it.[21]

This divided world is the world of William Shakespeare as much as it is the world of John Payne, Anne Line, and William Cecil, and it forms the backdrop to the poems and plays he produced during this time of prolonged crisis.

Before we leave Mr Payne, one last extract from Allen's account:

> After all, very meekly, when the ladder was about to be turned, he said, JESUS, JESUS, JESUS; and so did hang, not moving hand or foot. They very courteously caused men to hang on his feet, and set the knot to his ear, and suffered him to hang to death, commanding *Bull*, the hangman of Newgate, to despatch (in the quartering of him), lest he should as they said revive, and rebuked him that he did not despatch speedily. All the town loved him exceedingly, the keepers and most of the Magistrates of the shire. No man seemed in countenance to mislike him, but much sorrowed and lamented his death; who most constantly, catholicly, patiently, and meekly ended this mortal life to rise triumphantly, his innocency known to all the world.[22]

This, of course, is Allen's verdict, but the ideological divide between those for and against the seminary priests was as extreme as the punishments that were applied. Cecil was scathing in his description of them as 'these seditious seedmen and sowers of rebellion'.[23] 'Seminary' means seedbed, and as he would also be aware, such men would sometimes refer to close companions as 'beadsmen', meaning that they would pray for each other using their rosaries.[24] We have an example of the term in Shakespeare's *Richard II*, where the words of Sir Stephen Scroop seem to prefigure Cecil's sentiments: 'The very beadsmen learn to bend their bows / Of double-fatal yew against thy state' III.ii.116f.[25] He meant that the King was now so unpopular that even

---

[21] Alford, 243.
[22] Allen, 137f.
[23] Alford (249), quoting from *The Execution of Justice*.
[24] The Jesuit superior Henry Garnet signs himself 'your most humble & devoted beadsman' in a letter copied into the recusant Brudenell Manuscript (2.133). *The Act Against Bulls from Rome*, 1571, had banned blessed 'Agnus Dei, or any crosses, pictures, beads, or suchlike vain and superstitious things' from being brought into the realm (13 Elizabeth c.2; see Tanner, 149).
[25] Shakespeare's only other use is in *The Two Gentlemen of Verona*. Proteus says, 'Commend thy grievance to my holy prayers, / For I will be thy beadsman, Valentine.' I.i.17f. Yew is 'double-fatal' because it is both poisonous to eat and used to make the longbow. If rebellion extends to the clerics it is doubly dangerous to the King because both spiritual and temporal powers are ranged against him.

lowly clerics devoted to prayer were turning against him, which is rather different from Cecil's blanket denunciation of Catholic priests. However, it is noteworthy that by the time Scroop gave this unwelcome message to his sovereign, the fate of Richard II was already sealed and he was soon forced from power. William Cecil always feared that the Catholics with their foreign-trained priests would somehow engineer the downfall of his Queen, and his own fate as chief minister was ineluctably linked to hers.

5

The Guldeford Connection

I have introduced you to one woman with two names: Anne and Alice. The next piece of the puzzle involves two women with the same name. The clue is to be found in the tiny village of Woodham Mortimer, the centre of which is just a mile or so from the equally diminutive Hazeleigh – Anne Line's home parish. Close by the church in Woodham Mortimer can be seen to this day the impressive façade of Mortimer's Hall (eerily similar to the Clock House). The blue plaque on the wall proclaims proudly that this was once the home of Peter Chamberlen, the inventor of obstetric forceps who was born in 1601. But we need to look back a little further. The frontage of the house is thought to date to the seventeenth century, but parts of the structure behind are old enough to have echoed the footsteps of Sir Robert Mortimer, the last male inhabitant to bear the name that is immortalised in that of the surrounding village. Sir Robert was slain at the Battle of Bosworth on 22 August 1485. His widow Isabella was the daughter of John Howard, the Duke of Norfolk, who perished in the same battle. Isabella and Sir Robert had no male heir, and so Mortimer's Hall passed to their daughter Elizabeth Mortimer, who married George Guldeford (or Guildford), a gentleman from Kent. The Guldeford star was rising as the Mortimer name was fading: both George Guldeford's father and grandfather had fought at Bosworth on the side of the victorious Henry Tudor, and Guldeford fortunes prospered accordingly. George Guldeford's half-brother Henry became a celebrated companion of Henry VIII, serving as his Master of Revels and later as his Master of Horse. In due time, Elizabeth Mortimer's inheritance of Mortimer's Hall was combined with her husband's inheritance of the principal Guldeford estates in Kent and Sussex, and together these estates were passed on to their son, Sir John Guldeford.

Sir John died in 1565, but there had been two women in his life who, I suggest, also played a crucial role in the life of St Anne Line – namely, his second wife, Mary Fitzwilliam, known as Lady Guldeford, and, somewhat surprisingly, one of his two sisters, who had the married name Anne Line. This, we can assert with confidence, is the original Anne Line – the woman who had legal right and title to the name, as opposed to Alice Higham, who merely adopted it. I shall refer to the former as Anne Line (snr), as she was probably at least 30 years older than her more widely known namesake. These two obscure individuals are the only gentlefolk referred to as Anne Line who have so far been identified anywhere in the surviving records of the second half of the sixteenth century, and at Woodham Mortimer the faint traces of their lives intersect.

Just to recap a little, the documentary evidence places St Anne Line at Jenkyn Maldons, the manor belonging to her father (who also owned land in Woodham Mortimer), and it connects Anne Line (snr) to Mortimer's Hall, a house that had been owned by her mother, Elizabeth Mortimer, and where she may well have been born and brought up.[1] These two manor houses, though separated by about a two-mile walk across the fields and lanes, were effectively neighbouring properties. Sir John Guldeford mentions in his will an existing agreement to grant a certain manor to his wife as her jointure (i.e. to provide for her needs should she be left a widow), and although he neglects to name the manor in question, it was very likely Mortimer's Hall, since this was in Essex, as was his wife's family, the Fitzwilliams, and also it was isolated from the main Guldeford estates in Kent and Sussex, making it the obvious choice.[2] If this is so, it would have come into Lady Guldeford's sole possession on Sir John's death in 1565, and this suggests a scenario that would account for several hitherto unexplained scraps of information about Anne Line's upbringing. Henry Garnet wrote mysteriously that 'she was for some time at Court (in the service of some ladies)'. These ladies have never been identified, but the connection with Mortimer's Hall suggests that the elderly Lady Guldeford may have been one of them. Garnet also remarked on Anne Line's refined upbringing, stressing that she 'knew every point of her duty perfectly and was thoroughly conversant in all matters an educated lady should be.' The scenario that presents itself is this: some years after Lady Guldeford was widowed and moved to Mortimer's Hall she received the young daughter of neighbouring landowner William Higham to wait on her and to be educated 'in all matters an educated lady should be'. Lady Guldeford would have seemed well connected indeed to the more lowly William Higham. In the unlikely event that he had heard rumours of the Catholic sympathies of certain relations, such as the offspring of her first marriage to Sir John Shelley of Michelgrove, or the late husband of her

---

[1] For Elizabeth Mortimer as the heir to the Mortimer estate, see Burke, *Extinct and Dormant Baronetcies*, 231.
[2] The assumption that he held this manor is derived from Burke's assertion that Sir John's mother, Elizabeth Mortimer, was the heir to the Mortimer estate (Burke, *Extinct and Dormant Baronetcies*, 231).

sister-in-law, Owen West, he could reassure himself that on her own side of the family she was related to the Sidneys and was a first cousin to Lord Burghley's wife, Mildred Cooke.[3] Notable among Anne Line's abilities was needlework, a skill that she would later use to provide the Jesuits with items that included 'two palls for chalices of her own work' (a pall is a cloth used on the altar during mass to cover the chalice).[4] Such work was obviously very far from what William Higham had in mind for his daughter. For Calvinists like Higham, palls were appalling and typical of the popish trumperies that accompanied the idolatry of the Catholic Mass. No, if William Higham sent his daughter to Woodham Mortimer Hall, he would surely have entertained the hope that along with the usual sought-after accomplishments, his daughter might one day acquire a respectable husband through her association with this new mentor. If so, he was to be first delighted and then aghast because it was presumably through Lady Guldeford that Anne Line was first introduced to Anne Line (snr), Lady Guldeford's sister-in-law, and Anne Line (snr) had a suitably eligible young relation called Roger Line of Ringwood, who was her husband's nephew. As Anne Line (snr) and her husband Richard had no surviving children, Roger Line was the heir to their handsome estate in Hampshire as well as to that of his own father. This was the Roger Line who would become Anne Line's husband. Of course, this adds another dimension to the name change from Alice to Anne, because it suggests rather strongly that it was through Anne Line (snr) that Alice Higham met the love of her life and became Anne Line. Probably more to the point, Anne Line (snr) may have been instrumental in bringing about her namesake's conversion to Catholicism, and it was common practice in the sixteenth century for a child to be named after a godparent. Indeed, a recent study has found that in the 1550s almost 90 per cent of girls shared their forename with a godmother.[5] Anne Line would not have needed a new godmother when she became a Catholic because it was not the practice to re-baptise under such circumstances; however, if Anne Line (snr) had played a significant part in the process, Anne Line may have seen her in something like that role. One way or another, it seems, A Line made A Line by the joining of two families – a curious circumstance indeed.

On paper, Alice Higham had made the perfect match to the eldest son of a landed family and one that offered all the security and future bounty one

---

[3] Lady Guldeford was also a first cousin to Sir Philip Sidney, though he was much younger than her. Owen West was the great-uncle of Thomas West, second Baron De La Warre, after whom the State of Delaware was named. Both Thomas West and three of his sons all served terms as governor of Virginia.
[4] Garnet's letter in Foley VII, 1355.
[5] Smith-Bannister, *Names and Naming Patterns in England 1538–1700*, 40.

could realistically hope to obtain by marriage. In happier times, her father William would have rejoiced in his daughter's good fortune – and perhaps he did for a while – but in the Guldeford house at Woodham Mortimer, his daughter, I suggest, had been catechised in the Old Faith as well as in good manners. Little is known about Anne Line (snr), but although her husband Richard Line was decidedly Protestant, she was herself a Guldeford with some most definitely Catholic relatives. Her sister had the married name Lady Mary West, and by the 1580s was a widow appearing with 'all her family' on a list of recusants in St Thomas parish, Winchester in 1583.[6] In the December of that year her house was raided after the Privy Council gave warrants 'for the searchinge and findinge of Jesuit Priestes'.[7] The searchers found no Jesuits, but a high altar in the 'Ladies chamber' was a bit of a giveaway, and then there was the 'secret place enclosed with bordes' in which were discovered 'divers newe and olde papisticall bookes, printed and written'.[8] As the search continued, a treasure trove of Catholic paraphernalia came to light:

> In another place more secret, ... underground was found a chest bound with iron, wherin was all manner of massinge apparell, a chalice of tyne [tin], a box full of singinge cates [Communion breads] a riche canopy of silver of Goldsmithes work, needell work ... uppon velvet for the altar, corpus cates, a paxe [pyx] of ivorie sett in woodde, there was also wrapped in greene sifte two Agnus Dei ... in satten broken in manie peeces, yet one of them so ioyned together as the superscription is easie to be redde. One [on] the one side is written. Ecce agnus dei qui tollis peccata mundi with the printinge of the lambe, on the other side not altogether so playne seemeth to be written Pius.v.papa pont:maximus.[9]

Other goods included beads, catechisms, priest's manuals, about forty service books for the Mass, and various items presumed to be 'hallowed thinges' because they were hidden with the rest. A few weeks after this raid, in the February of 1584, the spy Thomas Dodwell (to his family's lasting shame) identified no less than five different priests who had been sheltered

---

[6] Identified as 'The ladie West', she appears in a document entitled 'The names of the Recusants within the county of Southampton' (SP 12/160 f.56).
[7] SP 12/164 f.24.
[8] SP 12/164 f.24.
[9] SP 12/164 f.24,25. Chalices would normally be made of silver, but so many were pilfered from priests in various prisons that it became the practice to have a 'chalice of tyne'.

by Lady Mary West, all of whom subsequently died either in prison or on the scaffold.[10] Lady Mary herself seems to have been treated with relative leniency, perhaps on account of her age. As well as a recusant sister, Anne Line (snr) had a recusant nephew called Richard Guldeford who fled into exile with his wife Benedicta in the summer of 1583. To go into exile on the orders of the authorities was an act of humble submission, but to go voluntarily without the requisite permissions was treated as an act of defiance, and Richard and Benedicta were duly denounced as traitors and their lands in Kent confiscated.[11]

Anne Line (snr)'s sister-in-law, Lady Guldeford, was from the predominantly Catholic Fitzwilliam family, but we have to be a little careful in tracing her as there were two Lady Guldefords in the 1580s who appear in various documents, and it is not always apparent in individual records which one is being referred to. As it happens, they were mother and daughter. Mary Fitzwilliam, who became the elder Lady Guldeford on her second marriage, had first married into another Catholic family, the Shelleys of Michelgrove, and a daughter from this marriage – Elizabeth Shelley – later married Sir Thomas Guldeford, who by then was her mother's son-in-law. Confusing as this may be, it is clear that both Lady Guldefords were presented for recusancy between 1577 and 1588, and one of them was imprisoned, a fact that may be deduced from a 1584 letter that recommends 'the enlargement' of Lady Guldeford – a way of referring to her release from the confinement where her recusancy had presumably landed her.[12] A son of Lady Guldeford (snr) from her first marriage, William Shelley, was imprisoned for recusancy in 1580, then imprisoned again and apparently tortured for alleged involvement in the Catholic Throckmorton Plot of 1583. He was subsequently attainted.[13] Another son, Richard Shelley, died in prison after approaching the Queen in Greenwich Park and handing her a petition pleading for Catholic toleration, an episode to which Shakespeare is thought to have

---

[10] SP 12/168 f.82. The priests were Robert Holmes, Robert Nutter, Gregory Gunn, Thomas Pilchard and Roger Dickenson.
[11] Richard and Benedicta Guldeford were attainted (had their property confiscated to the crown) under the 1571 statute 'An Acte agaynst Fugitives over the Seaes', 13 Elizabeth c.3 (*Statutes of the Realm* IV.531ff). See Loseley MSS., LM/A.6.7.
[12] See *CRS* 22: 10, 44, 81, 120; *O'Dwyer*, 80; *VCH Essex*, Vol 6, [1973] 223; letter dated 27 October 1584 (*Lansdowne MSS*, Vol.40 f.148).
[13] According to Burke (*Peerages*, 582.) William Shelley was married to Mary Wriothesley the aunt of Shakespeare's patron Henry Wriothesley, the third Earl of Southampton.

alluded in *Titus Andronicus*, and the Jesuit poet Robert Southwell in his *Humble Supplication to her Majesty*.[14]

The Guldeford connection to the Highams may have had another twist unconnected to religion. In 1506 the Crown granted to Richard Guldeford a manor on the Kent/Sussex border called Higham, a property that stayed within Guldeford hands throughout the sixteenth century.[15] Is this just a coincidence? Today, 'Higham's Farm' is located two miles south east of the village of Kenardington, where the manor of that name was owned by the Richard and Benedicta Guldeford, who fled into exile in 1583. Could it be that the heralds who traced the Higham family back to Cheshire were mistaken and in fact they came from this Higham in the South-East that had been linked to the Guldefords for several generations? The physical landscape suggests as much, for the fertile Cheshire plain with its prime agricultural land is a far cry from the fly-bitten marshlands of the Dengie peninsula, but Higham Farm stands on the edge of Romney Marsh, where farming conditions are virtually identical to those found further up the coast near Maldon.

The Guldeford connection provides a way into Catholic networks that both Anne and Roger Line could have been influenced by and welcomed into.[16] With the existence of two Lady Guldefords and Lady Mary West, it also provides a possible explanation for Garnet's remark about Anne Line being present 'at Court (in the service of some ladies)', to which he attributes Anne Line's 'truly excellent knowledge' of the accomplishments of a gentlewoman.[17]

In 1597 a Guldeford son would marry a daughter of the Earl of Worcester, giving us a link to the Catholic trio of Byrd, Worcester and Petre that we know spent time together at Petre's house in Essex, and no doubt met in town at Worcester's house on the Strand, where Anne Line is reported to

---

[14] See John Klause, 'Politics, Heresy, and Martyrdom in Sonnet 124 and *Titus Andronicus*', 225–226. Titus, dismayed at the injustice inflicted on his family, sends a clown as a messenger to appeal directly to the emperor, but his efforts backfire: the hapless clown is dismissed with the words 'take him away and hang him presently' (IV.iii.98; IV.iv.44). Southwell alludes to Richard Shelley as he writes of his own petition: 'neither daring our selves to present them in person, being terrified with the president of his Imprisonment that last attempted it' (*Humble Supplication*, 45, quoted in Klause). Shelley was evidently sent on his mission by leading Catholic nobles, in particular Lord Montague.

[15] Bindoff, *The Commons 1509–1558* Vol II, 87f, 262, 265, 267, 434.

[16] On Anne Line's mother's side there was also a significant Catholic connection. Her great-uncle, Sir Christopher Alleyne 'of the Mote' (at Ightham in Kent), Member of Parliament, was named on a list of potential supporters of Mary Queen of Scots drawn up in 1574. He married Audrey Paget, daughter of Lord Paget, and was accused of keeping 'a vile papistical house'. He died in 1586, and his wife died a recusant the following year (see Hasler, *The History of Parliament: The House of Commons, 1558–1603*). Audrey Alleyne was the sister of the well-known Catholic exiles Thomas and Charles Paget.

[17] Garnet, letter 11 March 1601, f.179v.

have heard Mass. Some years later, Worcester played a significant role at the accession of James I, particularly in the vital initial stages of establishing the new administration:

> Worcester's son Thomas was sent by the Privy Council immediately after Elizabeth's death to inform James of his accession, and Worcester's wife went to accompany the new Queen to London. Note also that one of Worcester's sons-in-law, William Petre, was knighted by James on May 3, and another, Sir Henry Guildford [Guldeford], was given a Crown lease on May 8, 1603, the day after James's arrival in London.[18]

Within two weeks of James I's arrival in London, and probably on the same day, William Shakespeare and company had become 'The King's Men', and Worcester's long-serving secretary William Sterrell had also received a welcome royal appointment:

> [Sterrell] was made keeper, and then landlord, of the Palace of St. John of Jerusalem, Clerkenwell, which housed the Office of Revels. These buildings were central to the arranging of court entertainments, and there year after year, the King's players must have spent almost as much rehearsal and preparation time as they did at the Globe.[19]

William Sterrell, we may recall, was the double agent who has been identified as the linchpin of the Catholic intelligence network in England during the 1590s and early 1600s.[20] Among his more important contacts were the Earl of Worcester, who sat on the Privy Council; Garnet, the head of the Jesuits in England; Persons, the most influential English Jesuit abroad who had the ear of both the Pope and the King of Spain; and his fellow agent Phelippes, who remained the best code-breaker in the country. Anne Line, together with her husband and her brother, skirted the periphery as these bigger beasts played their games. Somewhere not far away, Shakespeare was doing the same.

---

[18] Finnis and Martin, 'Thomas Thorpe, "W.S.," and the Catholic Intelligencers', 30 n73.
[19] Finnis and Martin, 'Thomas Thorpe, "W.S.," and the Catholic Intelligencers', 30.
[20] See Finnis and Martin, 'The Identity of "Anthony Rivers"', esp. 62–63.

Part Two
Anne

'That the selfe was not the same'

6

The Bells of St Clements

Roger Line married Alice Higham on 3 February 1583 at St Clement Danes Church on the Strand, and we may assume from this that the Highams and perhaps the Lines had a town house in this bustling parish, bordered on the east by the City of London and on the south by the river Thames.[1] The Inns of Court were nearby, with Lincoln's Inn Fields to the north. The Strand was both the finest thoroughfare in the parish and constituted the principal route west from the City of London to Westminster. The Earl of Worcester had a house here, and on the other side of the street from St Clement Danes stood the magnificent London residences of the Earl of Essex and the Earl of Arundel. It must have seemed a grand venue for the joining of two proud families of albeit relatively minor landed gentry. Just a few minutes' walk from St Clement Danes, east up Fleet Street and north up Fetter Lane, was the room where the bride would later be arrested. According to a later prison list, the groom, Roger Line, would have been under the age of sixteen at the time of the wedding, but there is good reason to doubt the veracity of this record, and both he and the bride were more likely to have been seventeen or eighteen, perhaps older.[2] The bride's younger brother William was sixteen or seventeen. Perhaps Anne Line (snr) was there among the wedding party with the other ladies who had taught the bride the necessary etiquette. Whether bride and groom had already been secretly reconciled to the Catholic Church is not known (Catholics were obliged to get married in Anglican churches for their marriages to be legally recognised), but if not, they would be in the coming months.

It would be nice to think that all was peace and harmony at the wedding

---

[1] WCA, Parish Register, St Clement Danes (entry reads: 'Roger Lyne & Alice Higham' and the date is recorded as 3 February 1582, as the year was reckoned from 25 March).
[2] Shanahan claimed that the baptism of Roger Line is recorded in the Ringwood Parish Register with the date 30 August 1564 (Shanahan 'Anne Line, nee Heigham: where was she born?', 24); however, this is probably a misreading of a 'Roger Bissopp' next to a 'Thomas Lynde'. I suspect that Roger Line was baptised in his father's parish of Fordingbridge, the records for which do not extend back to the 1560s. William Higham was born in 1566, according to Jesuit records.

itself, but when the respective families learned of the conversions to the Catholic Church the reaction was extreme. William Higham (snr) cut off his daughter and refused to hand over her dowry. He treated her brother, his son and heir, in the same way, taking legal action to disinherit him. Amazingly, the same thing happened to Roger Line, who was heir both to his father and to his uncle Richard, husband of Anne Line (snr), but was cut out of it by his family. This kind of reaction, whilst extreme, was by no means unique. The Catholic Edward Walpole, eldest son and heir to the Walpole estate, was disinherited by his Calvinist father as the latter lay on his deathbed in 1588. The property was divided between Edward's mother and his younger brother Calibut, through whom it passed down to his great-grandson, Robert Walpole, Britain's first prime minister.

The fact of disinheritance is all the more extraordinary with respect to Anne Line's father, because he disinherited his *only* son, a measure of how keenly he must have felt the betrayal of his values by his own offspring. The sacred bond between father and son by which name and honour has been perpetuated from time immemorial had broken on the rocks of religious incomprehension, the alienation profound. With the family of Roger Line, Anne's husband, we find almost a mirror image of the story: Roger Line was the heir to his aunt and uncle – Anne Line (snr) and her husband Richard – because they had no children of their own. Richard Line of Chichester had been the first Line to receive a grant of arms, an achievement of enormous significance for such a family, but he somehow managed to ensure that the title went to Roger Line's younger brother despite Roger having the prior claim. Richard Line's land at least went to good use as he made it an endowment for a grammar school that he founded at Ringwood.

In the introduction to this book I described it as a biography, but of an unusual kind, and it is at this point that I am going to break the normal rules and introduce some Shakespeare. The justification for doing this is, first, that it is hard for us to think ourselves back into the sixteenth century and to relate to the issues and tensions of that time, but it is not hard for Shakespeare to do so for obvious reasons. Second, I wish to invite the reader to observe in particular the parallels between the fictional Imogen and the factual Anne. We could have turned to the opening scene of *A Midsummer Night's Dream* where a wilful daughter is threatened with death by her father – or 'to endure the livery of a nun' – if she continues to hold to her love for Lysander against his wishes, but it is in a later play that we have a more exact parallel as a newly wed couple is confronted by an angry father – Cymbeline, the king of the Britons. If some of my suggested allusions seem over-subtle, please remember the admonition from the preface to the First Folio: 'Reade him, therefore; and againe, and againe : And if then you doe not like him, surely you are in some manifest danger, not to understand him.' Shakespeare's text is meant to be read and pondered as well as performed from the stage. We begin with the father's furious reaction to the groom:

> Thou basest thing, avoid! hence, from my sight!
> If after this command thou fraught the court
> With thy unworthiness, thou diest: away!
> Thou'rt poison to my blood.

In a modern context, if someone were 'banished' we might imagine them being forcibly deported by being taken onto a plane by armed guards. In Elizabethan England and in Shakespeare's imagined ancient Britain, the banished person was ordered to leave on pain of death, having been given a certain number of days to settle their affairs and make their own arrangements for the actual journey. This was almost certainly the situation that was faced by Roger Line in 1586.

Cymbeline's son-in-law, Posthumus Leonatus, is moderate, even gracious, in his response:

> The gods protect you!
> And bless the good remainders of the court! I am gone.

There then follows an exchange between Imogen and her father, the King:

Imogen: There cannot be a pinch in death
More sharp than this is.
Cymbeline: O disloyal thing,
That shouldst repair my youth, thou heap'st
A year's age on me.
Imogen: I beseech you, sir,
Harm not yourself with your vexation
I am senseless of your wrath; a touch more rare
Subdues all pangs, all fears.[3]

---

[3] By 'a touch more rare', Imogen suggests that she has been touched by love, and that overcomes all fear. But in a recusant context, the word 'rare' is a loaded term associated with the Jesuit martyr Edmund Campion, and the phrase 'more rare' may be a pun on *orare*, meaning prayer. A similar pun is used in Ben Jonson's epitaph in Westminster Abbey: 'O RARE BEN JOHNSON [*sic*]'.

Cymbeline: Past grace?[4] obedience?[5]
Imogen: Past hope, and in despair; that way, past grace.
Cymbeline: That mightst have had the sole son of my queen!
Imogen: O blest, that I might not! I chose an eagle,
And did avoid a puttock.[6]
Cymbeline: Thou took'st a beggar; wouldst have made my throne
A seat for baseness.
Imogen: No; I rather added
A lustre to it.
Cymbeline: O thou vile one!
Imogen: Sir,
It is your fault that I have loved Posthumus:
You bred him as my playfellow, and he is
A man worth any woman, overbuys me
Almost the sum he pays.[7]
Cymbeline: What, art thou mad?[8]
Imogen: Almost, sir: heaven restore me! Would I were
A neat-herd's daughter, and my Leonatus
Our neighbour shepherd's son![9]
Cymbeline): Thou foolish thing!
[Re-enter QUEEN]
They were again together: you have done
Not after our command. Away with her,
And pen her up.[10]

---

[4] In their own eyes Puritans stood for *grace*, as opposed to the *works* of Catholics with their vain devotions.

[5] Anne Line's husband and brother were fined and imprisoned under the 1581 statute entitled *An Act to retain the Queen's Majesty's Subjects in their due Obedience* (23 Elizabeth, c.1.).

[6] The eagle was associated with the Spanish crown, from which Roger Line would receive a pension. A puttock is more commonly known as a kite, a bird of prey with associations of gluttony, in the sense of insatiable and ravening, suggesting that the similarity between the rapacious 'Cloten' and 'glutton' is probably intentional.

[7] Anne could well have been Roger's playfellow at Mortimer's Hall. If so, William Higham had only himself to blame for sending her there. Roger Line overbuys his new wife 'almost the sum he pays' because the Line estates were approximately twice the extent of the Higham estate in terms of productive land (not including an additional 200 acres of heath belonging to the Line estates), making this potentially a remarkably precise reference.

[8] Religion has been described as a form of madness since the time of Socrates.

[9] Oh the irony! Anne Line *was* a neat-herd's daughter, for neats are cattle and it is clear from Camden that the land in this area was used predominantly for sheep and cattle, the land being too poor and boggy for arable farming. To be precise, under the scenario outlined above, Roger Line was a neighbouring livestock farmer's sister's nephew.

[10] *Cymbeline* I.i.125–152.

King Cymbeline is angry with his daughter because he had someone else in mind for her to marry – namely, Cloten, 'the sole son of my queen'. It is not impossible that this could reflect Anne Line's circumstance quite precisely because there is a possibility that her mother had died and her father remarried. This is suggested by a marriage of a William Higham to an Edyth Griggs recorded in the parish of Woodham Ferrers in 1560, and Woodham Ferrers is only about six miles from Jenkyn Maldon. If Anne Line was the daughter of Higham's first wife, the Higham household could have been very like of that of King Cymbeline in the play. Did she come under pressure to marry the son of Edyth Griggs from a previous marriage? It is impossible to know. But regardless of whether Shakespeare's play reflects Anne Line's circumstances quite so neatly, it is not difficult to imagine William Higham raging at his daughter that she should have found a more suitable match than the Catholic Roger Line – one that would have made her father proud rather than being the cause of anxiety and grief in his old age. When the awful reality dawned on William Higham that his daughter had married a Papist, it might have occurred to him that if he could part his daughter from her husband he could bring her to her senses. Then she could procure a divorce – it was not impossible – and marry a man of suitable means and respectability. Perhaps Higham had a local gentleman in mind who attempted to woo Anne Line while her husband Roger was detained elsewhere. The following dialogue is from *Cymbeline* Act II scene iii. Cloten has been encouraged by his mother the Queen and his father-in-law Cymbeline to woo Imogen in the absence of the banished Posthumus. This is rather odd, as Imogen is clearly married to Posthumus and is very much in love with him. However, this does not deter the crass and doltish Cloten from serenading Imogen with music early in the morning (*aubading*, to be precise) and battering on the door of her bedchamber:

Cloten: I am advised to give
her music o' mornings; they say it will penetrate.
[Enter Musicians]
Come on; tune: if you can penetrate her with your
fingering, so; we'll try with tongue too: if none
will do, let her remain; but I'll never give o'er.
First, a very excellent good-conceited thing;
after, a wonderful sweet air, with admirable rich
words to it: and then let her consider.
[SONG]
Hark, hark! the lark at heaven's gate sings,

> And Phoebus 'gins arise,
> His steeds to water at those springs
> On chaliced flowers that lies;
> And winking Mary-buds begin
> To ope their golden eyes:
> With every thing that pretty is,
> My lady sweet, arise:
> Arise, arise. (*Cymbeline*, II.iii.11–25)

The song has a distinctly Catholic feel to it that hints at the Catholic identity of Imogen. The 'winking Mary-buds' are the most obvious example, but note also the preceding line, 'On chaliced flowers that lies'. 'Chaliced flowers' evokes, in the first instance, the campion flower with its chalice form and five heart-shaped leaves, and then Edmund Campion, the Jesuit martyr arrested by George Eliot who discovered him *lying* in a loft space at *Ly*ford Grange. So, why is it that Cloten appears to produce a Catholic song? There are two possibilities. The first is that the musicians are surreptitiously revealing the Catholic identity of Imogen under the nose of a dull-witted Cloten. The second and darker interpretation is that Cloten is cynically using Catholic imagery in an attempt to ensnare Imogen. This would anticipate the development later in the play when he will determine to rape Imogen while wearing the clothes of Posthumus.

At first there is no response to Cloten's efforts, but the King advises his son-in-law to persist:

> *Cymbeline:* Attend you here the door of our stern daughter?
> Will she not forth?
> *Cloten:* I have assailed her with music, but she vouchsafes no notice.
> *Cymbeline:* The exile of her minion is too new;
> She hath not yet forgot him: some more time
> Must wear the print of his remembrance out,
> And then she's yours.[11] (II.iii.36–43)

When she finally emerges she runs the gauntlet of her unwelcome wooer but outsmarts and outfaces him.

> *Cloten:* Good morrow, fairest: sister, your sweet hand.

---

[11] 'Minion' is a word often used of a male favourite of a king, and so had particular resonance in the Court of James I who doted openly on a Robert Carr, a 'gentleman of the bedchamber'. There is irony in its use here.

THE BELLS OF ST CLEMENTS

Imogen: Good morrow, sir. You lay out too much pains
                 For purchasing but trouble; the thanks I give
                 Is telling you that I am poor of thanks
                 And scarce can spare them.
Cloten: Still, I swear I love you.
Imogen: If you but said so, 'twere as deep with me:
                 If you swear still, your recompense is still
                 That I regard it not.
Cloten: This is no answer.
Imogen: But that you shall not say I yield being silent,
                 I would not speak. I pray you, spare me: 'faith,
                 I shall unfold equal discourtesy
                 To your best kindness: one of your great knowing
                 Should learn, being taught, forbearance.[12]
Cloten: To leave you in your madness, 'twere my sin:
                 I will not.
Imogen: Fools are not mad folks.
Cloten: Do you call me fool?
Imogen: As I am mad, I do:
                 If you'll be patient, I'll no more be mad;
                 That cures us both. I am much sorry, sir,
                 You put me to forget a lady's manners,
                 By being so verbal: and learn now, for all,
                 That I, which know my heart, do here pronounce,
                 By the very truth of it, I care not for you,
                 And am so near the lack of charity—
                 To accuse myself – I hate you; which I had rather
                 You felt than make't my boast.
Cloten: You sin against
                 Obedience, which you owe your father. For
                 The contract you pretend with that base wretch,
                 One bred of alms and foster'd with cold dishes,[13]
                 With scraps o' the court, it is no contract, none:
                 And though it be allow'd in meaner parties—
                 Yet who than he more mean? – to knit their souls,

---

[12] The exchange here and following seems to reflect the debate about religious toleration. The recusants would no longer be 'mad' (i.e. religiously transgressive) if they were allowed to practise their religion in peace.

[13] Roger Line was bred of *arms*, as in the arms of his family that he was entitled to wear, but he was 'fostered on cold dishes' as he was obliged to live on the leftovers of the Spanish Court in the form of his meagre Spanish pension.

	On whom there is no more dependency
	But brats and beggary, in self-figured knot;
	Yet you are curb'd from that enlargement by
	The consequence o' the crown, and must not soil
	The precious note of it with a base slave.
	A hilding for a livery, a squire's cloth,
	A pantler, not so eminent.
Imogen:	Profane fellow
	Wert thou the son of Jupiter and no more
	But what thou art besides, thou wert too base
	To be his groom: thou wert dignified enough,
	Even to the point of envy, if 'twere made
	Comparative for your virtues, to be styled
	The under-hangman of his kingdom, and hated
	For being preferred so well.
Cloten:	The south-fog rot him![14]
Imogen:	He never can meet more mischance than come
	To be but named of thee. His meanest garment,
	That ever hath but clipp'd his body, is dearer
	In my respect than all the hairs above thee,
	Were they all made such men. (II.iii.85–135)

It is quite possible, even likely, that Roger Line was 'named' – i.e. informed on – either by Anne Line's father or by someone close to him, and it was this that resulted in his arrest and subsequent banishment, a subject we shall come to presently. The fact that Roger Line was treated differently to William Higham (jnr), who was able to stay in the country, suggests the intervention of William Higham (snr). Certainly the actions of William Higham (snr) were harsh. Indeed, they call to mind the extreme reaction of Shylock when he learns that his single offspring, his beloved Jessica, has left him in order to convert and marry a gentile: 'I would my daughter were dead at my foot' (*Merchant of Venice*, III.i.87f) and 'she is damn'd for it' (III.i.31). However, in William Higham's defence, we must take into account the sincerely held view of many Puritans that Catholicism was essentially demonic. From their theological perspective, witchcraft and Catholic practices belonged in the same category, and either would clearly have been an appalling thing to

---

[14] The 'foggy south' is attested elsewhere (cf. *As You Like It*, III.v.52); nevertheless, Cloten's curse may be intended to recall either the proximity of Ringwood to the south coast of England or Roger Line's death in exile on the southern side of the English Channel.

discover about one's daughter. By the 1580s William Higham may have already buried both his youngest child and his first wife, making the loss of his only remaining daughter to the clutches of Satan all the more traumatic. When he turned to his Puritan friend Giles Alleyne, or to Reverend Gifford, the expert on witchcraft who preached in Maldon, what would they have suggested? The answer is surely prayers and fasting, but possibly exorcism too. During the 1580s exorcism certainly featured in both Protestant and Catholic practice, though accounts of such events differ sharply in terms of their reflection of the polemical issues of the day. For example, an exorcism conducted by a Catholic priest at Hackney and described in the Brudenell manuscript has various notes in the margin for the less observant reader, such as: 'The divel sweareth: & speaketh as Protestants use to doo'; 'The divel cannot abide holy vestments'; 'The divel and Protestants cannot abide Hollywater'.[15] Thankfully, on this occasion, the Devil was 'expulsed' after being 'tormented' by 'Our B.Ladie'. Of course, for William Higham, on the other side of the fence, Catholics who invoked the Blessed Virgin Mary (such as his daughter) could be summoning a demon instead. Shakespeare parodies the too-ready resort to exorcism in *The Comedy of Errors*, but it would be a mistake to interpret this as a dismissive verdict on the existence of the spirit world.

Again in defence of William Higham, it is worth noting that Europe was being convulsed by a Christian civil war, and an increasingly nationalistic England was busy stoking it up on the Protestant side. By the 1585 Treaty of Nonsuch, England agreed to supply troops to the Calvinists in the Netherlands who had rebelled against their Spanish overlords. As a consequence, the Earl of Leicester, commander of the English force, was appointed governor of the United Provinces. The treaty was a response to the siege of Antwerp, the capital of the Dutch rebels, but it came too late to prevent the fall of that city to the Spanish. Thus, when Roger Line fled to Antwerp a year later, he was fleeing across no-man's land in the midst of a bitter conflict, and his father-in-law's Calvinist friends in Maldon are unlikely to have been impressed. Attitudes engendered by sectarian conflict could be very extreme. The 1572 St Bartholomew's Day massacre and the 'Spanish Fury' of 1576 (when rampaging Spanish troops had sacked the city of Antwerp) confirmed in Protestant minds the Catholic propensity for treachery and violence, but without engendering a notably more peaceable response on their own side. Inevitably, violence hardened theological divisions whereby each side saw the other as the enemies of God. In 1580, when a force of Spanish and Italian

---

[15] Brudenell, 1.485–491 (on the exorcism of Sara Cheney at the house of Lord Vaux, 1585).

troops surrendered to the English under Lord Grey at the Irish town of Smerwick, not only were the soldiers massacred in cold blood, but the priests and the women and children inside the surrendered fort were killed as well. Grey wrote to Queen Elizabeth of his success, 'so hath it pleased the Lord of Hosts to deliver your enemies into [your] highness hands', and his words were echoed in popular depictions in which such victories were not merely over enemies, but over 'Roman enemies', against whom such atrocity was clearly felt to be understandable, if not thoroughly well deserved.[16] Over the following decades, Catholic Ireland would be subjected to a scorched-earth policy, whereby famine was used as a weapon to kill tens of thousands of people, significantly reducing the native population.[17]

Let us return from the world of sixteenth-century warfare, whether of spiritual or temporal varieties, to the pleasantries of St Clement Danes Church in the Strand. In its present incarnation it was built by Sir Christopher Wren and is now the Church of the Royal Air Force. The parish is proud of its association with various notable figures, including William Webb Ellis, the inventor of rugby football, who was rector of the parish for twelve years. The medieval church that once stood on the site has not survived, but the sixteenth-century parish registers have, and they include entries for the marriage of 'Roger Lyne & Alice Higham', and, as it happens, the christening of Robert Cecil, 'sonne of the Lord high Treasurer', whose mother was Lady Guldeford's cousin. These echoes from a conflicted time seem to have been entirely lost from the accepted parish history, apart from what may be a rather curious remnant. The parish celebrates its connection with a well-known nursery rhyme whose origins are unknown, but which is thought to date from the seventeenth century:

> 'Oranges and Lemons,' say the bells of St Clement's;
> 'You owe me five farthings,' say the bells of St Martin's;
> 'When will you pay me?' say the bells of Old Bailey;
> 'When I grow rich,' say the bells of Shoreditch;
> 'When will that be?' say the bells of Stepney;
> 'I do not know,' say the great bells of Bow;
> 'Here comes a candle to light you to bed,
> Here comes a chopper to chop off your head,
> Chip chop chip chop – the last man's dead.'

[16] Cooper, *The Queen's Agent*, 249.
[17] Cooper, *The Queen's Agent*, 249ff.

This is the rhyme with an accompanying game in which two children make an arch with their arms like the entrance of a church and the other children singing the song dance through it round and round until the last ominous lines, when the arch becomes a trap that catches a child on the word 'dead'. There is a dramatic contrast between the happy start and the harsh ending that is very obvious, but there is a more subtle hint early on of the turn that will come at the end. Old Bailey was not a church: 'Old Bailey Lane' was the name of the street where the Sessions House was located, and on the other side of the road stood Newgate prison. Eventually, both buildings were replaced and the court that became known as the Old Bailey was built on the site of the old prison. In the seventeenth century, the court house on Old Bailey Lane did not have a peal of bells, so the 'bells of Old Bailey' must refer to the bells of the church of St Sepulchre, also on Old Bailey Lane. It was the bell of St Sepulchre that would signal to the condemned in Newgate prison that the time had come to begin the three-mile journey to the Tyburn gallows. Bells rung at a wedding or to celebrate national rejoicing are a happy sound, but on other occasions they had a melancholy resonance. Shakespeare would write: 'It was the owl that shriek'd, the fatal bellman, / Which gives the stern'st good-night', and Donne would title his best-known meditation with a death-divining epigram:

Nunc lento sonitu dicunt, Morieris.
Now, this Bell tolling softly for another,
saies to me, Thou must die.[18]

Anne Line would have heard the bell of St Sepulchre many times, as her lodgings in Fetter Lane were less than half a mile away.

It has been pointed out many times that 'Oranges and Lemons' may have something to do with the journey from Newgate prison to the execution site at Tyburn, and it would be remiss of us if we failed to consider the possibility that it may refer specifically to Anne Line and to the executions of the two priests who died alongside her and who were killed by being cut into pieces. To my knowledge this has never been suggested before, but it fits the poem and the game that goes with it to a remarkable degree. The general objection to the Tyburn interpretation has been that there are a number of variants of the poem, including the earliest published version from 1744, that do not have the final two lines. Moreover, similar rhymes featuring the voices of various church bells occur in other places in England and other countries in

---

[18] *Macbeth* II.ii.3f; Donne, 'Meditation XVII', in *Devotions upon Emergent Occasions*, 86.

Europe. However, it may be the case that around the time of Anne Line's death, an existing rhyme was adapted to make it fit her particular circumstances. This would explain the radical twist to the more conventional tradition that we see in the well-known version given above. There is a shocking element to it as though it commemorates shocking events, and certainly a rhyme could perform the function of keeping historical events alive in the collective memory – witness 'Remember, remember, the fifth of November, gunpowder, treason and plot'. As it happens, the year of the Gunpowder Plot, 1605, recorded the earliest known instance of a play about Dick Whittington, whose story may also have some relevance to this discussion. Whittington was a historical figure who prospered as a merchant in the late fourteenth and early fifteenth centuries and served several times as the Lord Mayor of London. The folk-tale version of his life has him travelling to London as a poor young man, to seek his fortune in the town where he has heard that the streets are paved with gold. Having failed to find any gold, a downhearted Whittington begins to make his way home, and gets as far as Highgate Hill when he hears the bells of Bow. They seem to speak to him, saying 'turn again Whittington, Lord Mayor of London', prompting him to turn back to the town, where he subsequently becomes rich – though the efficacy of his cat – and eventually is made Lord Mayor. What has this to do with Anne Line? Well, Anne Line's most distinguished antecedent was her mother's uncle, Sir John Alleyne, who was twice appointed Lord Mayor of London during the reign of Henry VIII, and gave in his will a 'rich collar of gold' to be worn by the Lord Mayor and his successors.[19] This brings us neatly to another link between Anne Line and Dick Whittington, because a significant bequest in Whittington's will was used to fund a major refurbishment of Newgate prison – Anne Line's home in the weeks before her execution, and where she could have seen for herself Whittington's symbol, the cat, carved above one of the archways. Perhaps somewhere among these associations was the element that prompted a rewrite of a poem about talking bells, done in such a way that it could serve discreetly to commemorate a martyr, and a woman whose fortunes in London led not to riches but, from the joyful wedding bells of St Clement's, via the ominous bells of Old Bailey, to the payment in blood demanded at Tyburn. She died with two young priests who had travelled to England – like the oranges and lemons – from Spain, where they had been at the seminary at Valladolid. She was lighted to her final rest by the candles of Candlemas, the feast she was

---

[19] Stow, quoted in, Elizabeth Furdell, 'Allen, Sir John', ODNB. Among Sir John's bequests was £10 for poor maidens' marriages (*ibid.*).

celebrating when she was arrested. The five farthings would recall in recusant ears the five wounds of Christ, symbolising the price Anne Line was made to pay for her faith. The theme of payment of a debt due, which seems to be the main concern of the bells, fits the Candlemas cross-quarter day when rents traditionally came due, and the use of 'rich' in relation to 'Shoreditch' may be a reference to Anne Line's Puritan cousin and collector of rents Giles Alleyne, owner of the Shoreditch site of The Theatre. How appropriate that a woman who instructed young children should be commemorated in such a way. Then again, all this could be mere coincidence. And that, precisely, is the beauty of hiding subversive material in a children's rhyme.

7

To the Counter in Wood Street

John Gerard

The Jesuit priest John Gerard had at least this much in common with William Shakespeare: they were both born in the year 1564, making them similar in age to Anne and Roger Line. A tall dark man with curly black hair and a ready smile, Gerard drew eyes that looked straight through Garnet, his Jesuit superior, but this very stylishness could prove a stunning disguise. He concealed himself thus: 'for the most part attired costly and defencibly in buff leather garnished with gold or silver lace, satin doublet, and velvet hose of all colours with clocks corresponding, and rapiers and daggers gilt or silvered'.[1] When the wife of Sir Everard Digby resolved to become a Catholic she asked a friend to find her a priest and was astonished to be informed that her house guest (John Gerard) would suffice. 'How can he possibly be a priest?' she exclaimed. 'Why, the man lives like a courtier. Haven't you watched him playing cards with my husband?' But while Gerard was at ease in such company he was also a deeply serious man who proved resolute under torture, and had the gumption to escape from the Tower of London on a rope slung between the window of the Lanthorne Tower and his waiting friends on the other side of the exterior wall. This was the unlikely priest who would draw Anne Line into the service of the Jesuits. By 1609 he had left England for good, and at the behest of his superiors wrote an absorbing account of his experiences on the English mission that is a prime source for what we know of Anne Line's family.[2]

The Indenture

John Gerard writes of Anne Line's brother: 'When his father learned that he, too, had become a Catholic, he sold the estates that formed his patrimony, in

---

[1] *Hat. Cal.* xi.365.
[2] Gerard, *Autobiography of an Elizabethan*, translated from the Latin by Philip Caraman.

order to keep him out of them. Their yearly income was reckoned at six thousand florins.'[3] Intriguingly, the legal document (called an indenture) relating to this disinheritance survives in the collection of the British Library. It consists of a slightly yellowing piece of vellum measuring approximately 24 by 20 inches, covered on one side with writing, and neatly folding up to show the following description on the outside: 'Mr Heigham his lease to Mr Lewyn for 2000 ... of Maldon Hills', and the words 'Per me Guilihelmn Higham parrens' [By me William Higham father].[4] Among the list of witnesses is one Roger Line. It is this document that enables us to identify beyond any reasonable doubt that Anne Line is the same person as Alice Higham of Jenkyn Maldons.

Several place names occur in the legal document: William Higham senior is described as 'of Jenkyn Maldon in the parish of Hastleighe', and the principal piece of land adjoins 'the manor or house called Fflanderswick in the parish of Purloughe' (Purleigh); Fambridge Ferry and Woodham Mortimer are also mentioned. These are the land holdings that once belonged to the Hospital of St Giles. There is a separate parcel of land at 'Woodham Mortymor', a little closer to Chelmsford. Roger and Anne Line are also mentioned, though Anne is called Alice, as in the marriage record: 'Roger Lyne of Ringwood in the countie of Southt [Southampton] gent & Alice nowe his wief daughter of the said William Higham'. There follows a specific preclusion from them pressing any future claim on the property or from taking any action against the new leaseholders, implying a prior agreement that a portion of the property would form Alice's dowry. It is witnessed thus: 'Sealled & delivered by the within named William Higham the father, in the presence of William Higham Junior' and, in addition to four other names, 'Roger Lyne'.

The principal holding is described as being bounded to the west by the road from Maldon south to 'Ffambridge fforrie' (Fambridge Ferry, a distance of six miles) and on the east by a property in the parish of Purleigh. Curiously enough, on the east side of the Fambridge road today and due east from Purleigh village, is a property called Clockhouse Farm.[5]

The land was transferred by the indenture to a certain William Lewyn,

---

[3] Gerard, 83.
[4] British Library, *Additional Charter 5982*, noted by Shanahan in 'Anne Line, nee Heigham: where was she born?'
[5] The house in Dunmow that is said to have belonged to William Higham is called the Clock House. In *Cymbeline*, Imogen weeps, ''twixt clock and clock' (III.iv.42).

'doctor of law', and his sons.[6] This William Lewyn, or Lewin, is well known from other sources as an ecclesiastical lawyer who rose to considerable heights through the patronage of a certain William Cecil, the Lord Burghley.[7] He may have been the tutor to Cecil's daughter Anne, and when she married the Earl of Oxford in 1571, Lewyn was appointed receiver of the revenues to the earl, who had significant holdings in Essex. Lewyn's father-in-law had a similar role because, as foedary of Essex, he was responsible for collecting revenues for the Court of Wards. These circumstances gave Lewyn specialised legal knowledge, an inside track to land sales, and friends in the highest places, a combination both intimidating and lucrative from time immemorial. There is no suggestion of foul play in his transaction with William Higham – he was merely the willing participant in the disinheritance – but this was not the first time Dr Lewyn had used legal means to try and get his hands on land claimed by Catholics, and not always honestly. In 1580, a dispute had erupted between Lewyn (acting for a man called Anthony Luther) and the recusant musician William Byrd over the rights to a lease of a manor called Battyshall. Lewyn's case seemed to depend entirely on hearsay, but when it came to court, Lewyn packed the jury with kinsfolk and various associates who consequently 'gave ther verdicte against Wm Byrd Whereuppon. he and all his. is lyke to be undone'.[8] The case went to arbitration, and at this stage Byrd was in a stronger position, as one of the arbiters was his friend Sir John Petre. In the event, the case lapsed when Byrd's brother purchased the property and then sold it on; however, according to the statement of the arbiters, William Byrd could have faced financial ruin had his brother not done so, and had the case gone against him.[9]

William Higham (snr) had money to spend from the disposal of his son's inheritance and his daughter's dowry, and it is said that the Clock House at Dunmow was rebuilt in 1586 or 1589, and in grand fashion. Having lost one child and disowned the other two, perhaps he made this fine house, with its Dutch-style frontage of brick and its new-fangled one-handed clock, into something he felt he could be proud to leave to posterity.

---

[6] Ownership of the neighbouring manor of Flanderswick had been obtained by William Lewyn, Anthony Luther and Thomas Gooch in 1582 (British Library. *Additional Charter* 5981).
[7] See Houlbrooke, 'Lewin, William (*d.* 1598)', ODNB.
[8] SP 12/157/59–61. Quoted more fully in Harley 82f. Luther appears to have been Lewyn's brother-in-law from his first marriage; Gooch, named re Flanderswick, was probably a son-in-law from his second – see Nina Green [http://www.oxford-shakespeare.com/Chancery/C_54–1145_Part_25_Le.pdf]. Battyshall and Flanderswick were both properties previously owned by the Earl of Oxford. As Member of Parliament for Rochester, Lewyn served on the committee for the bill against recusants of 1593.
[9] See Harley, 54f, 81–84.

The Counter in Wood Street

It is clear that the threat of disinheritance was initially just that, a threat designed to induce a change of heart in the three young converts. The Higham indenture was signed on 1 July 1585, and the Lines were still hoping for Roger to reconsider his position the following year. But by this time the stakes had been raised even higher, as Roger and his brother-in-law William were arrested at a Catholic Mass.[10] Subsequently, as John Gerard records with some pride,

> [Roger's] father, or perhaps his uncle (he was heir to both), lay on his death-bed and sent him a message in prison.[11] In it he begged him to conform and attend church at least once, for otherwise his patrimony would go to his younger brother. The good man replied firmly: 'If I must desert either the world or God, then I desert the world, for it is good to cleave to God.' So both his father's and his uncle's estate went to his younger brother.[12]

The arrests are recorded in a list relating to the Counter prison, of 'Prestes and Recusants ... nowe ther remanynge'. The list appears to have been made in June 1586 but the arrests must have been before 3 February of that year. The relevant record is as follows:

> Willm Highame and Roger Lyne gent. they were taken wythout byshopsgate at Masse wth blackborne Alias tomson that was hanged: they are in execucyon ffor C [100] Marks a pece they have been dyvers tymes examyned before Mr Justys Yonge.[13]

Gerard says of William that 'he kept a priest in his house, a Father Thomson, whose martyrdom I witnessed later'.[14] And, according to Challoner, Richard Thomson, alias Blackburn, had been Anne Line's confessor and was executed at Tyburn on 20 April 1586 (we have here a typical example of

---

[10] The precise location of the arrests is unknown. Anstruther suggests the house of Robert Bellamy (*Seminary Priests*, Vol.1, 351) but Bellamy apparently lived 'at the sign of the Tambourin' in Holborn, (*CSP Foreign*, Jan-July 1589, 365) which conflicts with the report of the men being taken outside Bishopsgate.
[11] It was in fact his uncle (husband of Anne Line senior) who was dying.
[12] Gerard 83. Much of Richard Line's inheritance was in fact used to endow the Ringwood Grammar School that had been founded by him in 1577. This school continued for 399 years, eventually closing down in 1976 after a fall in pupil numbers.
[13] SP12/190 f.78 (transcript in CRS 2, 249f).
[14] Gerard, 83.

Elizabethan spelling: Blackborne is Blackburn, Tomson is Thomson, etc.). The phrase 'in execucyon' is probably less ominous than it looks, and we may assume it refers to the execution of a writ. The two young men would have been charged under the statute of 1581 entitled, rather petulantly, 'An Act to retain the Queen's Majesty's Subjects in their due Obedience', according to which, 'every person which shall willingly hear mass shall forfeit the sum of one hundred marks and suffer imprisonment for a year'.[15] They were treated leniently, for under the same statute it was an act of treason for a Protestant to be reconciled to the Catholic Church, a charge both men were open to. The record of the incident does not tell us whether Roger Line and William Higham were arrested at William Higham's house, although the fact that they were arrested with Higham's chaplain suggests as much. It would be interesting to know this for certain because it would place Higham's home in London, not far from The Theatre in Shoreditch and the haunts of actors and playwrights.

In one fell swoop, Anne Line had husband, brother and priest taken from her, and we might have supposed that she could at least take some comfort in the fact that she had escaped arrest herself. However, it seems she had aspirations that readers today might struggle to understand. Challoner writes approvingly of her 'desire ... of ending her days by martyrdom; on which account she bore a holy envy to priests and others, who seemed to be in a fairer way to that happy end than she, or any other of her sex'.[16] He continues: 'She also related to her confessor a vision which she had seen of our Lord in the Blessed Sacrament, bearing His cross and inviting her to follow him.'[17] The priest to whom she imparted this information – William Thomson – promised that in the event of facing martyrdom himself (as he did on 20 April 1586), he would 'pray for her that she might obtain the like happiness'.[18] This desire for martyrdom is also attested by Gerard, who was told in no uncertain terms, 'I naturally want more than anything to die for Christ, but it is too much to hope that it will be by the executioner's hand.' She surmised, 'Possibly Our Lord will let me be taken one day with a priest and be put in some cold and filthy dungeon where I won't be able to live very long in this wretched life.' When she was in due course condemned, 'her delight was in the Lord, "and the Lord granted the petitions of her heart"'.[19] It is tempting to pass over this embracement of suffering because it can

---

[15] 23 Elizabeth, c.1., see Tanner, 150–154; 153.
[16] Challoner, 258.
[17] Challoner, 258.
[18] Challoner, 258.
[19] Gerard, 84.

seem so outlandish to modern ears, and yet this is the authentic voice of Christian martyrdom, a tradition that goes back to the earliest days of the Church. The suffering of the martyr has power to redeem, because it is the will of God that the sufferings of the believers be united to the sufferings of Christ in the great sacrifice that redeems the world. This is the sense in which Catholics understood St Paul's teaching that we make up in our own bodies what is lacking (incomplete) in the suffering of Christ (Col 1:24). The sacrifice of Christ is incomplete until the believers unite their own sufferings to his. This makes a little more sense of the enthusiasm for martyrdom; otherwise meaningless suffering takes on a positive value as an offering made to God and becomes powerfully redemptive.

Challoner has little more to say about Anne Line's spirituality, but he tells us that 'her soul was strong and vigorous, and ever tending to exercises in Christian perfection'. He continues, 'Her devotion was unfeigned; she received the Blessed Sacrament at least once a week, and always with abundance of tears.' These are things noted by priests. Her conversation, he declares, 'was edifying, willingly discoursing on spiritual subjects, and not on worldly vanities'.[20]

Early in February 1586, no less a personage than Secretary to the Queen, Francis Walsingham, was involved in the case of Anne Line's husband. It is thought most likely that the actual arrest took place sometime in January, though this is conjecture and it is quite possible that the arrests happened sometime before. All we have is the following, in another list of people held on account of religion at the prison called the Counter in Wood Street: 'Roger Line comitted by S^r ffra Walsingham the iij^d of ffebruary 1585.'[21] For legal purposes the year was held to start on 25 March, so a date recorded as 3 February 1585 actually corresponds to the year 1586 in modern reckoning.[22] This means that Roger's committal took place on the third anniversary of his marriage. This may be sheer coincidence of course, but it could also imply that the defiant marriage of a pair of recusant gentlefolk had attracted the attention of Secretary Walsingham and he was using the wedding anniversary to show his disapproval.[23] If so, it may indicate a broader awareness of this story in the 1580s than is evident from the history books.

---

[20] Challoner, 258.
[21] SP 12/195 f.95.
[22] It was probably an error in the publication of these records in 1906 (CRS 2, 271), putting the committal date as 3 February 1583, that led Clara Longworth (*Shakespeare: A Portrait Restored*, 240) to conclude that William and Roger were arrested during the nuptial mass. Her information came from the Catholic historian Fr. Newdigate – presumably he was aware of the 3 February wedding.
[23] NB: legal proceedings were likely to take place around this date due to the Candlemas cross-quarter day, so the coincidence is perhaps less surprising than it may at first appear.

Be that as it may, while Roger Line was sent to the Counter, it appears from the following remarks by Gerard that William Higham was initially sent to a notorious prison near Blackfriars:

> [William] ... was put in Bridewell with the priest who lodged with him. This is the prison which they use for vagabonds, making them do hard labour under the lash. There I visited him and found him working the great tread-mill dripping with perspiration.[24]

Another Jesuit, the priest Robert Southwell, wrote a graphic description of this prison in a letter in 1590:

> Almost all who are taken now may expect to taste of Bridewell, that place of shame; it is a slaughter-house where the cruelties inflicted are scarcely credible. The tasks imposed are continuous and beyond ordinary strength, and even the sick are driven to them under the lash. Food is not only of the scantiest, but so disfigured that it cannot be swallowed without retching ... Bedding is straw matted with stinking ordure ... It is the one Purgatory that all we Catholics dread, where Topcliffe and Young, butchers, have complete licence to torture. Yet whatever happens to us, I know we shall be equal to it ... and our Lord will speak peace to His people that His glory may dwell in our land.[25]

---

[24] Gerard, 83. Gerard is known to have visited another prisoner at Bridewell sometime between 17 May 1584 and Easter 1586.
[25] Letter of Southwell to Aquaviva, Jan 1590, see *CRS* 5: 329f; Devlin, *The Life of Robert Southwell*, 211.

8

The Babington Plot

During the summer of 1586, it seems that William Higham was released from the purgatory of Bridewell to join Roger Line and a handful of other religious prisoners in the Counter, his name appearing under his brother-in-law's in the list quoted above: 'Willm Higham comitted by his honor also the xxxth of July 1585'.[1] This date appears to be anachronistic. We know that William Higham was not in the Counter for a whole year because he was in Bridewell in the spring. It could be that the agent Nicholas Berden, who was responsible for producing the list, has invented this committal date to make it easier to get Higham released early by making it look like he had completed the full year of his prison sentence. Berden, also known as Thomas Rogers, had been a servant to a gentleman called Gilbert Gifford who converted to Catholicism and attended the seminary of Douay. Rogers/Berden also became a Catholic and was accepted into Catholic circles in London, but both he and Gifford were turned by Walsingham and worked as government agents.[2] By helping or appearing to help Catholics like William Higham to get released from prison, Berden could reinforce his cover at the same time as elicit bribes. Meanwhile, the Catholics thought he was their man in Walsingham's household.

Roger Line and William Higham appear in a third list from the Counter, but with some additional information:

Lyne   ) gentilmen under
Higham) xix yeares[3]

This list is in a paper filed under 'December ?' [*sic*] in the Calendar of State Papers, and contains an explanatory note thus: 'Prisoners about London for

---

[1] SP 12/195 f.95.
[2] Cooper, *The Queen's Agent*, 183–185.
[3] SP 12/195 f.133, pub. in CRS 2: 255. Roger Line would actually have been 21 in the spring of 1586 when this list was compiled, and William 19 or 20. Again, this comment could be designed to facilitate their release in order to collect a bribe.

Relligion, which are mete to be banished or otherwise disposed of'. This led to the assumption that both these young men were banished in December 1586, but this is not the case. They certainly ended up abroad – William was in Rome by 1598 and Roger in Belgium in 1593 – but we now have information that enables us to clarify the sequence of events.[4] The reason for the filing under December is unclear (it may relate to a discussion in the Privy Council), but the papers actually contain data from the previous summer, and we know that the summer of 1586 was an exceptionally interesting one for Secretary Walsingham, as the events known as the Babington Plot that would lead to the execution of Mary Queen of Scots were beginning to play out.

Walsingham had contrived by the use of a double agent to set up what to Mary Queen of Scots and her supporters appeared to be a secure line of communication from her place of confinement at Chartley Hall. Various messages passed back and forth, and every single one was intercepted and deciphered with the aid of an expert code-breaker called Thomas Phelippes. Now Phelippes was also a skilled forger, and this meant that he could make copies of the original messages that could be passed on to the intended recipients, while the originals that might prove useful as evidence at a later date could be retained. An additional bonus was that a message could be embellished in the process: an incriminating postscript, for example, could be carefully encoded and added in what appeared to be the original handwriting. A more satisfactory arrangement for a spymaster could hardly be imagined. Secretary Walsingham had only to wait for his targets to incriminate themselves, and if they declined to do so, or he wished to hurry the process on, he could simply invent the incriminating evidence himself. The details of the Babington Plot are beyond the scope of this book, but there are certain aspects that are relevant. The first is that the crucial letters that would lead to the beheading of Queen Mary, widespread arrests, and the hanging, drawing and quartering of fourteen men were sent during the July of 1586, and this gives us a reason why Walsingham suddenly required a list of 'Prisoners about London ... mete to be banished or otherwise disposed of': he needed to free up prison space to accommodate expected new arrivals.[5]

The second noteworthy fact about the Babington Plot is that one of the

---

[4] According to the records of the Jesuit order, William Higham was enrolled on 20 December 1598 in Rome and then early in 1599 obtained permission to go to Spain, where he served as a brother at the English College at Valladolid, dying there in 1625. His birth is recorded as 1566, in the diocese of Colchester, Essex (McCoog, *English and Welsh Jesuits, 1555–1650, Part 2*, 206).

[5] Hence, *CRS* 2: 253.

fourteen men executed was Thomas Salusbury, elder brother of John Salusbury, the gentleman from North Wales to whom *Loves Martyr* was dedicated ten years later. *Loves Martyr* was the book that contained 'The Phoenix and the Turtle' as Shakespeare's contribution. Thomas Salusbury was a close friend of Babington and was accused of pledging to raise a rebellion in North Wales in support of Babington's wider scheme. From the scaffold he urged that Catholics should not attempt to change the religion of the country by force, but left the crowd in no doubt about his own faith, declaring, 'I have lyved a catholique and so will I dye.'[6] The rebels were executed in two batches at St Giles' Inn Fields, the first seven on 20 September being castrated and disembowelled while still alive. These were the ones who had supposedly pleaded guilty, and included Babington. According to Stow's Chronicle, Salusbury was among the seven who pleaded not guilty and were executed on the following day, when they were permitted to hang until unconscious before being cut down and cut up. After his death, his younger brother John was able to inherit his lands and title. This privilege was denied to another of the executed men, a gentleman called Edward Jones, who was treated more harshly. He had apparently become a Catholic under the influence of Thomas Salusbury; like the Salusbury family, he came from Denbighshire in Wales. Despite his pleas that his 'posterity' should not be punished on his account, his lands were attainted to the Crown (i.e. confiscated) and a substantial portion later granted to Robert Cecil. Among the peripheral figures who were imprisoned as a result of the affair was a certain Thomas Gerard, thought to be the father of John Gerard, who was abroad at this time training as a Jesuit.

One of the men who shared the fate of Thomas Salusbury in September 1586 was a Robert Gage whose brother was affianced to a young woman called Margaret Copley, who duly became Mrs Gage. Fourteen and a half years later, in February 1601, Mrs Gage was arrested with Anne Line at a house in London, in Fetter Lane. Back in 1586, Robert Gage appears to have been a friend of Anne Line's brother William, as we see from a report by a spy called Francis Milles to Secretary Walsingham that reveals, rather alarmingly, the company that William Higham was keeping at the very time Walsingham was preparing to make his arrests:

> At the Castle there supped with Anthony Babington one Thornborough a merchant, one Savage a young gentleman of Staple Inn, and Pooley [*spy*], known to him, a man, as [Berden] thinks, discovered a

---

[6] Kenyon MSS, 614. Quoted in Roberts, 'Salisbury [Salesbury], Thomas (1561x4–1586), conspirator', ODNB.

good while since by Babington. With [Berden] supped Edward Shelley, who brought with him Carleton the priest [*Richard Sherwood*], one Higham lately condemned for hearing a mass, and enlarged out of the 'Compter,' [*the Counter on Wood Street*] and one Robert Gage. He assures [Berden] that Ballard was on Tuesday last in the city – the day that the messengers told him [Milles] they had by attending on himself lost a great booty of him – but by the name of Black Foskewe, and that he himself brought the said Ballard on Wednesday last towards night to his house to ride into Sussex. From thence Gage expects him assuredly in the city again to-morrow or Monday next, and promises to bring [Berden] and him together.[7]

This letter is dated 30 July 1586, and Milles tells us that his information 'was sent by Berd. yesternight, at 7 o'clock. Preparation was made for the apprehension, but the party was in neither of the places supposed.'[8] John Savage had allegedly sworn an oath to assassinate the Queen; John Ballard and a secular priest were the first to be detained. Both were among the first batch to be put to death on 20 September.

The third pertinent fact about the Babington Plot is that Catholics believed there had been a frame-up. The following sentence from *An Epistle of Comfort* (1587–88, p. 21) has been taken as Robert Southwell's verdict on Walsingham's scheming:

> For so the devill when he seeth, that by open pursute he can not overthrowe us, he covertly cowcheth him selfe in the shadowes, & bryers of worldlye vanityes, and delightsome allurements, therby to entrapp us ere we preventne his traynes.

In a private letter to the Catholic exile Verstegan, Southwell was rather more specific: 'The matter of Babington was wholly of their plotting and forging, of purpose to make Catholikes odious and to cut of[f] the Queen of Scots. The chief plotters were the Secretary [Walsingham], Lecester and the Treasurer [Cecil]'.[9] In a later edition of Southwell's *The Humble Supplication*, in which he pleads the Catholic case, we find, 'It is further known that the coppie of that letter which *Babington* sent to the Queene of Scots was brought

---

[7] SP 53/18 f.185. Black Foskewe is John Ballard, who went by the name of Captain Fortescue.
[8] SP 53/18 f.185.
[9] Verstegan, *The Letters and Despatches of Richard Verstegan*, 3.

ready penned by Poolie from Mr Secretary.'[10] The possibility that Shakespeare was in sympathy with such views is suggested by his furious play *Titus Andronicus*, which features a forged letter planted by that purest of villains, Aaron the Moor, who then 'finds it' and brandishes it in feigned horror. This concocted evidence condemns two innocent brothers to death. Was he thinking of two victims of the Babington debacle in particular? I think he probably was, perhaps the two Bellamy brothers, who lost their lives in the aftermath despite having no part in the plot itself. Shakespeare barely conceals the identity of Aaron the Moor, as 'the Moor' was Queen Elizabeth's nickname for her Secretary Walsingham. Shakespeare was at the very least touching a raw nerve. The Babington Plot and its aftermath evoked horrific memories for Catholics, as is plain from the Jesuit William Weston's description:

> [a] sudden hurricane of persecution ... it raged for several months in its wild fury and its savagery beyond human endurance, now (I hear) it is less severe. It is not that they are sparing any Catholic, man or woman, but simply that it is impossible for such a violent disturbance of property not to bring with it great disorder in all parts and the imminent ruin of the whole country.[11]

The numerous arrests and alarming reports stemming from the government were accompanied by a more general aggression towards 'the papists', that was exploited by sundry cattle thieves and those who had scores to settle. While many Catholics had their own stories of loss, such as the Bellamy family losing one son through being tortured to death in prison and another on the scaffold, these private griefs found a collective focus in the dramatic execution of Mary Queen of Scots. When Verstegan published his *Theatrum crudelitatum haereticorum nostril temporis* in Antwerp in 1592 – a book designed to illustrate to a continental audience the horrors of the persecution of Catholics in England – it was the execution of Mary Queen of Scots that formed the climax.[12] Back in England, Southwell would write of her in the poem 'Decease Release':

> Alive a Queen, now dead I am a saint;
> Once Mary called, my name now Martyr is;

---

[10] Verstegan, 37.
[11] W.W. to C.A. 10 May 1587. F.G. 651, f. 48. quoted in Caraman, *Henry Garnet*, 38.
[12] See Dillon, *The Construction of Martyrdom in the English Catholic Community, 1535–1603*, 272–276.

> From earthly reign debarred by restraint,
> In lieu whereof I reign in heavenly bliss ...
>
> Rue not my death, rejoice at my repose;
> It was no death to me but to my woe;
> The bud was opened to let out the rose,
> The chain was loosed to let the captive go.[13]

Robert Southwell landed in England with Henry Garnet in July 1586, just as the storm of the Babington Plot was brewing. They separated on arrival and Southwell headed for London, where he made contact with his fellow Catholics by quietly entering the Clink prison as a visitor, having bribed the jailer. The authorities had wind of his arrival in London, but he quietly slipped out of town to attend a gathering at a country house at Hurleyford in the Thames valley, that included Garnet, Gerard and William Byrd. By the time the authorities had put out that he had left London he was heading back in again, in response, it is thought, to an invitation to preach the sermon at the Marshalsea prison where Catholics had arranged a Mass for the feast of St Mary Magdalene (22 July). Walsingham would receive a report from a spy who was at this Mass, identifying various members of the congregation but not the priest. No doubt the rapidly developing Babington affair was drawing every ounce of attention, and matters of less immediate concern were disregarded. The incriminating letter that would be the death of Mary Queen of Scots was in Walsingham's hands as early as 19 July, and the first arrest took place on 4 August. By this time William Higham had been freed on surety and Roger Line had also been released from prison, but in his case it was into banishment, implying perhaps that his marriage had drawn a special kind of spite and Anne Line's father had achieved a bitter victory over the deprived heir of Ringwood. It is possible, though less likely, that Roger Line was released on a similar bond of surety to William Higham's but chose to flee to the Continent. Whatever the case, Roger's eyes had met Anne Line's for the last time, and it seems that in that brief period between his release from jail and his enforced departure, Anne had become pregnant. The son to whom she gave birth would never set eyes on his father.

---

[13] Robert Southwell, 'Decease Release', in Miola, *Early Modern Catholicism: An Anthology of Primary Sources*, 197 (lines 13ff.).

9

Separation

We have seen that King Cymbeline was so angered by his daughter's marriage that he ordered the banishment of her new husband. In *Cymbeline* Act I, Scene iii, Posthumus has sailed into exile on a boat, leaving his servant to report the news to his distraught wife:

Imogen:	I would thou grew'st unto the shores o' the haven,
	And question'dst every sail: if he should write
	And not have it, 'twere a paper lost,
	As offer'd mercy is.[1] What was the last
	That he spake to thee?
Pisanio:	It was his queen, his queen![2]
Imogen:	Then waved his handkerchief?
Pisanio:	And kiss'd it, madam.
Imogen:	Senseless Linen![3] happier therein than I!
	And that was all?
Pisanio:	No, madam; for so long
	As he could make me with this eye or ear
	Distinguish him from others, he did keep
	The deck, with glove, or hat, or handkerchief,
	Still waving, as the fits and stirs of 's mind
	Could best express how slow his soul sail'd on,
	How swift his ship.
Imogen:	Thou shouldst have made him
	As little as a crow, or less, ere left
	To after-eye him.[4]

---

[1] A close friend of Roger Line wrote to Anne's brother William and the paper was indeed lost, as it is now in the collection of State Papers, suggesting that it was intercepted en route. Discussed below.
[2] The word 'queen' (cwen) occurs in old English poetry, meaning wife, especially of a nobleman or important individual.
[3] Linen may be a pun on Line. See Epilogue.
[4] There is some evidence of Papists being referred to as crows. It may be a codeword here.

Pisanio:	Madam, so I did.
Imogen:	I would have broke mine eye-strings; crack'd them, but
	To look upon him, till the diminution
	Of space had pointed him sharp as my needle,
	Nay, follow'd him, till he had melted from
	The smallness of a gnat to air, and then
	Have turn'd mine eye and wept.[5] But, good Pisanio,
	When shall we hear from him?
Pisanio:	Be assured, madam,
	With his next vantage.
Imogen:	I did not take my leave of him, but had
	Most pretty things to say: ere I could tell him
	How I would think on him at certain hours
	Such thoughts and such, or I could make him swear
	The shes of Italy should not betray
	Mine interest and his honour, or have charged him,
	At the sixth hour of morn, at noon, at midnight,
	To encounter me with orisons, for then
	I am in heaven for him; or ere I could
	Give him that parting kiss which I had set
	Betwixt two charming words, comes in my father
	And like the tyrannous breathing of the north
	Shakes all our buds from growing.[6] (I.iii)

By 16 August 1586, Roger was in Belgium and William and Anne were still in England, and we know this from a letter of that date written to William Higham from Antwerp by the priest called Richard Sherwood who had been his fellow prisoner in the Counter on Wood Street.[7] This letter was obviously intercepted ('twere a paper lost), which is why it is preserved in State Papers. The transcript, with my boldface highlights, modernised spelling and punctuation, is as follows:

---

[5] Anne Line was known to be handy with a needle.
[6] The 'encounter ... with orisons' refers to the Divine Office prayed by devout Catholics at various hours of the day and night.
[7] SP12/249 f.142. The relevant entry in the Calendar of State Papers implies that Roger Line was still in England, but the letter itself shows the contrary. Sherwood appears in the same prison lists as Roger Line and William Higham – for example, 'Richard Sherwood als Carlton to be banished being so at the L. commandement', plus marginal note: 'discharged', SP12/190 f.89, published in *CRS II*, 273; see also *CRS II*, 255.

My good sweet friend, neither **distance of place nor length of time** can make me to forget you whom I have once so dearly loved and be assured that my love to you absent is no less. This present I have great joy to hear of your perseverance in virtue ... prove God ... **I have been earnest with Mr Lyne** to write to you to come over but I doubt he hath not urged you ... And therefore I thought good to write to you myself proving and ... from ... you upon the old love professed between us ... all ... your ... you will not fail to **come to Antwerpe** where you shall be sure to find Mr ... by him you shall **hear of your brother**... Assuring you that ... I have already made means that you shall be provided to your contentment. For your coming use the help of the gentleman by which means you have this letter and ... not that by him I may hear ... presently answer from you. But in ... of ... speedy coming ... if you find not contentment trust me no more. **Commend me most heartily to your good sister and tell her from me that I would gladly she were here with her husband** where I trust **she should better recover her health than where she is**, and she should find me ready to do her all the comfort and pleasure I possibly can ... you shall ... find ... to satisfie my desire I will ... your ... nor ... for ... I would. And so my owne deare friend I hope to have your speedy presence. I take my leave for this time with a thousand hearty ...

Antwerp the 16th of August 1586.
Your most faithful friend
R. Sherwood.

The letter is addressed thus: 'To my assured dear friend
Mr Willm Higham give
this in London.'

The letter has a postscript as follows:

I understand if you have made some scruple of your coming by reason of your sureties who stand charged for your ... payment of your ... nobles a year but ... you for your coming shall be a means ... you shall ... discharge them of the whole... thereof have no doubt.

If William breaks his bail, those who have stood surety for him will have to pay up, and Sherwood reassures William that a way will be found to reimburse them. In fact, the Spanish were regularly disbursing money to English

Catholic exiles in the Netherlands, and Roger Line was to be one of the beneficiaries. Perhaps Sherwood is hinting at the same source of funds for William.

There was a gold coin called a 'noble', minted in London and Calais.[8] The design on the obverse was a ship and on the reverse a cross and the inscription, 'IHC AUTEM TRANSIENS PER MEDIUM ILLOR IBAT'. This is taken from Luke 4:30, which refers to the occasion when Jesus was seized by an angry crowd and taken to the top of a hill with the intention of throwing him off a cliff. The phrase translates as: 'But Jesus, passing through their midst, went on his way'. Does this make the reference to 'nobles' a subtle message of encouragement to William Higham, written with a nod and a wink? The man Catholic prisoners most feared was the sadistic Richard Topcliffe, whose lair, with its blacked-out windows, was at Bridewell, but Higham had now escaped from his clutches.

The original postscript is a paragraph written in the middle of a sheet of paper leaving a space above. However, in the letter as we have it, this space has been filled in with a similar but slightly different script. Is this a note by Roger Line perhaps? Or has an agent like the code-breaker Phelippes or his associate Berden used this gap to add material to the letter? The contents of the addition, reproduced below, are not particularly interesting in themselves – it could be an attempt to use William to flush out a certain Michael Huggenson who plays no further part in the story – but it may be an indication that the modus operandi of Phelippes was applied to much smaller fry than the Queen of Scots:[9]

> doubt not to trust ye gent by whose means you have this letter and request his help in your coming for my sake. There is one Michael Huggenson who sometime did serve my Lord Throckmorton and afterwards Mr Jenkinson the sower and since has been in prison. I pray you enquire him out and bring him with you if you can.

---

[8] Hence Hostess Quickly in *2 Henry IV* (II.i.153f): 'Pray thee, Sir John, let it be but twenty nobles; / i' faith, I am loath to pawn my plate.' Although although nobles remained in circulation, they were last minted in 1470, since when the equivalent gold coin was known as the angel.
[9] A note in the margin of Berden's prison list (relating to Richard Sherwood) reads, 'A man to no accompte meet to mak a stale to tak byrds of his kynd' – in other words, a man of no particular interest in himself but suitable for use as a bait to catch others (SP12/195 f.134).

The practice of releasing recusants on surety or bond is known from many other examples.[10] For instance, Swithun Wells, the schoolmaster from Hampshire who was eventually hanged outside the door of his house in 1591 for allowing Mass to be said there, had been one of those rounded up for questioning at the time of the Babington Plot: a report of November 1586 reads, 'Swythen Weells Released uppon bond'.[11] Now, Swithun Wells is one of those connecting pieces in the Catholic Shakespeare jigsaw. Wells is associated with the Second Earl of Southampton, for whom he had worked as a tutor.[12] It was the Second Earl's son, Henry Wriothesley, to whom Shakespeare dedicated his first published works, the poems *Venus and Adonis* and *The Rape of Lucrece*. When he was seven his father died and he became the Third Earl of Southampton. Many of Southampton's relatives, and at this time Southampton himself, were Catholics. His mother was Mary Browne, and just as a Wriothesley held the earldom of Southampton title, so a Browne held the title of Viscount Montague. Moreover, Clare Asquith argues that the members of this wider Montague/Browne clan became important patrons of Shakespeare and it was their discreet protection that enabled him to avoid the level of pressure from the authorities that might otherwise have been applied.[13] On the one hand, Swithun Wells was connected to the Wriothesley and Browne circles known to Shakespeare, and on the other, he was connected to a personal friend of Roger Line, because the priest arrested at his house and executed alongside him was a former servant of Richard Sherwood before both men became priests.[14]

This brings us back to the three lists of recusant prisoners at London jails found in the State Papers. The first is thought to have been written by Walsingham, who wanted some recommendations from Phelippes as to how to dispose of surplus detainees. The second is a copy made by Phelippes and handed on to a spy called Nicholas Berden, who was sub-contracted this task. Berden writes instructive comments on his list, including the following postscript:

---

[10] Gerard tells of an occasion when he was released in this manner and had to report to the prison every three months and renew the surety. This he did three or four times before he made plans to flee to the Continent after Whitsun 1586. The final surety was provided by a 'very dear friend' who, Gerard observes, 'after I had left England, ... paid more than the surety – he forfeited his life, being one of the most distinguished in that group of fourteen gentlemen who were executed in the cause of Mary Queen of Scots'. According to Caraman, this was Anthony Babington himself (Gerard, 5,6; 5n).
[11] SP/195 f.42.
[12] Questier, 64. Wells links also to the entourage of the Montagues, Questier 204.
[13] Asquith, *Shadowplay*, 36–46. The London house of the Montagues, which may have been frequented by Shakespeare, was in Montague Close just on the south side of the bridge at Southwark and a few minutes' walk from the Clink prison. A little further on was the site where the Globe Theatre was located from 1599.
[14] This was Edmund Gennings. Questier, 267.

Soche persons as I have noted to be hanged are of most trayterous myndes and disposicions[.] Soche as I have marked for banyshement are most meete for the same puerpose for thatt they are excedinge pore & contentious.[15]

That last remark carries some irony as it is clear that Berden's own finances were somewhat strained. When Phelippes received the list back from Berden he copied it out again with his own comments, and this forms the third and final version that would be returned to Walsingham. Now, some of the names on the list are marked for banishment or hanging but many are not, including those of Roger Lyne [*sic*] and William Higham. The name Richard Sherwood actually has the word 'released' written next to it in the margin,[16] and Berden tells us the probable reason in a note:

Richard Sherwood Alias Carlton pryson[r] in the Counter in Wood Strete; And Ralphe Byckley semenary priest prysoner in ye gate house for whose libertye I beseche you to move his honor [i.e. Walsingham] assuringe you that they bothe shall do good service & some what my present nede shall be supplyed by them [i.e. by a bribe].[17]

Berden knew that Walsingham wanted prisoners out, and he also knew that friends of the prisoners wanted them out and were willing to pay to facilitate their release. A more satisfactory arrangement for an impecunious spy could hardly be imagined. He seems to have deliberately underestimated the ages of Roger Line and William Higham, describing them as under nineteen, in order to make it easier to engineer their release and obtain his reward. Berden reveals what he was up to in a letter to Phelippes, as well as telling him of a likely source of funds:

Sir, if it please you to procure me the liberty of Ralph Bickley, Seminary priest in the Gatehouse, at his honour's hand, it will be worth 20*l*. [£20] to me; and the liberty also of Richard Sherwood, *alias* Carlton, prisoner in the Counter in Wood Street, will be worth 30*l*.[£30]. They crave their liberty upon bonds with sureties to appear again at twenty days warning. The money will do me great pleasure, being now in extreme need thereof; neither do I know how to shift longer without it. In

---

[15] SP12/195 f.130 (transcript in CRS II, 275).
[16] SP 12/190 f.89.
[17] SP12/195 f.134 (transcript in CRS II, 256).

which suit I earnestly pray your furtherance, not only for the gain, but also to make them beholden unto me and thereby to make them instruments to do her Majesty good service, though against their will ...

From Bedlam, this Saturday night.[18]
Yours to command NICHOLAS BERDEN.[19]

Earlier in the same letter, this inhabitant of Bedlam informs his handler that on the previous Thursday he was 'at the French Ambassador's ... where there were Lady Compton and Lady Strange, with young Thomas Jarret attending upon them. There was also Francis Tresham, son of Sir Thomas Tresham.'[20]

Sir Thomas Tresham was a well-known landowner and a stubborn recusant from the county of Northamptonshire, where he farmed rabbits, among other things.

THOMAS TRESAM
Knight: a man of rare wisdome and learning, having paid for his Recusancy (as it is said) 9000^l & suffered much: a man most remarkable, and stoute in defence of the Cath. cause: England lost her Jewell when he died at his Manor of Rushton the xj [11th] of September 1605[21]

Tresham regarded the Pope as having authority in spiritual matters, but in temporal affairs he insisted that he was a loyal servant to the Queen, such that when as a Catholic he was deprived of the right to bear arms, he

---

[18] Bedlam, the hospital for the mentally ill in Bishopsgate, was administered by the governors of the Bridewell prison, which may explain Berden's presence there.
[19] SP 12/195 f.135, quoted in Morris, *Troubles II*, 161f, (filed in CSP under 'March?' 1586).
[20] SP 12/195 f.135. It is more likely that this information actually came from William Sterrell, who is known to have been a friend of the ambassador. Young Thomas Jarret is probably John Gerard's older brother Thomas, who would have been 25 or 26 years old and was a friend of Lord Strange. Lord Compton's name occurs in a list catalogued as 'Names of knaves, Papists and harbourers of priests. Five of them the Lord Montague's household servants; another five, household servants of Lord Lumley; two servants of Lord Compton' (CSP cxcv, 107 [SP 12/195 f.184]). Lady Compton (née Anne Spencer), was the sister of Lady Strange (née Alice Spencer).
[21] Brudenell MS, 1.752.

declared that he would fight for her with his bare hands. Despite being imprisoned in the Fleet, held under house arrest for several years and paying a small fortune in recusancy fines, he designed and built a number of unusual buildings which survive to this day, including the extraordinary Triangular Lodge. This compact stone-built edifice literally has three sides, each 33 feet long and displaying various numbers and words, some of which, rather like Shakespeare's phoenix poem, have tended to baffle interpreters. However, it is generally agreed about Triangular Lodge that it is a monument in stone to Tresham's Catholic faith and was obviously more than simply accommodation for his warrener, as he claimed. The narrow underground passage leading several hundred metres from the Lodge to Tresham's magnificent Rushton Hall residence and the branch off to the neighbouring chapel rather point in that direction. The entrance to this tunnel, behind a wall in the Rushton Hall cellar, was discovered as recently as 1979, and no doubt there are more mysteries yet to be revealed. Thomas Tresham, assisted by his daughter Mary, is now thought to have been the pseudonymous Jollet and thus responsible for the most complete contemporary account of the last days of Anne Line.[22] If money was provided to facilitate the release of Richard Sherwood, Roger Line or William Higham from prison, Tresham, via his son Francis, could well have been the source. The Earl of Worcester is another possibility. Sterrell is known to have facilitated the release of other Catholic prisoners at a later date, including Nicholas Owen, the lay-Jesuit who was particularly important to the mission because he was the master hide-builder, responsible for constructing the most ingenious priest-holes.

However, there was someone else at the French Embassy whose presence seems to have caught the attention of the authorities. This was Lady Strange, the wife of Ferdinando Lord Strange, who had a theatre company that a few years later is believed to have provided Shakespeare with his introduction to the London stage.[23] The authorities may have suspected that the presence of Lady Strange in the company of known Catholics at the French Embassy touched very sensitive matters of state, and the reason for suggesting this is a curious fact about the letter from Antwerp – namely, that it has passed largely unnoticed until now because the letter itself is filed in State Papers under August 1594, eight years after it was written. Why was this? The answer may lie with the series of interrogations that took place in August 1594 of Catholics suspected of returning from the Continent to facilitate an

---

[22] See Kilroy, *Edmund Campion: Memory and Transcription*, 13f.
[23] E.K. Chambers, *The Elizabethan Stage*, Vol. II, 122ff; Honigmann, *Shakespeare: the 'lost years'*, 59–76.

attempt to put Ferdinando on the throne of England. Any evidence of possible connections between Ferdinando's wife and Catholics, either through the French ambassador or a seminary priest such as Sherwood, was liable to attract attention.

The conclusion that William Higham was released on surety accords with Gerard's comment that 'after he was freed' he became a tutor to the son of a Catholic lady: 'besides the rudiments of Latin he taught the boy the harp, an instrument which he himself played with great skill'.[24] Gerard reports that he visited him at this time and 'had a long talk with him about his vocation', pleased no doubt that he had encouraged such thoughts in a young man who was to become a Jesuit lay-brother. That William remained for several years in England is confirmed by letters dating from 1594. Finnis and Martin believe this correspondence shows that the Earl of Worcester's secretary William Sterrell 'organized permission for Ann Line's brother to leave the country for Flanders'.[25] Certainly the request 'I pray you get over Mr. Higham by [any] means you can' appears in a postscript to a 1594 letter addressed to a Catholic servant of the Earl of Essex called Henry Wickham.[26] According to Finnis and Martin, Henry Wickham (or Wicham) was one of the many aliases adopted by William Sterrell to facilitate intelligence-gathering activities for clients who included the Earl of Essex and the decipherer Thomas Phelippes. In 'The Secret Sharers' (p. 207), Finnis and Martin list the following aliases used by Sterrell during the 1590s and early 1600s: 'Henri Saintmain, Robert Robinson, Harry Wicham, George Fenner, Francis Cordale, Ortelio Renzo, Thomas Neevell, Anthony Rivers, [Vincent?] Orwell, and Peter Hallins'. His clients thought they had a man on the inside of the Catholic networks, and so they did, but Sterrell was a double agent who carefully controlled the flow of information in both directions. Be that as it may, the main content of the Wickham letter concerns some dealings involving Richard Sherwood, Sterrell, William Allen ('the principal merchant') and 'the traffic of Arbella' (Arbella Stuart had a claim to the throne and was unmarried), but William Higham seems to have been incidental to such dark manoeuvrings – the postscript is an afterthought featuring a request to purchase a musical instrument, a 'bandora or orphtrye of the new fashion ... the best you can find' for a man called Throckmorton,

---

[24] Gerard, 83.
[25] Finnis and Martin, 'Another Turn for the Turtle', 14. The secretary, William Sterrell, refers to 'Mistris Line'. Finnis and Martin claim he would have met Roger Line in Flanders and, '[f]rom the mid-1590s, at latest, he worked secretly as a close confidante with Fr Garnet; Gerard, and other priests using houses entrusted to Ann Line's management, would have been well known to him' (*ibid.*).
[26] Letter of Francis Derrick to Henry Wickham, 29 September 1594, *Cal. Hat. Mss*, Vol. 4, 1439, p. 625.

who also requires lessons and a 'most cunning man in that instrument'. Unless this is all some elaborate code, we must conclude that William Higham was in demand for his ability to provide musical entertainment rather than for plucking the strings of international intrigue. We next hear of him in Rome, where he was enrolled as a Jesuit lay-brother in 1598, and from Rome he was transferred in 1599 to the English Seminary at Valladolid, where he served until his death in 1625.[27] As for Roger, whether he had gone voluntarily into exile, fleeing the gathering storm of the Babington broils, or, more likely, was banished, any attempt to return would have been fraught with difficulties. It had been about three and a half years since the wedding, and at least six months since his arrest. We know nothing of Roger Line's life in Belgium except that Gerard tells us 'the King of Spain gave him a pension, part of which he sent to his wife', and that he attended the Douay/Rheims seminary.[28] Gerard's testimony is supported by a Spanish record dated 1596 that lists a 'Roger Lynne' among other English pensioners.[29] He is recorded as deceased by this date but had been receiving 30 escudos a month. This was about average; some received as little as 12 escudos, but William Stanley, Colonel of the English regiment, received 200. Another name on the same list is Richard Gage (rated at 20 escudos) the brother-in-law of the Mrs Gage who would be arrested with Anne Line at Fetter Lane.

Douay

There had been quite a community of English Catholic exiles at Douay, and many of both the faculty and the students of the recently founded university (established in 1562) were English, including the first Chancellor, Dr Richard Smith from Oxford. William Allen's seminary was unlike modern seminaries in that full-time studies were not restricted to candidates for the priesthood. In practice it operated as an English college of the university, but with a decidedly evangelical bent. Allen's hope was primarily that priests would be trained who would return to their homeland as missionaries, but also that lay students studying humanities, law or philosophy 'may be employed in promoting the Catholic cause in England even at the peril of their lives'.[30] The

---

[27] McCoog, *English and Welsh Jesuits, 1555–1650, Part 2*, 206.
[28] Gerard, 83; *Douay Diaries*, vol. I, 280.
[29] Archivo General de Simancas, *Seccion de Estado*, 612/125-27, quoted in Loomie, 253.
[30] *Douay Diaries*, xxviii.

missionary zeal of these Douay/Rheims exiles was felt by certain travellers and friends of students visiting the college. Such people were described in the *Douay Diaries* as 'for the most part devoid of all religion or at least schismatics', but they were 'pressed to remain a few days with us … until they knew the chief heads of the catholic religion, had learned to confess their sins properly, and were reconciled to God'.[31]

The *Douay Diaries* record in the list of those matriculating from the college in April 1593 one '*Rogerus Lyne, Southantoniens*'.[32] This brief, seemingly innocuous entry in fact incriminates Roger Lyne as a traitor according to the same 1585 act of Parliament by which Fr Richard Thomson had been condemned. This act, while aimed primarily at priests, had also specifically addressed the case of anyone studying at 'any college of Jesuits, or seminary … out of this realm in any foreign parts' who was not an 'ecclesiastical person' – in other words, lay-people like Roger.[33] Increasing numbers of young Catholics had in fact been going abroad to study in order to avoid the Oath of Supremacy required to matriculate at Oxford and Cambridge. The government attempted to counter this by decreeing that those studying at such colleges must return to England within six months of the 1585 act being passed and must then present themselves within two days of their arrival and take the very same oath that they had been going abroad to avoid. The penalty for failing to comply was to 'be adjudged a traitor, and suffer, lose and forfeit, as in case of high treason'.[34]

The seminary established by Allen at Douay had to be relocated to Rheims between 1578 and 1593 due to the conflict in the Netherlands. It then returned to its former location. This is why the first Catholic translation of the Bible into English, produced by the college, became known as the *Douay Rheims* version (the New Testament was published in 1582 and the Old Testament in two volumes in 1609 and 1610). Roger Lyne finished his course in 1593 and therefore must have been a student at Rheims, perhaps for a period of six years.[35] The Catholic seminaries were much commented on in England, so when Shakespeare referred to a 'young scholar, that hath been long studying at Rheims' in the *Taming of the Shrew* (II.i.917), this could only mean to an English play audience a Catholic exile from the banned seminary. As we have seen, such people had been cast as traitors by the law

---

[31] *Douay Diaries*, xxxivf.
[32] *Douay Diaries*, vol. I, 280.
[33] 27 Elizabeth c.2; see Tanner, 154–159.
[34] 27 Elizabeth c.2; see Tanner, 154–159.
[35] According to the *Catholic Encyclopedia* the course of studies lasted six years, but the *Douay Diaries* suggest that studies of two years were possible.

of 27 Elizabeth, and therefore when Shakespeare treats such a character sympathetically we have one of those hints, 'hugely politic', of where his sympathies lie.[36] His character has two names, Lucentio and Cambio. The Jesuit mission to England was dedicated to St Luke by Southwell and Garnet, and it may be that Shakespeare characters with names such as Lucentio are referencing this.[37] Cambio is the Latin word for 'change', suggesting that the young scholar is a convert like Roger Line. It seems unlikely but is not impossible that Shakespeare had Roger specifically in mind. At the end of the play Lucentio's wife famously does not come when he calls her as she is too busy. Did Roger Line call his wife to join him in exile? Richard Sherwood certainly urged her to join him, but for whatever reason she did not go.[38]

While we are in the realms of speculation and on the subject of Douay we may point out that the German scholar Hildegard Hammerschmidt-Hummel has argued that Shakespeare himself may have studied at Douay from 1578 to 1580.[39] This is quite a claim to make. The brilliant Christopher Marlowe, who may have been sent as a spy to the college in the late 1580s, illustrates the reputation it would come to have: 'Did he not draw a sort of English priests / From Douai to the seminary at Rheims, / To hatch forth treason 'gainst their natural queen?'[40] By the end of the century the college would have sent around 300 priests to England, about a third of whom were executed. Both John Payne and the two priests who would be hanged with Anne Line had crossed its portals. For one of them, Mark Barkworth, it was the place he was received into the Catholic Church and the place his remains would be taken after his death; the other, Roger Filcock, studied there for two years before being transferred to Valladolid in Spain.

The idea that England's bard may have studied in such a place is not as

---

[36] Sonnet 124; *The Taming of the Shrew* remained unpublished until the First Folio, eight years after Shakespeare's death, perhaps because it may have been seen as too obviously Catholic.

[37] Cf. *The Comedy of Errors, Titus Andronicus, The Taming of the Shrew* (Asquith, *Shadowplay*, 294). Mikalachki, (*The Legacy of Boadicea*, 174) notes that, according to Geoffrey of Monmouth, King Lucius of the ancient Britons, grandson of Cassibelan, 'converted Britain to Christianity, making it the first nation to publicly confess the new faith', and this is assumed by the Jesuit Robert Southwell (*Humble Supplication*, 29). Jesuits placed their mission to England under the patronage of St Luke (L. *Lucae*).

[38] The point being made by Shakespeare would be that if the unruly and violent Protestants, personified in Kate, could be tamed/reconciled to Catholicism, their devotion would exceed that of even an exemplary couple such as Anne and Roger Line. This suggestion depends on Asquith's interpretation of the play (Asquith 54f).

[39] The suggestion was made previously by Alan Keen and Roger Lubbock (*The Annotator*, 103). Hammerschmidt-Hummel (*William Shakespeare*, 78–82) also argues for the authenticity of three possible signatures of Shakespeare, dated 1585, 1587 and 1589, in the records of the English College in Rome, suggesting that he visited the college in these years.

[40] Marlowe, *The Massacre at Paris*, sc. 21, ll. 100–103.

bizarre as it may first appear. The universities of Oxford and Cambridge had suffered a significant setback during the first years of Elizabeth's reign as a number of the best lecturers chose voluntary exile over conformity.[41] The old universities' loss was Douay's gain and standards were high. Hammerschmit-Hummel points out that the humanities course had five components – Rhetoric, Poetry, Syntax, Grammar and Rudiments – that seem designed to train a wordsmith. Moreover, the Jesuit influence was strong, and what is often overlooked is the emphasis the Jesuits placed on drama, which they used both in teaching and in missionary work. The original layout of the Douay college is not known, but the modest English College at St Omer, founded in 1593, has two theatres in it and a large room for storing props, indicating the importance placed on such activities. Jesuit drama in fact became well known throughout Europe in the seventeenth century, prompting an English spy to comment, 'The Jesuits being or having Actors of such dexterity, I see no reason but that they should set up a company for themselves, which surely will put down The Fortune, Red-Bull, Cock-pit and Globe.'[42] Their work, like Shakespeare's, blithely ignored the classical rules which segregated comedy from tragedy, and there are other parallels. Hammerschmidt-Hummel notes that 'the latest theatrical techniques were used in the performance of exciting historical dramas and plays about the lives of the martyrs, in which the individual found himself caught up in a conflict between the material and spiritual world'.[43]

If, as Hammerschmidt-Hummel suggests, Shakespeare studied at Rheims from 1578 to 1580, he may, as a number of other scholars have suggested, have progressed further under the tutelage of Edmund Campion, travelling with him to Lancashire and residing at Hoghton Tower.[44] If this still unproven theory is correct, it fits with the tradition that he spent some time at the nearby Rufford Hall with the Heskeths, and that some years later these Lancashire contacts led to him arriving in London as a member of Ferdinando Lord Strange's theatre company – Lord Strange being of the great

---

[41] This was particularly true of Oxford, whose mayor reported to the Privy Council in 1561 that there were 'not three houses in it free of papists' (quoted by McConica 'The Catholic Experience in Tudor Oxford' in McCoog, *The Reckoned Expense*, 51), and this 'was the background to the steady stream of Oxford men who made their way throughout the 1560's and 1570's to the seminaries of Louvain, Rheims and Douai' (*ibid.*). 'All told, something over a hundred fellows and other senior members left Oxford during the first decade of the reign of Elizabeth, a great percentage of them into the priesthood and the work of the English mission' (*ibid.*, 51f.).
[42] John Gee, *New Shreds of the Old Snare etc.* (1624), quoted in Hammerschmidt-Hummel, 50.
[43] Hammerschmidt-Hummel, 48.
[44] Built by Thomas Hoghton, who helped to found the Douay seminary and who married John Gerard's aunt Katherine.

Stanley family of Lancashire and the Isle of Man.[45] If Shakespeare was at Douay from 1578 to 1580, he would have been contemporary with John Gerard.[46]

From the possibilities of Shakespeare's movements we return now to the imponderables of Anne Line's. Why Anne did not follow her husband abroad we will probably never know, but Gerard describes them admiringly as truly living a life 'of poverty and holiness'.[47] Perhaps it was this poverty – a gospel virtue to a Jesuit – that prevented such a course, or her chronic ill health, or perhaps she was expecting her husband to make the hazardous return home once he had completed his studies. Whatever the reason, within months of matriculating at Douay, Roger Line died. This was in 1593 or 1594, when he was around 30 years old. Although the sources do not say how he died, it is perhaps worth noting that the theatres were closed in London throughout 1593 due to an outbreak of plague that reportedly killed over 10,000 people. After briefly opening in January 1594 they were closed again (on the Lines' anniversary, 3 February), and stayed closed for another two months. Tragically, it is clear from a letter written by William Sterrell, the Earl of Worcester's secretary, that Roger had attempted to obtain a passport to return to England in the months preceding his death. He writes (spelling modernised):

> I can do nothing for your friend Roger Line because I dare not move the Earl of Essex for any such warrant for any such man. Yet such a thing might be procured by the means of some of the Lord Treasurer's [Burghley's] secretaries but it is costly to deal in unless Line have money, but if he will write to any friend he hath I will convey it to them for your sake, and fisk what they will send. He will have honesty, God willing. More than this I can not promise.
> Harry Wicham [alias William Sterrell][48]

The letter has a date on it of 20 July 1605, that was presumably added later because it is clearly wrong, as is its filing in State Papers under 1602.

---

[45] For the Lancashire connection and the 'Shakeshafte theory', see Honigmann.
[46] Enos (Shakespeare and the Catholic Religion, 37) suggests that John Gerard's servant, Richard Fulwood, was related to William Shakespeare, giving us another possible connection between the two men. Certainly, if Shakespeare knew Gerard, it would explain a great deal. The suggestion is that Richard Fulwood's brother was married to the daughter of Shakespeare's step-grandmother – in other words to someone that Shakespeare would have seen as a cousin.
[47] Gerard, 83.
[48] SP 12/183a f.154 (CSP 283.75.III.). The letter is addressed to Francis Derrick, the writer of the letter dated 1594 containing the request to 'get over Mr Higham as soon as you can' (as noted above, p. 75, 76).

Fortunately there are enough details in the contents to date it with some confidence to between late 1593 and early 1594 – Sterrell notes that the 'King of Scots is taken by Bothwell ... We know not whether he was taken willingly, but Scots are Scots', and 'My Lord Admiral is going to relieve Brest'. A force of more than 2000 English troops were landed in Brittany in early 1594 to aid the Protestant defenders of Brest, and the Bothwell reference is presumably to an incident at the end of July 1593 when Bothwell and his supporters forced their way into the King's chamber at Holyrood and came away with a pardon for various prior misdemeanours. Clearly, a friend of Roger Line attempted to get him back to England in the months before he died. Was this return always the plan after Roger had completed his studies at the Douay–Rhiems seminary? Or had he some intimation of his own death and was trying to find some way to see Anne again before he became too sick? Perhaps it is no coincidence that it was in early 1594 that Anne Line, accompanied by a cousin, Mr Shelly, was noted among those attending Mass at the Earl of Worcester's house.[49] For the sacraments there were other places Mr Shelly could have taken her, but to find someone with more influence at Court who might facilitate a passport, there were very few. If this was the hope, it was either too late or the papers unobtainable, but it certainly brought Anne Line to the attention of the Worcester household at an acutely sensitive time.

---

[49] *CSP Addenda 1580–1624*, 32.64.

10

The Bells of Shoreditch

The original lease to Burbage for his theatre at Shoreditch had an option for renewal after ten years – in other words, in 1586 – and Burbage duly approached Alleyne in 1585 with a view to taking advantage of this provision.[1] Burbage was therefore actively negotiating with Giles Alleyne at precisely the time that dramatic events were taking place in the life of Alleyne's neighbour in Hazeleigh, William Higham (snr), that culminated in the drawing up of the indenture now in the British Library and the selling of the land due to Anne Line for her dowry. Bearing in mind that Anne Line was not only a neighbour of Giles Alleyne but related to him as the daughter of his first cousin, he could not escape involvement in the drama of the family split that was occurring. Thus, land, leases and truculent Puritanism meet in Hazeleigh and Shoreditch in 1585/86, and it is not unreasonable to suppose that if Burbage knew what was going on in Hazeleigh, it was a story he is likely to have regaled his associates with because it shows what manner of a man he had to deal with. The Burbage in question here is James Burbage, the entrepreneurial actor and theatre manager who built The Theatre at Shoreditch and died in 1597. However, the story could as easily have been passed on by either of his sons, Cuthbert and Richard, who dealt with the renewal of the Giles Alleyne lease after their father's death and were responsible for dismantling the old theatre and building the Globe. William Shakespeare was a fellow shareholder with the Burbage brothers, both in the Globe and later in the Blackfriars theatre, and it would be hard to find someone more closely associated with him than Richard Burbage, a starring actor in the Lord Chamberlain's Men. Indeed, it has been suggested that Shakespeare did his theatrical apprenticeship in the 1580s alongside Richard Burbage and under his father James, the 'effective founder and leader' of first Leicester's and then Lord Strange's men, according to Ian Wilson.[2] During the 1585/86 renewal negotiations, Giles Alleyne was offered free

---

[1] See Chambers, *Elizabethan Stage*, vol. II, 383–400, esp. 398.
[2] See Wilson, *Shakespeare: the evidence*, 65–77.

seats at The Theatre, for himself and his family, at any performance at which they arrived while seats were still available; however, he declined Burbage's terms.

The Burbages were a conduit by which the Lines' story could have been gossiped around Shoreditch. Quite apart from the diffuse and often overlapping networks of Catholics and people involved in the theatre that provided myriad ways for news to travel, two immediate neighbours of Giles Alleyne at Shoreditch also provide us with some intriguing links. Immediately to the south was land leased from the Crown by the Earls of Rutland (which at one time included the location of Richard Burbage's home on Holywell Lane). The fifth earl, Roger Manners, was a close friend of Shakespeare's patron the Earl of Southampton (in 1599 Manners would engage in his own legal dispute with Giles Alleyne). Later, after Shakespeare had retired from his theatrical career, he and Richard Burbage are known to have worked a commission for the Sixth Earl of Rutland, Francis Manners, the brother of Roger. Both earls had Catholic wives, and Francis Manners eventually became a Catholic himself. The Rutland link with Anne Line is that one of the three most extensive contemporary accounts of Anne Line's death is to be found in the Rutland papers, though it is not known who wrote it.

There was another set of litigious neighbours of Giles Alleyne at Shoreditch who cannot be passed over without mention – namely, Sir George Peckham and his offspring. In addition to his continuing ownership of neighbouring property, Sir George had once been in possession of the Holywell site itself, possibly as the jointure of his first wife, who died in childbirth.[3] He sold it in 1555, and after a short time in the hands of another owner, it was acquired by Giles Alleyne. However, the children of Sir George's first wife challenged the legality of the original sale and in 1582 brought a case that caused considerable anxiety to Burbage, whose players 'for sooke the said Theater' for a while, 'to his great losse'.[4] Now, the Catholic Sir George Peckham remarried, and who should he take as his bride but the sister of the Jesuit John Gerard, who would play a crucial role in the next phase of Anne Line's life. What does this mean? John Gerard knew the story of the disinheritance early on, as he had a long discussion with William Higham in prison in the spring of 1586. He is also known to have visited the

---

[3] Sir George's first wife was called Susan Webbe and it has been noted that Shakespeare had first cousins called Webbe and that two of his fellow actors, Augustine Phillips and Thomas Pope, were also related to Webbes. However, 'Whether or not all of these people were of the same "web" has yet to be proved' (Enos, 154).
[4] Quoted in Chambers, II, 394.

Peckhams' house at Denham around this time. The fact that John Gerard's brother-in-law was the former owner of the Holywell site and retained a neighbouring property certainly suggests another tight little network through which gossip could spread about the shocking treatment of Giles Alleyne's young relative on account of her conversion.[5]

---

[5] Sir George Peckham was the nephew of Thomas Wriothesley who was the grandfather of Shakespeare's patron the Third Earl of Southampton who was a close friend of the Earl of Rutland. The Catholic Sir George had much in common with his father-in-law and fellow Catholic, Sir Thomas Gerard. Both had suffered in prison – Sir Thomas for attempting to free Mary Queen of Scots and Sir George for sheltering priests – and in the early 1580s they worked together on a scheme to establish a Catholic colony in the Americas at Rhode Island. The scheme foundered amid shipwreck and straitened circumstances but Peckham's *True Reporte of the Late Discoveries and Possession of the New-Found Landes,* published in 1583 in an attempt to drum up support, remains an important source for historians of the early attempts at colonisation.

Part Three
Martha

'Grace in all simplicitie'

11

Relieved by the Jesuits

Anne Line was one of many widows of the plague years who had to make the best of their circumstances. Her health was precarious and her finances a world away from the rich endowment of the Ringwood estate. She could sew, but it would not be easy to replace her husband's remittances by her dexterity with a needle, and she must have felt very much alone, as this was not the only loss she had suffered. For more than 400 years, Garnet's hint about the Roman Matrons passed historians by, and then the wills of Roger's parents were discovered and it was realised that, like Perpetua, Anne Line had been parted from her only child. The boy was called John and was raised by Roger's parents, but he is unmentioned in any of the previously known contemporary sources.[1] We have to assume that there was no contact between Anne Line and her in-laws because Roger's father was still unaware of his son's death in July 1595, over a year after it had occurred.[2] Garnet gives us the briefest of indications of Anne Line's caring attitude towards children: 'By the assistance of good Catholics, we took a lodging for herself, very comfortable, and capable of accommodating a few children she instructed.'[3]

How exactly Anne Line's child was taken from her remains a mystery, but the sad truth is that in the conflicted atmosphere of the time, it was being seriously advocated that *all children* of recusant Catholics should be taken from their parents. This was debated in Parliament in the spring of 1593 as one of several proposals to tighten up the laws:

> Recusant heiresses were to lose two-thirds of their inheritances; recusant wives were to lose their dowries and jointures. In addition, *all children aged seven and over were to be removed from their recusant parents' care*

---

[1] That John Line was raised by Roger Line's parents in Hampshire is inferred from the wills; Christine Kelly in the ODNB entry for Anne Line concurs.
[2] This is evident from the will.
[3] Garnet's letter (Foley VII, 1356).

and given to selected families to raise – at their parents' expense (such was the pernicious influence of recusant mothers on the next generation) [my italics].[4]

Initially the bill that contained these ideas addressed the issue of recusancy in general, but this meant that its provisions could be applied to Puritans as well as Catholics, and the House of Commons proved to be not so keen on that idea. After much debate, most of the clauses were dropped from the final draft (including those mentioned above) in favour of a more limited measure to hold householders liable for the recusancy of their members. The bill became law in April 1593 as the 'Act against *Popish* Recusants' [my italics] – a sop to Puritan sensitivities.

Anne Line, grieving and bereft, was assisted by John Gerard. He surely exaggerates when he writes that she was 'without friends in the world', but she had certainly reached a dimly lit fork in the road. Gerard tells us, 'I introduced her to the house where I was staying, and the family gave her board and lodging while I provided her with whatever else she needed', and from this time on, Anne devoted herself to the mission of the underground Catholic Church under the direction of the Jesuits.[5] The house where she stayed initially, although not named by Gerard, may have been the Wisemans' at North End, two miles south of Little Dunmow. The Black Chapel at North End (still extant) was also in the gift of the Wiseman family. This very unusual wood-framed chapel, with living quarters attached, was a peculiar, meaning that it did not come under the jurisdiction of the local bishop. In effect it was a private Wiseman chapel. There was another Wiseman house near Thaxted, where Gerard barely evaded capture in 1593, and London houses on the Strand and at Golden Lane. The Wisemans of Essex were noted for the redoubtable Jane Wiseman, who was sentenced to *peine fort et dure* in 1598 for assisting a priest, but mercifully was later released:

> The sentence is that the said Jane Wiseman shall be led to the prison of the Marshalsea of the Queen's Bench, and there naked, except for a linen cloth about the lower part of her body, be laid upon the ground, lying directly on her back: and a hollow shall be made under her head and her head placed in the same; and upon her body in every part let there be placed as much of stones and iron as she can bear and more; and as long as she shall live, she shall have of the worst bread and water

---

[4] Hogge, *God's Secret Agents*, 208f.
[5] Gerard 83f.

of the prison next her; and on the day she eats she shall not drink, and on the day she drinks she shall not eat, so living until she die.[6]

John Gerard was arrested on St Georges Day 1594 (23 April), and it is clear from his autobiography that Roger Line had died prior to this date.[7]

The Wills of Roger's Parents

The will of John Lyne (dated 17 July 1595) reads in part as follows:

> ... son Roger's son John, then under the age of 18; ... if my son Roger come into the country within fifteen years after my death of before then my will and meaning is that he shall have the use of John his son's lands and annuity until (John) come to the age of 21; to son Roger, 100 marks if he come into the country within fifteen years after my death but if he come not or be departed out of this world then I will that the aforesaid 100 marks be paid unto Roger's wife, his son John, my son Richard's children Richard and Margaret Lyne, Richard Cooke and Christian Oviatt equally.[8]

His 'daughter-in-law Alice' is also left a gold ring.

The will of Agnes Lyne, Roger's mother (dated 9 October 1600), has the following:

> £10 and three silver spoons to son Roger's son John Lyne at 21; ... item, I give to Alice Lyne the wife of my said son Roger Line my best cloth gown, a red moradoc petticoat and a kirtle of silk grograine.[9]

These wills confirm the Anne/Alice identification because it is evident (1) that Roger is out of the country, and (2) that he has been passed over for the inheritance as Gerard has told us. Perhaps there was a message in the quantity – 100 marks – to be left to Roger *if* he returns, because this was precisely the fee he was obliged to pay for the offence of hearing Mass when he was arrested ten years before. The hint, or assumption, may be that if

---

[6] Indictment, 30 June 1598. *CRS V*, 367.
[7] As suggested in the ODNB article (see Kelly).
[8] PCC Prob 11/87: sentence 18 May 1609 [*sic*], Prob 11/114.
[9] PCC., 27 January 1603, Prob 11/101. For the unearthing of the wills we are indebted to Michael Andrews-Reading. Note the variant spelling Lyne/Line within the same sentence.

Roger returned to England it would be because he had returned to Protestantism. Whatever the intention, the wills reassure us that the rift with Roger's family was not a complete break, and certainly by the mid-nineties some affection still remained for the wife they knew as Alice.

The discovery of the wills also allows us to make sense of records in the *Visitations of Hampshire* from 1622 and 1686. The latter has a 'ROGER LYNE of Ringwood' who married an Anne (yes, *Anne*, not Alice), 'and had issue'. The next entry is for John Lyne, their son, who died around 1640 aged 52. This entry is accompanied by the note of an exasperated scribe complaining, 'This Descent no way peices to the former Entry of the Lynes of Ringwood', and yet, he indicates, that 'Mr Lyne is a Branch of that family is the fame of the county' (i.e. is well known).[10] When we examine the 'former Entry' from the 1622 visitation we see what his problem is, because Roger Lyne is simply not mentioned – we see his brother Richard instead.[11] However, this is because the 'former Entry' *only traces the line of inheritance*, and as we now know, Roger was passed over. The latter possibility obviously did not occur to our 1686 scribe.

---

[10] *Visitation of Hampshire and the Isle of Wight, 1686*, 27.
[11] *Visitation of Hampshire Pedigrees 1530, 1575, 1622–34*, 203.

12

Mrs Martha

As if the two names Alice and Anne were not enough, the Jesuit superior Henry Garnet tells us that 'we gave her the name of Mrs Martha'.[1] This recalls the gospel story of the sisters Martha and Mary who welcomed Jesus to their house as a guest (Lk 10:38–42). Mary sat at the feet of Jesus listening to his words, while Martha did all the work of preparing food. When Martha complained at the unfairness of this, Jesus gently rebuked her, saying that Mary had chosen the better part. In the Catholic tradition, Martha and Mary had come to symbolise the *actives* and the *contemplatives* respectively among religious orders, with the implicit recognition that both are needed. Anne would later play host to women staying in London on their way to join contemplative convents in Flanders. Rather than join them, she chose the perilous role of an *active* in the English mission, rather like a religious sister. Meanwhile, her brother William was to take vows of poverty, chastity and obedience as a Jesuit in Spain. Gerard tells us that Anne also took a vow, following her husband's death. He writes: 'At this time she made a vow of chastity, a virtue she practised even in her married life.'[2]

The Guldeford Connection

John Gerard's assertion that Anne Line was 'without friends in the world' is perhaps a little misleading, though no doubt she was at a loss as to which way to turn.[3] Gerard neglects to mention her connection, through her late husband, to the Guldefords and a whole network of inter-related Catholic families. The 1593 report that Mistress Line visited the Earl of Worcester's house to attend Mass may indicate that Anne Line was associating with her

---

[1] Caraman, *Garnet*, 278.
[2] Gerard, 86. Finnis and Martin (13) translate this as 'a virtue that even as a wife she had valued greatly'. The original is in Latin.
[3] Gerard, 83.

Guldeford relatives and that it was they who introduced her to the Worcester household.⁴ Certainly, three years later, the Guldeford heir, Henry Guldeford, married a daughter of the Earl of Worcester.⁵ The links through the Guldefords to other Catholic families are too numerous and complex to spell out in detail, but among the more significant names are the Browne/Montagues, the Gages, the Copleys, the Shelleys, Robert Southwell, the Cottons of Warblington Castle, the Fitzwilliams, the Brudenells, the Mores, the Ropers, the Paynes and, distantly, the Howard Dukes of Norfolk. In fact, virtually all the named individuals who appear in contemporary sources in association with Anne Line appear to have been related to her in some way. For example, two women mentioned by Gerard as present with Mistress Line during a raid – Mrs Vaux and Lady Lovell – turn out to be two sisters of the Roper family that employed John Payne as their chaplain. The Ropers were related both to the Mores and to the Guldefords. The woman arrested with Anne Line in Fetter Lane, possibly in a house belonging to the Payne family, was a Mrs Gage, née Copley, again related to the Guldefords. At the Earl of Worcester's house, Anne Line was accompanied by a Mr Shelley, probably a son of Lady Guldeford from her first marriage. There were no doubt other relatives not mentioned in the sources who also played a part in her life. For example, through Lady Guldeford, Roger Line was related to the extraordinary Jane Dormer who married the Spanish ambassador and became the Duchess of Feria; thereafter, she played a pivotal role in organising English Catholic exiles in Spain and obtaining financial support from the Spanish Crown for those in particular need, and we know that Roger Line obtained a pension from the King of Spain. The most detailed contemporary account of Anne Line's last days was discovered in a manuscript that belonged to the Brudenell family, and so it goes on. The Guldefords had particularly strong familial and business links with the Gages of Firle in Sussex, who were linked in turn to the Browne/Montague family of Sussex and Hampshire, and to the Wriothesley family of Shakespeare's known patron, the Third Earl of Southampton. 'Among those noted as frequenting Southampton House in London were a Mrs Gage and a Mrs Banister who was probably [Robert] Southwell's sister Mary.'⁶ Clare Asquith has argued that the Montagues were the key patrons and protectors of Shakespeare from the early 1590s until around 1610, and that he probably resorted to

---

⁴ Shanahan suggests this possibility ('Anne Line nee Heigham: where was she born?' *Essex Recusant* 5, 22–26).
⁵ Another Worcester daughter married the heir of John Petre, the patron of William Byrd. This 1596 wedding, between Katherine Somerset and William Petre, took place at Essex House.
⁶ Hodgetts, *Secret Hiding Places*, 22.

Montague House, a place she describes as one of 'the most notorious dissident centres in London'.[7] We may excuse John Gerard a slight exaggeration in his remark about 'no friends in this world', given that by 1594, many of Anne Line's friends were not in *this* world but in the next. Nevertheless, he was clearly being disingenuous, and it is not unlikely that Gerard came to her rescue at the urging of one of these numerous Catholic relations who knew of her desire to serve the Jesuit mission.

Safe House

Anne Line rapidly came to play a vital role in the mission. As the persecution increased, so did the numbers of priests being ordained abroad, with new arrivals more than replacing the numbers arrested and executed. The Jesuits among them were few in number, at times no more than a handful in the whole of England and Wales, but in practical organisational terms they played the leading role in the Catholic mission during this period. The plan of action had been decided at a famous meeting in Hurleyford in 1586, shortly after the arrival of Fr Garnet, who would become the new Jesuit superior in England.[8] Among those present over a period of several days were Gerard and Southwell. They decided that newly ordained priests arriving in England would travel to London and make contact with the Jesuits, who would then send them out to the regions where they could lodge with a family. Incidentally, this meeting was also the first recorded encounter between Fr Garnet and the composer William Byrd, who was also there, presumably assisting with the music for the liturgical celebrations. As the Hurleyford plan began to be implemented, Fr Gerard tells us of his role:

> At that time also many priests of my acquaintance used to come to London. As they had no place where they could lodge in safety, they put up at taverns while they were doing their business. Also, the majority of priests coming from the seminaries over here [the continent] were instructed to get in touch with me, so that I could introduce them to their Superior and give them other help they might need. I had not always got lodgings ready for them and I could not always find a Catholic home to send them to. So I rented a house with a garden of its own in a suitable district... There I sent all the men who

---

[7] Asquith, *Shadowplay*, 126. See also 262, and throughout.
[8] Harley, 80f.

came over with letters of commendation from our Fathers abroad and other good people whom I thought would be useful to our cause...
In charge of this house I put a very good and prudent widowed lady, who was later to receive the honour of martyrdom.[9]

The prudent and good woman was Anne Line: 'her maiden name was Heigham and her husband's name Line'.[10] It is no wonder that Fr Garnet would later praise her prudence and discretion. These qualities were essential for this role at the heart not just of the Jesuit efforts, but of the whole Catholic enterprise of ordaining priests abroad and sending them back as missionaries to England. When Fr Gerard was arrested in 1594, Anne Line continued to manage this very special house. Held in the Tower of London, Fr Gerard was visited there by the Countess of Arundel and her daughter, who had passed through the gates under the pretext that they wished to view the lions that were kept there at the time. After three years, and having suffered repeated torture, Fr Gerard escaped from London's great citadel, resulting in the following report, sent to the Privy Council by Sir John Peyton:

1597, Oct 5 – This night there are escaped two prisoners out of the Tower, viz. John Arden and John Garret. Their escape was made very little before day, for on going to Arden's chamber in the morning I found the ink in his pen very fresh. The manner of their escape was thus. The gaoler, one Bonner, conveyed Garrett into Arden's chamber when he brought up the keys, and out of Arden's chamber by a long rope tied over the ditch to a post they slid down upon the Tower wharf. This Bennet is also gone this morning at the opening of the gates.... I have sent hue and cry to Gravesend and to the Major of London for a search to be made in London and all the liberties.[11]

There were two servants of the Jesuits at the other end of the rope, one of whom, John Lillie, had planned the escape and acted as go-between with the prison warder. Gerard tells us that after rowing a good distance down the Thames, 'I sent my fellow-prisoner with John Lillie to my house, where Mistress Line, that saintly widow, was in charge, while I took Richard

---

[9] Gerard, 82.
[10] Gerard, 82.
[11] Quoted in Caraman, Gerard, 139n. Again the spelling of names is confusing, but it is clear that 'Bennet' is the gaoler Bonner, and Garret/Garrett is Gerard.

MRS MARTHA

Fulwood and went with him to Father Garnet's house.'[12] It was not the last time that John Gerard was to benefit from John Lillie's courage and intelligence.

In July 1599, Gerard was giving a retreat at the London house of Mrs Vaux. He was alone in his room, and had sent his retreatants away for a period of private meditation. 'Suddenly,' Gerard writes, 'John Lillie rushed up the stairs and burst into my room without knocking. He held a drawn sword in his hand.' He notes coolly, 'I was a little taken aback by this sudden intrusion.'[13] The house was being raided. The usual clamouring and banging on the door that generally heralded such events had been avoided, as an unsuspecting servant had opened the door before he realised what was happening and the pursuivants had rushed past him. Within minutes they had found the chapel with Mass vestments all set out. Gerard was just yards away with John Lillie in his room directly opposite the chapel. He describes the searchers approaching and knocking at the door: 'As there was no bolt or lock on the door, we pressed down on the latch with our fingers. Then they knocked again, and we heard the mistress saying: "Perhaps the servant who sleeps here has taken the key away with him. I'll go and look for him." '[14] The searchers followed her downstairs but then became sidetracked by the discovery of two women whom they began to question. One was Mrs Vaux's sister Lady Lovell, the other 'Mistress Line' (Mrs Vaux and Lady Lovell were from the Roper family that had hosted John Payne in Beckenham). While this was going on, Gerard was able to scramble into a hiding place under the eaves of the roof, but when he gestured to his companion to follow him, Lillie whispered in reply, 'I can't come. There's no one to own the books and papers in the room, for they're after you. Just say a prayer for me.' Lillie's brave trickery worked, and he was assumed to be the priest and arrested, bringing an end to the search.

Gerard got away on this occasion, perhaps returning to Harrowden Hall, the Northamptonshire home of Mrs Vaux and her husband George, where he lived after his escape from prison. The Vaux family were intermarried with their neighbours the Treshams, and, three generations back, with the Guldefords. Jane Vaux of Harrowden was the second wife of Sir Richard Guldeford; their son Henry Guldeford was knighted first by Ferdinand of Aragon and then by Henry VIII, for whom he served as Master of Revels and later as Master of the Horse and also as Controller of the Household.

---

[12] Gerard, 137.
[13] Gerard, 151.
[14] Gerard, 152.

He spoke up in defence of Katherine of Aragon and was buried in the church at Blackfriars (see ODNB).

John Gerard would eventually board a ship for the Continent in the retinue of the Marquis of St Germain, the Spanish Ambassador. He died in 1637 aged 73. Lillie's identity was soon known to the authorities, but after some time in prison he managed to escape and made his way across the Channel. He became a Jesuit brother and died of consumption in 1609, at the age of thirty-six.[15]

---

[15] See Caraman, *Garnet*, 264n. Garnet also owed a debt to Lillie, who managed to smuggle a warning to him out of prison in a message written in orange juice when he learned that Garnet's house had been compromised and was about to be raided. He left Rome for England on 15 May 1609 and probably died shortly after arriving back in his home country (Foley I, 455).

13

Fetter Lane

Sometime after Gerard's escape from the Tower, Anne Line, he reports, 'gave up managing the house'. He feared that it was unsafe for him to visit any house where she lived as, by then, so many people knew her identity. Despite this, 'she hired apartments in another building and continued to shelter priests there'.[1] It was in this new location, in the ominously named Fetter Lane, that her much-vaunted prudence was perhaps overtaken by her generosity as a host, for on 2 February 1601, which was the feast of Candlemas, the large number of people who came to her house aroused the suspicions of neighbours. On this feast day, also known as the Purification, the rite of the blessing of candles would normally precede the celebration of Mass. Garnet describes what happened:

> The hour came when the room of the good lady was betrayed by some Judases (as they label many) on the day of the Purification of the Madonna and a furious band of men authorized by Popham entered. The priest was standing blessing the candles and one of that band nearly seized him when he ran in among the Catholics (the heretics take the guilt for bullying a lady Catholic of good faith as though she were a man). They tried to grab the shirt-tale of the tunic and it was torn as the priest made his escape. All the others were delivered to Popham. He commanded that the tunic be repaired but it stayed in rags. The source of this was the testimony of the other lady that was sentenced to death.[2]

Sir John Popham was the Chief Justice who would later pass sentence on Anne Line. The other lady 'sentenced to death' was the widowed Mrs Gage, who was spared the scaffold after an intervention by the Lord Admiral. Twelve years previously, Mrs Gage and her husband had been found guilty

---

[1] Gerard, 84.
[2] Garnet, 11 March letter, f.180.

of sheltering a priest and their land had been confiscated and granted to the said admiral. 'Since that time,' Garnet writes, 'he sustained their lives ... with a merciful heart.'[3] According to Challoner, a witness called Marriot, one of the 'furious band' of raiders, 'deposed that he saw a man in [Anne Line's] house dressed in white, who, as he would have it, was certainly a priest'.[4] We know little of the trial itself, but as Anne Line had been accused under the statute of 27 Elizabeth of assisting a priest, and the priest had got away, the evidence of the man in a white garment was presumably central.[5]

According to Gerard, the priest, Francis Page, dashed out of the room, shutting the door behind him, and 'rushed upstairs to a room where he knew Mistress Line had prepared a hiding-place and got safely into it. The whole house was searched but they did not find him.'[6] After the raid was over Fr Page emerged and left the house, but his frustrated pursuers had not given up and he was spotted as he made his way through the London streets and arrested. This time he regained his freedom through the intervention of a certain Ralphe Slyvell, whose name is recorded in the Rutland papers:

> There was executed also one Mistriss Lynde [Anne Line], condemned at the Sessions house the 26th day of February for the escape of a supposed priest ...
> There was condemned with her one Ralphe Slyvell for rescuinge the said supposed priest, but repryved [reprieved].[7]

According to Jesuit Records, Francis Page, who had been ordained as a secular, was admitted to the Jesuit Order by Henry Garnet soon after the death of Anne Line.[8] Anstruther (265) writes of Fr Page:

> He worked as a clerk in London and fell in love with the daughter of his employer. She was a Catholic and introduced him to John Gerard, SJ (q.v.) at that time (1594–7) a prisoner in the Clink. Francis not only became a Catholic but decided to become a priest. This seems to be the only record of a love affair of a future Elizabethan priest. He became a fast friend of Gerard.

---

[3] Garnet, 11 March letter, f.180.
[4] Bishop Challoner, *Memoirs of Missionary Priests*, 258 (from Champney's *Annales*). The Brudenell MS (2.113) confirms the proximity of a certain 'Marryot the notorius pursuivant' by noting that such a man was called to give evidence in the trial of Anne Line's fellow martyr Roger Filcock.
[5] Finnis and Martin, 14.
[6] Gerard, 84f.
[7] *Manuscripts of the Duke of Rutland*, 370.
[8] Foley I, 424.

Francis Page remained at liberty for over a year before he was arrested again, and then it seems he was imprisoned in the Tower of London, where, among the graffiti of prisoners carved into the walls of the Beauchamp Tower, is the following inscription: 'En Dieu est mon Esperance [In God is my hope] F. Page'.[9] On 17 April 1602, Francis Page was brought before the same notorious Judge Popham who had presided over Anne Line's trial. The Jesuit historian Foley writes:

> The ladies of the Court had, either in jest or in earnest, stormed against the Lord Chief Justice [Popham] and loaded him with maledictions because he had condemned a lady to be hung for receiving a priest into her house, yet had not apprehended and convicted the priest himself, but let him escape.[10]

Not surprisingly, when Popham finally had his quarry at bay, he was ruthlessly efficient and Francis Page died at Tyburn three days later, the last Jesuit to be martyred under Queen Elizabeth.

On her arrest, Anne Line was taken the short distance to Newgate prison, and at this point, Gerard, recalling the events several years later (1608), makes a mistake in his narrative. He claims that 'after some months' Anne Line was brought to trial. In fact the trial was a little over three weeks after the arrest, and took place on the 25th or 26th of the same month. On other details he is clearly more reliable. He tells us that, in prison, 'she sent, a short time before her execution, a letter to Father Francis Page, the priest who had escaped at the time she was caught'. Lest we doubt his memory, he tells us, 'I have the letter with me now', and his pride at his association with Anne Line is obvious: 'Three times she mentioned me in the letter, referring to me as her father.' This missive was evidently a kind of last will and testament, disposing of her possessions. To Gerard she gave 'a large finely wrought cross of gold which had belonged to her husband'. Gerard, her admiring mentor, tells us that later, by word of mouth, she left him her bed. Perhaps this conversation took place on the way to the scaffold when she had no further use for it. Unfortunately, as Gerard records, 'when I came to buy it back from the gaolers who had ransacked her cell after her death, all I could get was her coverlet, which I used afterwards whenever I was in London and felt safer under its protection'.[11] He clearly regarded her as a saint.

---

[9] Bayley, *The History and Antiquities of the Tower of London*, 163.
[10] Foley I, 427.
[11] Gerard, 85.

The arrest took place, as we have noted, at Candlemas, on 2 February 1601. 'Candlemas' is the popular name for the feast known more formally as 'the Purification of Our Lady' and also as 'the Presentation'. It commemorates the occasion referred to in Luke 2:22–38, when the baby Jesus was taken to be presented in the Temple in Jerusalem in accordance with Jewish tradition. The text given below is from the Rheims New Testament of 1582, the first approved Catholic translation of the New Testament to be published in English. In the margin is the subtitle, 'The gospel upon the Purification of our Lady or Candlemas day':

And after the daies were fully ended of her purification according to the Law of Moyses, they carried him into Hierusalem, to present him to our Lord (as it is written in the law of our Lord, *That every male opening the matrice, shalbe called holy to the Lord.*) and to give a sacrifice according as it is written in the Law of our Lord, a paire of turtles, or two yong pigeons. And behold, there was a man in Hierusalem, named Simeon, and this man was just and religious, expecting the consolation of Israel: and the Holy Ghost was in him. And he had received an answer of the Holy Ghost, that he should not see death unless he saw first the CHRIST of our Lord. And he came in Spirit into the temple. And when his parents brought in the childe IESUS, to doe according to the custome of the Law for him: he also tooke him into his armes, and blessed God, and said,

NOW THOU *doest dimisse thy servant O Lord,*
According to thy word in peace,
Because mine eies have seen, thy SALVATION,
which thou hast prepared before the face of al peoples
A light to the revelation of the Gentils, and the glorie of thy people Israel

And his father and mother were marvelling upon those things which were spoken concerning him. And Simeon blessed them, and said to MARIE his mother, Behold this is set unto the ruine, and unto the resurrection of many in Israel, and for a signe which shal be contradicted, and thine owne soule shal a sword pearce, that out of many hartes cogitations may be revealed. And there was Anne a prophetisse, the daughter of Phanuel, of the tribe of Aser: she was farre striken in daies, and had lived with her husband seven yeres from her virginitie. And she was a widow until eightie and foure yeres; who departed not from the temple, by fastings and praiers serving night and day. And she at the same houre sodenly comming in, confessed to our Lord: and spake of him to al that expected the redemption of Israel. And after they had wholly done al things according to the law of our Lord, they returned into Galilee, into their citie Nazareth.

This brief passage of scripture contains a holy widow Anna, a sacrifice of 'a pair of turtledoves', and, 'a sign that is rejected'. This is the only example of a woman called Anne or Anna in the whole of the New Testament, and likewise the only mention of turtledoves. Anne Line would be executed alongside two Catholic priests. Simeon's prayer is known as the *Nunc Dimittis*, and as part of the office of Night Prayer it was recited daily by priests and many of the Catholic laity, as it is to the present time. There is a comment on the 1582 text: 'Marke that *widowhood* is here mentioned to the commendation thereof' [my italics].[12] For obvious reasons, Catholics would have seen the arrest of Anne Line on the Feast of the Purification as providential.

Candlemas was not only a religious feast, it also marked a secular event. Since Magna Carta (1215) it had been determined that the undue delay of justice was itself an injustice, and consequently regular court sessions were established four times a year on what became known as the 'quarter days'. In England they were held on Lady Day (25 March), Midsummer Day (24 June), Michaelmas (29 September) and Christmas (25 December). On these days, as well as the court sessions, rents were due, debts were settled and a variety of other business was transacted. Over time it became necessary to have additional days with a similar function, and these were set approximately halfway between the quarter days, at May Day, Lammas, All Hallows and Candlemas. These became known as the 'cross-quarter days'. This may go some way to explain the coincidence of the dates of Anne and Roger's wedding (3 February 1583); Roger Line's committal (3 February 1586), and Anne's arrest (2 February 1601). To one of a poetic frame of mind, the irony of the arrest on such a day of someone who was about to set out on her own way of the *cross*, accompanied by two men who would literally be *quartered*, could hardly be missed – as though the dark providence of a shrieking harbinger was also gliding over proceedings.

Gerard gives only the briefest report of Anne Line's death, but there are three other contemporary accounts that are more detailed. One is the long letter by Henry Garnet to his superior in Rome, dated 11 March 1601; the

---

[12] In the margin is the title 'Holy Widowhod'. The full text of the comment is as follows: 'Marke that widowhood is here mentioned to the commendation thereof even in the old Testament also, and the fruite and as it were the profession thereof is here commended, to witte, fasting, praying, being continually in the Temple, even as S.Paul more at large for the state of the new Testament speaketh of widowhood and virginitie, as being professions more apt and commodious for the service of God.' See *The New Testament of Jesus Christ* (Rhemes, 1582).

second is the fairly terse report from the papers of the Duke of Rutland;[13] and the third and most complete is that found in the Brudenell manuscript, a source that only came to light in 1968 when it was purchased by the Bodleian Library. This meticulously hand-written and illustrated work consisting of two large leather bound volumes had been in private ownership and was hitherto unknown to scholarship. Gerard Kilroy (in *Edmund Campion: Memory and Transcription*, 199–204) has pointed out that Anne Line, Barkworth and Filcock receive considerably more attention in this 1800-page Catholic encyclopedia than any other martyrs. The account given below is taken from this source, except where otherwise stated.

Anne Line was held in the Newgate prison on Old Bailey Lane. She was first summoned to court in the neighbouring Sessions House on the evening of 25 February, which was Ash Wednesday, then again the next day. Anne was so ill that she had to be carried to the courtroom 'betwixt two men in a chair'. This *carrying* of Anne to the courtroom is mentioned several times and in different sources. It was obviously a feature of her story that was often repeated, perhaps as an illustration of the callousness of the Lord Justice Popham, who ordered her to appear in spite of her condition.

Sonnet 74

At this point we shall break from our narrative to consider what happens when we read Shakespeare's Sonnet 74 in the voice of Anne Line:

1 But be contented when that fell arrest
2 Without all bail shall carry me away,
3 My life hath in this line some interest,
4 Which for memorial still with thee shall stay.
5 When thou reviewest this, thou dost review
6 The very part was consecrate to thee:
7 The earth can have but earth, which is his due;
8 My spirit is thine, the better part of me:
9 So then thou hast but lost the dregs of life,
10 The prey of worms, my body being dead;
11 The coward conquest of a wretch's knife,
12 Too base of thee to be remembered.

---

[13] There is a discrepancy in the dates: Rutland has the arraignment at the sessions house as being on the 26th, whereas Brudenell has it on the 25th and the 26th. Brudenell provides the more detailed account.

13 The worth of that is that which it contains,
14 And that is this, and this with thee remains.

Commentary Sonnet 74 – Anne Line Hypothesis[14]

The sonnet is spoken in the voice of Anne Line. She is saying, (1) 'be contented', because she herself was *content* to die as a martyr for her faith. The Brudenell manuscript records her 'great joy and contentation of mind' after hearing of her impending death.[15] Note also that from this first line can be spelt 'fetter lane arrest'. She was taken with another gentlewoman, Mrs Gage,[16] who was given *bail* (2); Anne was not. Very unusually, due to her sickness, she was physically *carried* into court (2).

'This line' (3) is Anne's physical body, which will remain to be *inter*red, laid to *rest*. Catholics would take great care to retrieve the body and perform a *memorial* Mass (4). Garnet would record; 'Catholics took away the body of Mrs Martha and buried it another place not far off in order to *inter* it with great decorum at some more convenient opportunity' [my italics].[17]

The *memorial* (4) is, first, the physical body left behind, but also *this line* (3), meaning the poem itself. In other words, *Sonnet 74* functions as a memorial. Kilroy, in his study of how Elizabethan Catholics kept the memory of Edmund Campion alive, notes: '*Memoria* was the name given from the earliest times to the tombs of the saints', and furthermore:

> In the absence of a proper crypt with a *memoria* for the body of their martyrs, the recusant community preserved the memory of its martyrs in lovingly transcribed [or composed] poems. Language became a shrine, each phrase an act of homage to the beloved saint.[18]

When you see/review her body (5), you see the body of a 'Martha' who served God among the pots and pans doing physical work, rather than a

---

[14] Gerard Kilroy suggests an interpretation along these lines (*Edmund Campion: Memory and Transcription*, 22).
[15] Brudenell MS, 2.117f. For a full transcript of the Anne Line material, see 'Petticoats on the Gallows', D. Shanahan, *Essex Recusant* vol. 10, num. 3 (Dec 1968), 107–110.
[16] Margaret Gage née Copley was married to John Gage of Firle: 'both [were] sentenced to death, but respited on their way to the place of execution. One of their children was a Jesuit, another a secular priest' (*Chronicle of the Canonesses*, 91). Her father 'fled from England on account of religion, and died in Flanders in the service of the King of Spain' (*Foley VII*, 1357, quoting her brother John Copley). Mrs Gage was also related by marriage to Anne Line via the Guldefords.
[17] Caraman, *Garnet*, 281.
[18] Gerard Kilroy, *Edmund Campion: memory and transcription*, 86.

'Mary' devoted to contemplation. There is an underlying distinction between spiritual and temporal realms that is important to understand. Lay-helpers of the Jesuits, some of whom became lay-brothers in the order, were referred to as *'temporal* coadjutors'. They assisted priests who would do the *spiritual* works of preaching, administering the sacraments etc. Anne is one of the temporal workers; it was her physical labour and therefore her body that she *consecrated* (6) to the Church. Seeing her body refers to her corpse. We might have supposed the seeing of the body referred to the scene at the scaffold, but the word 'review' is used, and emphasised by repetition. This implies a seeing again at a later occasion, something that would certainly have happened when her body was retrieved from its temporary grave, and perhaps also at a requiem Mass.

'The earth can have but earth' (7) evokes words from the Ash Wednesday liturgy that Anne would have celebrated in prison two days before she died: *'Memento, homo, quia pulvis es, et in pulverem reverteris'* (Remember man that thou art dust, and to dust thou shalt return). This in turn evokes the creation of Adam/Man from the dust of the Earth. 'My spirit is thine' (8) is addressed to Christ, and at the same time to his mystical body the Church, which is here supposed to include the reader. Lines 9 and 10 suggest the body is merely 'the dregs of life' and therefore not such a great loss.[19] Anne was killed by hanging, not by 'a wretch's knife' (11), but following her death the hangman is described by Garnet as 'engaged in the *stripping*' of her body. If a knife was used to cut the stockings and bandages from her legs – said by onlookers to be 'as thin as the rope with which she was hanged'[20] – would this not be a cowardly conquest? We know from the Brudenell manuscript that the executioner had a knife, because Anne Line borrowed it to cut off her petticoat lace, which she flung into the crowd of onlookers.[21] Line 12 refers to the loss of dignity of the stripped body. 'The worth of that' (13) (i.e. the body) 'is that which it contains' (i.e. the spirit). 'And that is this' refers back to line 8, to Anne's spirit that she has given to Christ and His Church, and which 'with thee remains'; she is telling those that grieve for her that she is still present.

Now, all the above we might dismiss on the grounds that it a speculative and unnecessary account of a sonnet that has a universal meaning and is a

---

[19] Compare Macbeth (II.iii.95f): 'The wine of life is drawn, and the mere lees [dregs] / Is left this vault to brag of.' For Macbeth, the wine of life is the life of grace that he has lost by murdering Duncan; for the Anne Line of Sonnet 74, the life of grace is what continues in her immortal soul; but for both, the graceless body is mere dregs/lees.
[20] Caraman, *Garnet*, 281.
[21] See page 113.

meditation on love and death. However, if we interpret the poem in this more conventional way, we find something rather interesting: the love that is evoked is the kind we might associate with Anne Line. In this alternate reading, 'this line' (3) refers to the sonnet itself. When we 'review' the sonnet we see 'The very part was consecrate to thee'. This can only refer to line 8, 'My spirit is thine'. If it was the spirit, not the body, that was 'consecrate to thee', that implies we are not referring to a romantic love in which the body is given to the other – it rather implies a platonic relationship or religious devotion. This second reading is entirely compatible with the first.

Returning to our Anne Line interpretation, there may be more to discover in lines 2 and 3. First, the phrase *all bail* in line 2 – why use the word 'all'? Is this just to supply a syllable in the right place? Well, *all bail* sounds like *all hail*, and this evokes the persecuted Church in Rome, where Christians had suffered because they would not *all hail* the emperor as a god. Interest in these Roman Christians had grown since the rediscovery of the Catacombs in 1578, and harried English Catholics clearly identified with their oppressed forebears. Moreover, it was well known that vital in this early Church were a number of courageous women who hosted Christian gatherings in their homes, and paid the price of martyrdom for doing so. There is an obvious parallel here with Anne Line, but still the link between *all bail* and *all hail* might seem very tenuous if it were not for the fact that the priest most likely by order of precedence to have given the address at Anne Line's requiem was Henry Garnet, the Jesuit superior, and Garnet, as we have seen, explicitly links Anne Line to the Roman Matrons in his letter to Rome. One wonders if Shakespeare was present at the requiem Mass and heard Anne Line being compared to a Roman Matron.

We shall turn our focus now to the word 'interest' in line 3: 'My life hath in this line some interest'. I have suggested that 'this line' refers to Anne Line's own dead body and this implies the notion of 'interest' in the physical corpse. This may seem rather odd, but we find another example of this use of language in *Cymbeline*, in Lucius's question to Fidele when he discovers her next to the headless corpse of Cloten: 'What's thy interest in this sad wreck?' (IV.ii.365f). We have already suggested that 'inter' and 'rest' hint at burial, but a little digging in the *Oxford English Dictionary* and the *Oxford Latin Dictionary* reveals the following additional meanings:[22]

1. 'Right or title to spiritual privileges'. From a Catholic theological perspective, death by martyrdom carries considerable merit. So, for example,

---

[22] Taken from OED online.

members of the Jesuit Order shared in the spiritual privileges of the Order derived from the merits and prayers of fellow Jesuits. The fact that so many were martyred meant that this was valued more highly as a result. The use of language related to monetary value as a metaphor for grace or spiritual power was not uncommon. The Church referred to its *treasury of grace*, and it had biblical precedent in the Gospel story of the pearl of great price. Anne Line was very much aware of what a privilege it was to be counted among the Holy Martyrs.

2. There is a second range of meanings, that the OED tells us are related to the medieval Latin *interesse*: 'the indemnity due to any one for the damage and prejudice done to him', or, 'Injury, detriment'. Anne Line was certainly injured. Any financial redress would be the sort of thing likely to be set due at a quarter day or cross-quarter day such as Candlemas.[23]

3. There are several Latin translations of the English word 'interest': one of them is *faenus* (or *foenus*) – possibly a pun, if Anne Line is the *phoenix* of Shakespeare's 'The Phoenix and the Turtle'. The meaning is given as: interest (on capital); a debt carrying interest; increase, gain, profit.[24]

My life hath in this *line* some *phoenix*?

---

[23] A subsidiary meaning of the above relates specifically to the lending of money. The canon law of the medieval Church did not allow usury, which is generally understood as the charging of interest on a loan. However, the canon lawyers actually drew a distinction between charging for the use of money, which was disallowed as *usura*, and something they called *interesse*, or interest, which was compensation to the lender if a loan was not repaid on time. This was legitimate, and this is significant for understanding the dialogue between Antonio and Shylock in Act I Scene iii of *The Merchant of Venice*. The Jew Shylock does not charge his regular 'rate of usance' on his loan to Antonio, but demands his pound of flesh from the region of the heart as an agreed forfeit when the loan is not repaid on time. This is *interesse*/interest. This means that the vengeful Shylock actually has a legal right to his forfeit – the law, including Catholic canon law, is on his side. Of course, the audience feels for the good Antonio, for whom enforcing the law would mean death, and he is saved by the compassionate Portia, who it might be said gets him off on a technicality. Now, it has been pointed out that there are parallels between the predicament of Antonio and that of Catholics sentenced to death in the courts of England (Milward, 93ff., Asquith 118). If this seems somewhat far-fetched, consider that many in Shakespeare's original audiences and almost certainly Shakespeare himself would have been present at executions of priests such as the Jesuit Robert Southwell, where the executioner literally cut out the heart of the condemned man as part of the quartering process (Devlin, 324.) We have to ask ourselves how anyone who had witnessed such a scene could fail to recall it on seeing *The Merchant of Venice*.

[24] *Oxford Latin Dictionary* (Oxford, 1982).

14

A Gentlewoman Hanged

Anne Line was arrested on 2 February 1601 and held at Newgate prison, which was opposite the Sessions House on Old Bailey Lane. She was condemned under the statute of 27 Elizabeth (1585) and executed by hanging on 27 February. Her body was retrieved from a common grave and interred with appropriate ceremony by her fellow Catholics at a later date. The two main sources for the last days are Garnet's 11 March letter and the Brudenell manuscript, referred to below as G and B respectively.[1]

Both Gerard and Garnet note that Anne Line was often ill, but she feared that her sickness might rob her of the honour of dying a martyr's death, and 'she much lamented to Father Bernard' that she was unworthy of it [G]. Her fellow prisoners testify to her alarming state of health:

> She was a woman so weak of body that the same day seven-nights before, she fell sick and was revived from death to life about XX times in that one night, as divers that watched with her can witness, and by reason of her weakness she had kept her bed well nigh all that week continually. [B][2]

On Shrove Monday the ailing Anne Line kept to her bed while the other prisoners sat together and ate dinner. Roger Filcock, who would be executed with her, was among them when Anne called out:

> [She] told them she heard very sweet and pleasant music, whereupon they all listened with great attention but heard nothing: then she demanded the second time saying, Do ye not all hear it? They listened again and said, as the truth was to their hearing they heard no music at

---

[1] Garnet's letter is quoted from Foley's transcript unless otherwise stated (Foley VII, 1344–1367).
[2] When Imogen appears to die, this elicits from Arviragus the words, 'The bird is dead / That we have made so much on' (*Cymbeline*, IV.ii.197–198). She later revives.

all; and so upon her insistence one of the Catholiques went to the door where she affirmed it to be, but heard no such thing. [B]

Within three hours the priest Roger Filcock was called to the Sessions House.

> Noticing towards evening that Father Roger had been removed, she said she now understood that the meaning of the melody was to summon that happy Father to Heaven, though indeed it was also a call for herself. [G]

According to Jollet, Anne was anxious that she 'not be superstitious', but was certain that she had heard music and feared that it was a sign 'to call him [Roger Filcock] away from us'.[3] This was not the only strange occurrence noted by Jollet: he continues, 'Also one of those nights after her sickness, as she sat up in her bed at her Evensong, there appeared a light more resplendent than her own candle light (which stood accustomably every night burning before her).'[4] Again her caution is evident, and reminiscent of verses in *Hamlet* and *Macbeth*: she was careful not to jump to conclusions and make 'any regard of it more than that it might be an illusion as well as a true vision' [B]. Garnet also records this caution towards apparently supernatural phenomena (this caution is characteristic of the spiritual writers of the Catholic Reformation, such as Ignatius Loyola or John of the Cross, who both emphasise the need for discernment):

> Just at the moment when all were moving to go, she called Father Bernard [another priest in the prison] and told him that two days ago, while she was saying the Vespers of the Blessed Virgin, she had seen a great light which much surprised her, though she had treated it as a mere superstition. [G]

On the same day that both she and Roger Filcock were condemned, Anne Line addressed a letter to Henry Garnet. He had written to offer his assistance, and he records her reply as follows (the only words we have written by her):

---

[3] Belarius and Guiderius hear solemn music marking the death of Cloten and presaging the apparent death of Imogen (*Cymbeline*, IV.ii.186ff).
[4] 'Here is a candle to light her to bed' ('Oranges and Lemons').

> She was very thankful to me for the interest I took in her, but she wanted nothing and that God provided everything for her, and consequently neither desired, nor would she permit that I give her anything that belonged to the Society [the Jesuits], though, nevertheless, should anything of the common stock for distribution happen to pass through my hands, she would be very grateful to be remembered. The letter was dated 23 February. She added a P.S.... 'I am just warned to prepare myself for God, because my accusation (or, as we say, indictment) is already written out for the Lord Chief Justice, and I shall be condemned because I have harboured a Priest (as they say), and Mrs Gage, and Roldolfo Sliford, for having, (as they say), liberated the Priest.'
>
> Mrs Martha, or Mrs Magdalen, as we also wish to call her, because she acts the part of both,[5] continues her postscript: 'The rest of our party will be indicted for having heard Mass; but in reality there was no Mass, and we can also swear that, as far as we know, there was no Priest. Is it not so? Tell us if you please. Excuse my haste, and obtain of our Lord that I may be worthy, please God, through your holy prayers to attain to so good an end. I hope to write again in a longer letter'. Such was the promise of that holy woman but I have received nothing more from her. [G]

Here we see the famous doctrine of equivocation in action: 'and we can also swear that, as far as we know, there was no Priest'. Of course she knew very well that there was a priest, but she has been taught that when telling the plain truth could endanger someone's life, it was permissible to make misleading statements (according to the teaching on equivocation). She is obviously not quite sure about this though, as she invites Garnet to set her right if need be: 'Is this not so? Tell us if you please.'

As well as the only words Anne Line wrote, Garnet also supplies us with her only recorded joke, though the Catholic humour requires some explanation, as in the following passage:

> All Catholics know well that before the coming of the Son of God into this world, and up to the time of His Holy Resurrection, there was a place called Limbo. We do not now know for certain what is become of that Venerable receptacle of those holy Patriarchs and Progenitors of

---

[5] In the Gospel story Martha busies herself preparing a meal while Mary, traditionally equated with Mary Magdalene, sits at the feet of Jesus listening to him. The two parts the women took came to symbolise the 'actives' and the 'contemplatives' in the Church.

our Lord, and it has also been disputed whether or not it is now become the Paradise [or Purgatory]. But we have here a Limbo (for so it is called in both Latin and English), the place where they ordinarily confine all those who have been already condemned to death; and all Catholics under sentence of death have to go to that prison before execution, unless exempted by a particular favour as was shown to the holy Martha. [G]

The Limbo was a tiny, vermin-infested cell, with a roof so low and walls so narrow that it was impossible to stand up straight or lie out flat on the floor. Confinement in the Limbo was thus a torture in itself, but it was occupied in the hours before Anne Line's journey to Tyburn by the large frame of the priest Mark Barkworth. He would follow on behind her, dragged on a hurdle with Roger Filcock through the miry streets of London to the same destination. The joke was in Anne Line's response to the suddenness of the summons to the gallows: she expressed surprise as did not think she could get to heaven 'except by passing through Limbo'.

Somehow or other Barkworth had managed to make his preparations:

Father Mark had shorn his head after the manner of a monk, with a crown, because the Order of the Benedictines in Flanders used to receive the tonsure when the moment of death was approaching. [G]

Garnet notes in his letter that Filcock's wish to be accepted into the Society of Jesus before his death had been granted to him, and Garnet would know because only Garnet, the Jesuit superior, had the power to grant it.

Of Anne Line's trial before the Lord Chief Justice, Garnet records the following:

She had been dangerously ill, and to such an extent that she was unable to rise from bed, which was testified by keepers and guardians of the prison, and it was hoped that they would allow her to remain; but Popham gave orders that she should be brought by all means, and if necessary even in her own bed, and so she was placed in a chair and carried between two constables. She was content when demanded in the court (where she was kept all the day), to be tried in the ordinary course by a sworn jury of twelve men, and the general opinion was that she would not be condemned, because there was no evidence to prove that she had harboured any Priest whatever in her house; and even if there had been one, yet if not a Priest ordained beyond the sea (which

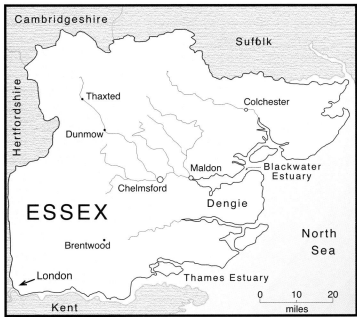

Above: Detail from Morant's 1768 map showing 'Maldon Jenkins'. Running past the house is the road from Maldon south to Fambridge Ferry. The bulk of the land allocated for Anne Line's dowry and her brother's inheritance is described as lying to the east of this road.

Below: County of Essex.

The Black Chapel at North End connected to the Wiseman family - a rare example of a medieval timber-framed chapel, it has living quarters attached.

Mortimer's Hall, Woodham Mortimer - brick frontage added in late 16th or early 17th century.

Hazeleigh Hall, home of Giles Alleyne. A footpath runs from the back of this property across the fields to Bury Farm, the site of Jenkyn Maldons, about fifteen minutes walk away.

The ruined chapel on Spital Lane, Maldon, once owned by Anne Line's father. Note the thin Roman bricks incorporated into the wall.

The heavily restored parish church of Woodham Mortimer, next door to Mortimer's Hall (seen on Morant's map).

The Clockhouse, Great Dunmow - brick frontage added in late 16th or early 17th century.

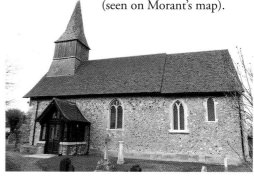

Saxon fish-trap in the Blackwater Estuary.
(©*Essex County Council*)

Commemorative medal (1588) celebrating the victory over the Armada.

Obverse (left): ships cracked like eggshells on British rocks.
Reverse (right): the Pope, almost splitting the sides of the world.
(*British Museum*)

Thomas More by Hans Holbein. He is wearing a 'collar of esses' that may be the chain bequeathed by Lord Mayor John Alleyne.
(©*The Frick Collection*)

Medallion from 1589 commemorating the victory over the Armada. Britain is depicted as a park in the midst of the sea.
(*British Museum*)

Left: Aureus of Nero and Agrippina held by the mayor of Maldon.

Right: One of the two examples of the same coin in the collection of the British Museum. *(British Museum)*

Coin of the Sybil Herophile with Sphinx on the reverse. *(Classical Numismatic Group Inc.)*

Coin of Cunobelin (Cymbeline) showing Janus and a wild boar. The letters CAMV are believed to stand for Camulodunum. *(British Museum)*

Coin of Postumus from Breamore Hoard A, found in 1998 about three miles from Fordingbridge, Hampshire. *(British Museum)*

Ducat of King Roger II of Sicily. Obverse: Christ. Reverse: Roger II and son Duke Roger. *(©www.cgb.fr)*

Coin of Postumus with lion grasping thunderbolt in jaws. *(British Museum)*

Coin of Postumus with famous beard. *(British Museum)*

Medal (1605) commemorating the discovery of the Gunpowder Plot and depicting the Jesuits as a snake hidden among roses and lilies. *(British Museum)*

Venetian silver ducat (1559-67). Obverse: Doge of Venice and St Mark. Reverse: the lion of St Mark - like the griffon it has eagle's wings. *(Classical Numismatic Group Inc.)*

they could not know) it was not a capital offence. But Popham warned the jury to be very much upon their guard, because this woman commonly received many Priests and Jesuits, as soon as they landed in England, and in addition he drew their particular attention to the fact that such Priests have shown that they very well knew her, and that Catholic things had been found in her house. And so they condemned her. [G]

At her trial at the Sessions House, Anne Line was accused of assisting a seminary priest, which of course she had done on numerous occasions. She had, in effect, dedicated the last eight years of her life to breaking the law which defined this as a felony. But the Catholic attitude when facing such accusations was that it was for the authorities to prove their case by due process in a court of law. According to Challoner, '[t]he evidence against her was very slender, which was the testimony of one Marriot, who deposed that he saw a man in her house dressed in white, who, as he would have it, was certainly a priest'.[6] This was, in all likelihood, Fr Francis Page dressed in a surplice, the white garment Catholic priests wear under the stole and chasuble that are donned for Mass. According to Garnet's account, the priest was 'standing blessing the candles' when the searchers burst in, and when they tried to sieze hold of him his white tunic was torn and left in their hands as he made his escape.[7] Popham 'commanded that the tunic be repaired but it stayed in rags' suggesting the intention, at least, to produce it in court.[8] Whether the evidence was slender or not, Anne Line was convicted on 26 February and sent back to Newgate prison.

Early on Friday, 27 February, Mr Muggins, the under-keeper of the jail, came and told Anne that she was called urgently to the Sessions House. He returned before she had managed to get herself ready with the news that she should prepare herself for death, 'for it was so determined'. Two priests, Fr Filcock and Fr Barkworth, were to die with her. Soon she was outside the iron gates of the jail, where the 'sergeant's catchpoles' were waiting with a cart, and she thanked her keeper:

'God a mercy good good Mr Muggins, I give you thanks with all my heart: I do still fear it is too good news to be true': this she repeated diverse times so most humbly and courteously saluted all her fellow

---

[6] Challoner, 258.
[7] Garnet, letter 11 March 1601, f.180.
[8] Garnet, letter 11 March 1601, f.180.

prisoners, desiring them to pray for her, and so with great joy and contentation of mind she hastened forth, thinking her preferment by God to be the greater in that she should yield her life for him in the company of such worthy and renowned men that she so highly honoured in her heart. And so in the open view of multitudes of people she was lifted up into the cart and being there she was not able to go one step without help: yet most cheerfully looking and courteously saluting the people, as well her own acquaintance as strangers, did heartily beseech God to bless them all and that they might have grace to live and die Catholics. [B]

When she was placed in the cart, together with some thieves who were heretics, she signed herself with the sign of the Cross, and her friends surrounded the cart expressing their desire for some token as a remembrance of herself ...

When the nursing woman [who was expecting to help her to dress] returned to the prison, she was astonished to see her in the cart [and] hastened towards her, and, taking her hand, they mutually recommended each other. [G]

The cart soon set off to cover the three miles or so to Tyburn, the execution site at the crossroads beyond the city to the north-west. They would pass by Fetter Lane near the start of their journey as they jolted their way though the parishes of London. At various points the cart was halted to allow ministers to preach to the condemned:

Then the minister willed her to confess the sins of her youth and of her middle age, and to thank God that he permitted her not to live to sin in her old. Whereunto she very meekly answered, yet with great resolution, saying: I came not hither to confess my sins but to die for the Catholique Religion, and I desire all this multitude of people to bear witness with me that I die only for the Catholique religion. Then quoth the minister, You have been a common receiver of priests. Sir, quoth she, where I received one I would to God I had been able to have received a thousand. [B]

One of the ministers annoyed her very much upon the way, endeavouring to pervert her from the Catholic faith, but in vain ... 'would God that where I harboured one, I had harboured a thousand'. [G]

The chronicler Stow has the following entries (note his reference to *the* statute):

> **Seminarie priests executed**
> The seven and twentith of February, Marke Bakworth, and Thomas Filcockes Seminarie priestes, were drawne to Tyborne, and there hanged and quartered for comming into the Realme contrarie to the Statute.
>
> **A Gentlewoman hanged.**
> And the same day a Gentlewoman called Mistresse Anne Lina, a widow was hanged in the same place for relieving a priest in her lodging contrarie to the said Statute.⁹

And so we come to the final section of the Jollet account:

> So she threw her handkerchief to one and gave much money among the common people; whereat divers of them gave regards and strived much for it. But when all her money was distributed she plucked out of her pocket half a biscuit loaf, which she distributed in like manner among the people, for which they strived greatly to catch the pieces: and when her bread was spent, she then called to the executioner for a knife to cut off her petticoat lace, which done she threw it among the people, saying: Take ye that I have now no more to give. [B]¹⁰

> When she was near the gallows she asked the executioner for a knife and with it cut off a piece of her gown and gave it to one of her friends. [G]

> So behaving herself most constantly to her last breathe, meekly saluting the people and earnestly praying to God that they might all die in the Catholique faith to the health and salvation of their souls: binding her garments beneath about her knees and putting a handkerchief about her face, pinning it fast: she meekly kissed the gallows tree, and both before and after her private prayers blessing her self with the signs of the cross, she commended her soul to the most holy blessed and glorious Trinity. [B]

---

⁹ Stow, 458f.
¹⁰ When Imogen is told by Pisano that he has been commanded to kill her, her speech in reply culminates in the words: 'Prithee, dispatch: / The lamb entreats the butcher: where's thy knife? / Thou art too slow to do thy master's bidding, / When I desire it too' (*Cymbeline*, III.iv.95–98).

When she arrived at the gallows at Tyburn, she kissed the gibbet, and prayed in private. The day was intensely cold, and it was snowing heavily, and all wondered that, being so very weak and exhausted, she did not perish. But at last, making the sign of the Cross, she was dead before the arrival of the two Fathers. [G]

Then a sergent came and called them for they had executed Mrs. Lyne. The day was extremely foul and the snow & wind beat very greatly uppon them, in ... that upon Father Barkworth; his shift [shirt] was very wet so that with their long stay he began to quiver and shake in that thynne attire: yet remembering himself he put away all quivering with resolution of mynde. Then a minister spoke unto them as the sled was drawn under the gallows. [B]

As soon as they arrived, Father Mark was the first to be put into the cart (from the hurdle); he instantly kissed the gown of his holy fellow-martyr ... He wore a hair-shirt under his clothes. Raising his eyes to Heaven, he made the sign of the Cross upon the gallows and the rope and kissed them, singing with joyful countenance and voice: '*Haec est dies Domini, gaudeamus, gaudeamus, guadeamus in ea* [This is the day of the Lord, let us rejoice, let us rejoice, let us rejoice in it]'; and kept repeating this, not allowing the ministers or any others to interrupt him, but always returning to his *gaudeamus*. He added also: *In manus tuas, Domine, commendo spiritum meum* [Into your hands Lord, I commend my spirit]. The minister called aloud to him to repent of his sins, to which he replied: 'Hold your tongue, you silly fellow'. [G]

The executions were at London's traditional venue and on the gallows known as the 'Tyburn Tree', a three-sided structure designed for triple executions. A small plaque, set in the tarmac at Marble Arch in London, is all that officially marks this Golgotha today.

15

Memoria

Henry Garnet wrote:

> When the crowd dispersed, my agent in London approached the corpse of Mrs Martha. Cutting the sleeve from her gown, he dipped it in the blood of the two Fathers, and he obtained also one of her stockings, notwithstanding the resistance of the executioner, who was himself engaged in the stripping; but he was appeased with a julio [a silver coin]. She used to have bandages on her legs, and thus her stockings were large, but they told me that her legs were as thin as the rope with which she was hanged. Perhaps I shall send these stockings to your Paternity if I find the opportunity.
>
> The head and the quarters of the two Fathers were first buried in a pit dug in the public road, and, later, the body of Mrs. Martha also; and above them all, three or four thieves: I do not know whether they were all women. But the Catholics took away the body of Mrs Martha and buried it in another place not far off in order to inter it with great decorum at some more convenient opportunity. The quarters of the martyrs have also partly been removed, and I believe they have now recovered them all.[1]

There is another reference to the burial in *The Lives of Philip Howard, Earl of Arundel, and of Anne Dacres, his wife.* This was not published until 1857, but reproduces material from manuscripts written by a chaplain to the Countess and passed down in the Howard family. It certainly reads like a contemporary Catholic 'life', extolling the virtues of its subjects and their exemplary sufferings, but this hagiography is spiced with authentic detail. Chapter VI is entitled 'The Queen's Hatred towards Her' and recalls an incident when Elizabeth visited Arundel Castle and the Countess (Anne

---

[1] Letter of Henry Garnet to Aquaviva. 11 March 1601 (ARSI, *Anglia 31*, II, ff. 172v-183v). Quoted in Caraman, *Garnet*, 281.

Dacres) was advisedly elsewhere. The Queen, 'espying in the glass of one of the windows a sentence written with a diamond insinuating hopes of better fortune', assumed it had been scratched by her absent hostess. Our observer notes disapprovingly that 'with her own hand she writ underneath another sentence expressing much passion and disdain. And this she did in all likelyhood to grieve and afflict the poor lady.'[2] The Queen was undoubtedly aware that this 'poor lady' was dedicated to supporting the Catholic cause, and particularly the Jesuits.[3] It is in this very personal account by the chaplain that we come presently to mention of Anne Line:

> Those finally whome she understood to have been constant and courageous in that cause, she endeavour'd to help and honour all she could both in their life, and after their death. As she did amongst others unto that happy gentlewoman Mrs. *Anne Line* who I saw put to death at *Tyburn* for having given entertainment to a Priest, in *February* 1600. For understanding that certain resolute Catholicks intended to take up her body in the night time out of the place where it was dishonourably buried in the same grave and under the bodies of diverse malefactors, she sent her coach with them, and therein brought the body to her own house where it was kept with reverence till it could be conveniently dispos'd of by those who had more interest therein.[4]

This report suggests that the Countess herself may have dressed the body – certainly she would have seen it at close quarters. Perhaps Shakespeare wrote Sonnet 74 for both of these brave women.

Garnet was not the only one to report Anne Line's death by letter. There is another letter, held among the state papers, that is signed by a mysterious Thomas in Liege.[5] Finnis and Martin conclude from the handwriting that this is another identity of the ubiquitous William Sterrell. Be that as it may, it is written by a Catholic who sets the execution within the context of the 'late troubles in England' – clearly the Essex Rebellion. He writes that 'it is evident the plot to have been layed by the puritaynes ... and principal actors thereof to have been more than ordinarily zealous in that proffession'. However, he admits, 'It is true that Sir Christopher Blunt died a Catholike

---

[2] Howard, *The Lives of Philip Howard, Earl of Arundel, and of Anne Dacres, his wife*, 193.
[3] Her husband Philip's conversion had been prompted by the trial and execution of Edmund Campion; Robert Southwell had been her chaplain; and we know also that she visited Gerard when he was in the Tower.
[4] Howard, 293f.
[5] SP 77/6/258.

(though he lived in schisme all his life time).' He complains that the authorities had contrived the following:

> to impose the crime upon innocent Catholikes, and thereupon in the midst of these tradgiche actions they have executed three or four poore priestes (the one condemned for or five yeares agoe) and a Catholike gentellwoman Mrs Anne Lyne for harbouring of priests onely.

He himself fears 'further perrill even the last stroke of death. But I am a foole to grieve my selfe, or write to you theis melloncully discourse', and concludes that 'these manners of proceedings are not the first that shall bene practised against us nor those previous the last we must suffer'.

Requiem

Francis Page had been Anne Line's confessor, he was the man to whom she confided her will, and he was the priest she was convicted for assisting – so he must surely have been at her requiem. Among the other priests were, almost certainly, the Jesuits Garnet and Gerard, and if all three were present, they probably all had roles in the service. By order of precedence, Garnet would have celebrated the Mass, but he may have preferred to preach, in which case Gerard could have been the celebrant and Francis Page, freshly clad in a new white surplice, could have played his part as cantor of the *Dies Irae*. To the select troop gathered for the occasion, his own part in the story – evading his pursuers twice within hours – must have seemed miraculous. As with Jesus when he slipped through the angry crowd intent on hurling him off a cliff, Page's time had not yet come.

At Warblington Castle on the south coast, 'part of the body of the martyr Mark Barkworth was found in a reliquary of crimson damask in John Cotton's study' during a search in 1613.[6] His head apparently made it to the Benedictine House at Douay, where it was kept until the time of the French Revolution, when it was lost. Anne Line's body may have been buried in the grounds, or beneath the cellar, of the Countess of Arundel's London house on the Strand, mere yards away from the church where she had been

---

[6] Hodgetts, 113.

married eighteen years before, and from the Earl of Worcester's house where she had heard Mass.[7]

Virtue's Steely Bones

Now that we have a historical account of the life of Anne Line that is as detailed as the sources allow, let us remind ourselves again of what prompted this investigation – namely, the possibility that something about this woman's life and death deeply moved William Shakespeare, that her story entered his imagination, illustrated perhaps by vivid memories of her tragic scene at Tyburn, and she became an unlikely muse. If this is so, it would not be surprising to find evidence of it beyond the confines of 'The Phoenix and the Turtle'. We have considered Sonnet 74, and will come on to the reference in *The Tempest*, but there is another text that may be worth adding to this collection. The following quote from *All's Well That Ends Well* (written between 1601 and 1609) is spoken by Parolles, an unsympathetic character speaking to Helena, the heroine.[8] In light of the fact that it was the Catholic Church that spoke up for virginity, in the form of clerical celibacy and the vows of religious life, the echoes of anti-Catholic polemic are obvious, but we may now see a rather more specific reference:

> To speak on the part of virginity, is to accuse your mothers; which is most infallible disobedience. He that hangs himself is a virgin: virginity murders itself and should be *buried in highways* out of all sanctified limit, as a desperate *offendress* against nature ... Besides, virginity is peevish, proud, idle, made of self-love[9] ... Out with't! within ten year it will make itself ten, which is a goodly increase;[10] and the principal itself not much the worse.[11]

---

[7] Catholics were accustomed to making special arrangements for burial as priests lived under assumed identities. Gerard tells us of a certain Fr John Curry, who died in London in the house kept by Anne Line, 'and there he lies buried in some secret corner; for those priests who live secretly on the mission, we are obliged also to bury secretly when they die' (unpublished letter, quoted by Foley, I 397n). Finnis and Martin suggest the Earl of Worcester's house, also on the Strand, as Anne Line's final resting place.

[8] Helena is described in Catholic terms: 'her dispositions she inherits, which makes fair gifts fairer ... she derives her honesty and achieves her goodness'. Note, in addition to the theology, we have the word 'fair' – according to Asquith, a coded marker of Catholicism. See Asquith, *Shadowplay*, 32–35, 292.

[9] This list is typical of accusations made against peevish recusant idol-worshippers.

[10] This is probably an ironic reference to *God's Arithmeticke*, a Protestant sermon by Francis Meres published in 1597 that argued against the Catholic practice of celibacy on the grounds that God loves multiplication.

[11] *All's Well That Ends Well* 1.1.136–149 (my italics).

Note the feminine 'offendress'.
Helena says of Parolles:

> And yet I know him a notorious liar,
> Think him a great way fool, solely a coward;
> Yet these fixed evils sit so fit in him,
> That they take place, when virtue's steely bones
> Look bleak in the cold wind: withal, full oft we see
> Cold wisdom waiting on superfluous folly.[12]

As Anne Line's thin limbs hung from the scaffold, stiffening in the cold wind, two priests shivered as they waited for their turn to die.

Barkworth's Passion

For Catholics in the crowd at Tyburn, the execution of the two priests Mark Barkworth and Roger Filcock would have been indelibly linked to the execution of Anne Line shortly before. Shakespeare also seems to make this same connection – including, I will argue, in *The Tempest*. In order to consider this, and for the sake of completeness, we will turn our attention to the men who died alongside Anne Line, and particularly to Mark Barkworth. Until the Brudenell manuscript came to light in 1969, there were only two contemporary accounts of any length of Anne Line's death; one was that contained in Garnet's letter to Rome of March 1601, and the other was a report found in the manuscripts of the Duke of Rutland held at Belvoir Castle. We know that Shakespeare had some connection with the Duke of Rutland in 1613, due to a unique reference to Shakespeare and his friend Burbage being paid 44 shillings each for producing the heraldic 'impresa', carried by the Duke at the Accession Tilt on 24 March. The Duke at this time was Francis Manners, the sixth earl, whose brother Roger had been the fifth earl in 1601 when both of them were imprisoned for several months following their involvement in the Essex rebellion.[13] It is to the anonymous

---

[12] *All's Well That Ends Well* 1.1.100–104.
[13] There is an intriguing unanswered question concerning Belvoir Castle, the seat of the earls of Rutland, because Belvoir is situated in an area of the East Midlands that from 1621 is referred to rather mysteriously in Jesuit records as *the residence of St Anne*. Could it be that Anne Line's remains are buried there? The most obvious alternative is that the Jesuits were making light-hearted reference to the house of the Catholic Queen Anne of Denmark in Grantham, also within the region known as the Leicestershire mission, but Queen Anne had died in 1619 and was buried in Westminster Abbey and she certainly had no reputation for sanctity. On the other hand, one of the three most significant accounts of Anne Line's death is preserved in the Rutland Papers, and certainly by 1609 a group of Catholics centered on the Countess of Rutland were being served by a Jesuit chaplain (McCoog, 'Wright, William (1563–1639)', ODNB).

account in the Rutland papers that we shall turn for an account of Mark Barkworth's execution:

> The execution of [MARK] BARKWORTH [alias LAMBERT, ROGER FILCOCK alias] ARTHUR alias NAYLOR, and [ANNE] LINE.
>
> [1600–1], February 27.] Mr. Barkwey cominge to the hurdle prayed and with a chearful voyce and smylinge countenance sunge all the waye he went to execution.
> The 27th daye of Februarie 1600, beinge the first Friday in Lent, the said Mr. Barkwey was brought to Tyborne there to be executed. Cominge up into the carte in his blacke habite, his hoode beinge taken of, his heade beinge all shaven but for a rounde circle on the nether parte of his heade, and his other garment taken of also, beinge turned into his sherte, having a pare of hose of haere, most joyfully and smylingly looked up directly to the heavens and blessed him with the signe of the crosse, sayinge, '*In nomine Patris, Filii et Spiritus Sancti, amen.*' Then he turned himself towards the gallowe tree whereon he was to suffer, made the signe of the crosse thereon and kissed it and the rope also, the which being put about his necke, he turned himselfe and with a chearfull smylinge countenance and pleasant voyce sunge in manner and forme followinge, viz.: '*Haec est dies Domini; gaudeamus, gaudeamus, gaudeamus in ea*' – usinge the same very often with these wordes, viz.: '*In manus tuas, Domine, commendo spiritum meum.*' Also he used these speaches to the people – 'I doe confesse that I am one of the Blessed Society after the holy order of St. Benedicte.' The minister called on him to be penitent for his sinnes, and he said 'Hold thy peace, thou arte a simple fellowe.' Then the minister wild him to remember that Christ Jesus dyed for him. And he, elevatinge his eyes to heaven and holdinge the rope in his handes – being festned together – so highe as he could reache, aunswered 'And so doe I for him, and I would I had a thousand, thousand lyves to bestowe upon him in this cause,' sayinge '*et majorem charitatem nemo habet.*' And then turninge himselfe againe, sunge as before, and desired all Catholiques to praye for him, and he would praye for them. And beinge asked if he would praye for the Queene he saied, 'God blesse her, and send her and me to meete joyfully in heaven,' and prayed also for Mr. Recorder who pronounced judgement against him, and for Mr. Wade, Ingleby, Parrat, and Singleton, who were the prosecutors of his death. And the carte beinge drawne awaye,

in his goinge of from the carte saied the same wordes as before, '*Haec est dies Domini; gaudeamus in ea.*' And beinge presently cut downe, he stoode uprighte on his feete and strugled with the executioners, cryinge, 'Lord, Lord, Lord,' and beinge holden by the strengthe of the executioners on the hurdle in dismembringe of him he cryed, 'O God,' and so was he quartered.[14]

The usual practice at Tyburn was for the prisoner to stand on the cart with the noose about his neck; the cart was then drawn away, leaving the prisoner hanging. Challoner records what happened on this particular occasion when the cart was withdrawn:

> some cruel wretch, fearing lest the weight of his body should put the martyr too soon out of his pain, for he was tall and bulky, set his shoulders under him to bear up at least some part of the weight, so that he was cut down whilst he was yet alive; and even when the butcher was seeking for his heart, he pronounced these words, O God, be merciful to me.[15]

About 30 years old when he died, Barkworth had been brought up a Protestant but converted to Catholicism at Douay when he was 22. While on a journey, he is said to have had a vision of St Benedict, who told him that he would die a martyr in the Benedictine habit. The Benedictine Order had played a vital role in the evangelisation of Europe, and particularly of England, as it was the Benedictine, Augustine of Canterbury, sent by Pope Gregory the Great, who had baptised King Ethelbert of Kent and begun the wholesale conversion of the Anglo-Saxon people.[16] Had Barkworth lived longer, he might have played an important part in the reconstitution of that order in England, but he was quickly captured and sent to Newgate. He had departed from the seminary at Valladolid in July 1599, and went from there to the Benedictine monastery of Santa Maria la Real de Irache (Hyrache), whose beautiful stone buildings (now no longer housing monks) can be found near Ayegui, between Lagrono and Pamplona. There, 'he was admitted as a member of the community and given the right, which later he exercised, to take the monastic vows at the hour of death and to be reckoned

---

[14] *Rutland Papers*, 369f.
[15] Challoner, 256.
[16] The role of King Ethelbert's French wife, Bertha, should not be forgotten – she had arrived from France a Christian and it was she who initially gave the monks a welcome. Part of the wall of her chapel still exists in the church of St Martin in Canterbury.

among the professed sons of St Benedict'.[17] At Valladolid he had studied with the son of William Byrd, with the nephew of Henry Garnet, and with Roger Filcock, who left for England in 1598 and became a Jesuit. Before he set off on his own journey, Barkworth had almost certainly made the acquaintance of William Higham, Anne Line's brother, who was given permission to travel from Rome in early 1599 to serve as a Jesuit lay-brother in the college at Valladolid.

The Brudenell manuscript contains the transcript of a letter written by Barkworth from prison shortly before his death in which he describes his interrogation and trial. He recounts that a witness who testified against him came secretly to him afterwards in prison to tell him that he had been bribed to testify, and to plead for his forgiveness. The misery and guilt of such a man can only be wondered at in the light of Barkworth's account of his sentencing:

> Then the Recorder having nothing els agaist me but that I was a catholique gave cruell sentence of deathe against mee: that I shoulde be half-hanged, the secrets of nature to be cutt of, and my neck by the shoulders, my entrails to be burned, my heade and quarters to be sett on poales. Which sentence when I hearde, I herat smyled, making signe of the crosse and rejoiced saying, *Te deum laudamus te dominum confitemur* [give praise to God and confess him to be the Lord]. And so I thanked the Recorder. [B][18]

The Tempest

We now have enough information about Barkworth to approach an oblique reference to his death in Shakespeare's *The Tempest*, but a few words of introduction are needed on the play itself. In the interest of simplicity and brevity we shall assume the basic interpretation given by Clare Asquith in her remarkable book *Shadowplay*, published in 2005.[19] She argues not only that Shakespeare was influenced by Catholicism, or that he was secretly a Catholic, but that more or less throughout his work there is a specific Catholic subtext. Moreover, the authorities were aware of his sympathies, if not with the detail of the allegory present in his work. Around the time

---

[17] CRS 30, p.44.
[18] Brudenell, 2.111, quoted in Kilroy, *Edmund Campion: memory and transcription*, 20.
[19] Asquith, 260–273.

1610–1611 there was an increase in the pressure on dissident writers, including Shakespeare, and it was this that Asquith claims effectively forced Shakespeare into retirement. On this view, *The Tempest*, written at this time, represents Shakespeare looking back on his career as a writer and signing off. The two subsequent plays – *The Two Gentlemen of Verona* and *Henry VIII* – were completed by another hand, probably that of Fletcher, and published without Shakespeare's consent. Asquith points out that when Shakespeare's colleagues arranged for his work to be published in 1623, seven years after his death, they put *The Tempest* at the beginning of the First Folio, as though, for them, it stood as both introduction and key to all that followed. The play itself, Asquith argues, is a *psychomachia*. In other words, we are seeing inside the head of the main protagonist, in this case Prospero, who represents Shakespeare himself. The airy spirit Ariel stands for his higher, creative faculties, and in stark contrast, Caliban represents the earthy, lower drives. There is a double allegory, in that Shakespeare is representing both himself and England as a whole, so that Ariel and Caliban also represent more cultured and more brutal aspects of England. As the play is being written, Shakespeare is feeling physically threatened by the Caliban authorities, and as a consequence, he lets Ariel go, symbolising his retirement from the stage.

We pick up the story in Act IV, scene i. Prospero has sent his spirit Ariel to the 'varlots'[20] Stephano and Trinculo, and when he returns Prospero asks where he has left them. Ariel's response links the varlots to the pursuivants who sought out Catholic priests: 'So full of valour that they smote the air for breathing in their faces; beat the ground / For kissing of their feet'.[21] The Catholic rite of ordination involves breathing into the face, symbolising the breath of the Holy Spirit, and it was the Pope whose feet were kissed. The invisible Ariel attracts the attention of Stephano and Trinculo with music, but curiously he reports this as 'they smelt music'.[22] The Catholic Mass was associated with both music and the characteristic smell of incense. They begin to follow the sound – as Ariel puts it, 'calf-like they my lowing follow'd'.[23] Prospero has already described Caliban as a moon-calf, echoing the words of Thomas More, who described Luther in this odd but memorable way.[24] Ariel describes leading the hapless Stephano and Trinculo

---

[20] *The Tempest* IV.i.170.
[21] *The Tempest* IV.i.172–174.
[22] *The Tempest* IV.i.178.
[23] *The Tempest* IV.i.179.
[24] More was referring to an incident in Germany in 1522 when a deformed calf was born with a flap of skin over its neck that looked like a monk's cowl. An astrologer from Prague was called upon to explain the significance of this strange occurrence and concluded that the monster represented Martin Luther. See Smith, 'The Mooncalf', *Modern Philology*, vol. 11, no. 3 (Jan. 1914), pp. 355–361.

'through / Tooth'd briers, sharp furzes, pricking goss and thorns which entered their frail shins: at last I left them / I' the filthy-mantled pool beyond your cell.'[25] Many a time pursuivants had been led a merry dance by a priest fleeing on foot across the countryside.

Prospero's response to Ariel's report is 'This was well done my bird'.[26] A bird is a creature of the air, fittingly for the airy Ariel, and could function as a symbol of the soul, from the parable of the birds of the air perching in the branches of the tree – understood as a symbol of the Church. Prospero then gives Ariel his next task: 'The trumpery in my house, go bring it hither / For stale to catch these thieves.'[27] This appears to confirm the recusant interpretation, as 'trumpery' was commonly used in a derogatory sense, referring to Catholic paraphernalia. Interestingly, in light of the name 'Trinculo', the word 'trinket' could have similar connotations ('fripperies' is another one). The OED quotes a 1591 anti-Catholic sermon as follows: 'Then they invented purgatory, masses, prayers for the dead, and then all their Trinkets.' When Ariel returns, 'loaden with glistering apparel, &c' (stage direction), Prospero says, 'Come hang them on this line.'[28] At this point Stephano and Trinculo enter led by Caliban, but they cannot see Prospero and Ariel because they are invisible. Stephano and Trinculo have determined on killing Prospero, and Caliban is leading them to his cell, where they suppose they can accomplish this while he is asleep.[29] Caliban urges his comrades to be silent as they are now drawing near to Prospero's habitation, and after some more banter, Caliban says:

> Prithee my king, be quiet. Seest thou here,
> This is the mouth 'o the cell: no noise, and enter,
> Do that good mischief which may make this island
> Thine own for ever, and I, thy Caliban,
> For aye thy foot-licker.[30]

This is a key moment as the murder of Prospero is anticipated, but what a contrast to the fevered agonising of Macbeth in the build-up to the murder of Duncan. Here, the audience is prepared for something ridiculous to

---

[25] *The Tempest* IV.i.179–182.
[26] *The Tempest* IV.i.184.
[27] *The Tempest* IV.i.186–187. See note on page 70 for the priest Sherwood described as 'a stale to tak byrds of his kynd' by the government spy Berden.
[28] *The Tempest* IV.i.193.
[29] The word 'cell' has obvious connotations of monasticism and therefore Catholicism.
[30] *The Tempest* IV.i.215–219.

happen – this is a comedy after all – but even so, the behaviour of Stephano and Trinculo at this point has audiences scratching their heads. The two would-be assailants notice the garments hanging on the line and immediately become distracted from their dastardly plan. Caliban is as baffled as the audience: 'Let it alone thou fool; it is but trash,' he says.[31] Stephano dismisses Caliban's repeated pleas with a 'Be you quiet, monster',[32] and we arrive at the key to this obscure vignette:

Stephano: Be you quiet monster. Mistress line,
is not this my jerkin? Now is the jerkin under
the line: now, jerkin, you are like to lose your
hair and prove a bald jerkin.

Trinculo: Do, do: we steal by line and level, an't like your grace.

Stephano: I thank thee for that jest; here's a garment for't:
wit shall not go unrewarded while I am king of this
country. 'Steal by line and level' is an excellent
pass of pate; there's another garment for't.[33]

If the 'Mistress line' in the text of *The Tempest* is the Mistress Line of Tyburn fame, what follows is some very dark humour of the gallows. The jerkin under the line was the jerking under the rope of a man with the shaved pate of a tonsured Benedictine monk.[34] When words are spoken from the stage, the audience is not distracted by the spelling, and 'steal' is the same as 'steel'. Line and level refer to the plumb line and level used by builders to check vertical and horizontal placement. Barkworth was cut into quarters, perhaps with the same steel knife that Anne Line had used to cut off her petticoat lace. It seems very likely that this scene in *The Tempest* recalls the tragic scene from ten years previously, including an acknowledgement that the sole evidence in Mistress Line's trial was allegedly the garment of a priest. According to Garnet, Anne Line was a skilled needlewoman who made vestments for the priests as well as certain items for the altar, and if this had become generally known, it would have added to the association between

---

[31] *The Tempest* IV.i.224.
[32] *The Tempest* IV.i.235.
[33] *The Tempest* IV.i.235–244.
[34] The repetition of 'jerkin' may suggest a reference to Jenkyn Maldons, and the reference to 'line and level' may be a double pun, 'line' referring to the land 'stolen' from Anne and Roger Line (the Ringwood estate) and 'level' referring to the 'levels' south of Maldon that would have formed Anne Line's dowry.

Anne Line and what pursuivants referred to as papist trash.[35] As well as recalling specific events, Shakespeare is surely alluding to the common complaint by Catholics that searches of their houses were often the pretext for simple thievery by those who leapt on the opportunity to rifle through the householder's property.

The incident with the line is problematic to say the least in traditional interpretations of *The Tempest*, but it fits much better within an overall recusant theme. It makes sense of Prospero's sudden anger when he recalls the plot against him and makes the famous announcement that is thought to presage Shakespeare's own retirement:

> Our revels now are ended. These our actors,
> As I foretold you, were all spirits and
> Are melted into air, into thin air;
> and like the baseless fabric of this vision,
> The cloud-capp'd towers, the gorgeous palaces,
> The solemn temples, the great globe itself,
> Ye all which it inherit, shall dissolve
> And like this insubstantial pageant faded,
> Leave not a rack behind.[36]

The scene following the line incident has Prospero considering the fate of prisoners confined in his 'line-grove', and he decides to be magnanimous.[37] Perhaps this represents the recusant fantasy of a return of England to the Catholic faith and the forgiveness that would be offered by a Catholic regime to repentant former persecutors. He says:

> Though with their high wrongs I am strook to th' quick,
> Yet with my nobler reason 'gaitist [against] my fury
> Do I take part: the rarer action is
> In virtue than in vengeance: they being penitent,
> The sole drift of my purpose doth extend
> Not a frown further.[38]

And, in what seems to be a hint of future toleration:

---

[35] Caraman, *Garnet*, 277f.
[36] *The Tempest* IV.i.148–156.
[37] Wilson, *TLS*, 15.
[38] *The Tempest* V.i.25–30.

> Go release them Ariel:
> My charms I'll break, their senses I'll restore,
> *And they shall be themselves* [my italics]³⁹

The implication is that English Catholics had learned the hard way what it was to be denied the right to be true to themselves and were now ready to grant freedom of conscience to their Protestant counterparts.⁴⁰

Lasting Memory

Whether sorrow at Anne Line's death was responsible for sparking Shakespeare's 'The Phoenix and the Turtle', we know from the 'Thomas in Liege' letter that such emotion spread beyond the select troop present at the requiem held in her honour. But we can only guess at the feelings of her father, or whether her son even knew who she was.

In December 1929, Pope Pius XI beatified Anne Line along with Mark Barkworth and others, including Robert Southwell, Philip Howard, and Nicholas Owen, the Jesuit lay-brother who constructed many of the ingenious hiding places used by priests such as John Gerard and Henry Garnet. Roger Filcock was beatified by Pope John Paul II in 1987. Anne Line was canonised in 1970 as one of the Forty Martyrs of England and Wales, whose collective feast day is 25 October, and today the Essex town of Basildon has both an infant school and a junior school named in her memory. If this is Shakespeare's muse, perhaps her greatest legacy lies in what she has to tell us about him.

---

[39] *The Tempest* V.i.30–32.
[40] For Shakespeare's plea for toleration in *The Tempest*, see Beauregard 'New Light on Shakespeare's Catholicism: Prospero's Epilogue in *The Tempest*', 171. Richard Wilson concludes: '[Shakespeare's] writings can be aligned ... with the politique faction which formed around Ferdinando, Lord Strange; took its philosophy of toleration from Florio's Montaigne in the library of the Montagues; split over the Essex rebellion; and at last regrouped behind the Howard project of religious détente' (*Secret Shakespeare*, 296).

Epilogue: The Symbol-Line Allegory

The House of Worcester

Anne Line was one of the almost hidden people of history. If Shakespeare has concealed her in the play *Cymbeline*, he did it for those in the know, for the coterie audience who could pick up his subtle allusions to the detail of her story. Just such a potential audience had been long in the making. When a government agent in 1593 noted the attendance of Mistress Line at Mass in the Earl of Worcester's house, his scant listing of her name left us a fat clue. After all, who would most remember Anne Line after her death, but people who had met her and for whom she had been both a trusted acquaintance and a fellow-believer in the underground Church? In Worcester's household, as in so many others, it was the women who played a vital role in keeping the faith alive, and among the women were five daughters of the Earl, named Frances, Catherine, Anne, Elizabeth and (oddly, but only from a modern perspective) another Catherine. In 1596, Elizabeth would marry Henry Guldeford, whose grandfather's sister was the original Anne Line (snr), creating a link by marriage between the Worcester family and Roger and Anne Line. We also have a link to a significant location in *Cymbeline*, because, while the Worcesters' London house was on the Strand, the family seat was Raglan Castle in Wales. Moreover, Frances, one of the Worcester sisters, would marry William Morgan of Llantarnam, a prominent Catholic neighbour of the Earl in Monmouthshire. In December 1607, Lady Frances Morgan, as she became, may have been at home in Wales, because her name is noticeably absent from a list of women drawn up in that month who were involved in an entertainment at Court, a list that does include the four other sisters named above. The presence of these four sisters is highly significant because they clearly represent, in the very Court of King James, just the kind of coterie audience that could appreciate a play featuring Anne Line in the subtext. December 1608 is about the mid-point of the various estimates by scholars of when *Cymbeline* was first performed (1606–1611).

Worcester had presided over the coronation ceremonials in 1603, and he would remain one of the King's four chief advisers for almost a decade, but it is easier to manage a state occasion than to marshal the tides of history. The world was changing, identities were shifting. After the union of crowns there was less talk of England, Scotland, Ireland and Wales, and more of the Empire of Britain; less talk of the English and the Scots, and more of the South Brittaines and the North Brittaines, and of the Welsh as the last remnant of the ancient Briton race. Religious as well as national identities were in transition with the disappointment of Catholic hopes either for Spanish military aid to restore Catholicism or for a sustained policy of toleration from the new king. This had been followed by the shock of the Gunpowder Plot and the hardening of the English Protestant identity in opposition to the Catholic threat. But Catholic hopes had not been entirely dashed by any means. Queen Anne of Denmark was rumoured to have a Catholic chaplain at Court, and increasing numbers of priests were operating secretly throughout England. Above all, there was still the hope that the young Prince Henry might in time adopt the faith of his grandmother, Mary Queen of Scots. It was into this shifting, uncertain and divided world that Shakespeare brought his play *Cymbeline*. It was entertaining but complex. Fundamentally, it is a very old-fashioned response to the question of identity, that looks beyond race and nationality to religion. It is about the triumph of love over hate, faith over despair, divine grace over human sin, and harmony over division, in Church, State, and Christendom. Perhaps that is one reason why Shakespeare chose to set a play about his own time in that of King Cymbeline, who was believed to have been the King of the Britons at the time of the birth of Christ. He is reminding his audience of a starting point.

The Tragedie of Cymbeline

> You do not meet a man but frowns: our bloods
> No more obey the heavens than our courtiers
> Still seem as does the King.

So begins *Cymbeline* with a very puzzling sentence indeed. It is almost as though Shakespeare was in a hurry when he wrote it and gabbled it out like an actor who does not quite understand his lines. As the dialogue proceeds, we get the gist of the situation – the King is unhappy and his courtiers are pretending that they are too – but this could have been said so much more simply. So, why was it not? Was Shakespeare slapdash – just having a bad day, perhaps – or is that first sentence wilfully obscure for a reason, and is Shakespeare challenging us to ponder it carefully? We expect the bloods *not* to be obeying the heavens and the courtiers *not* to be seeming-as-does-the-King, but actually the sense is quite different and subversive: the courtiers *are* seeming as does the King and therefore the bloods *are* obeying the heavens, which means they are in harmony with what is right and good, even if they have to pretend to put on another face for the benefit of the King who, by implication, is not. So, it appears, we have a roundabout and safely subtle way of saying that the King is not in harmony with heaven. This sentence is puzzling because it is meant to be. It is a carefully constructed riddle and it is the first indication that *Cymbeline* is related to Shakespeare's other carefully constructed riddle, 'The Phoenix and the Turtle', that has been interpreted as a eulogy for Anne Line. The connection will be made again later in the play with the use of the riddle of the eagle and the tree.

And so we come, via Shakespeare's phoenix, to the suggestion that Anne Line's story is in fact the crucial lost source for the puzzle that is *Cymbeline*, and in particular for the luminous Imogen: 'A shop of all the qualities that man loves woman for' (V.v.166–167). No one found it because it was not part of the published literature and, like a coin buried in a garden, it has remained a secret until the present day. The scholars simply never looked in the right place. In what follows, it will help the reader to have some familiarity with the play, but none is assumed and I hope none is necessary to follow the argument. For clarity's sake there is some minor repetition of material given earlier in this volume.

Given the sensitivity of her work for the Jesuits during the 1590s, Anne Line was necessarily a secretive figure. This clearly changed with her public trial and execution, when all London could have heard about her, including William Shakespeare. However, I contend that Shakespeare's writing suggests a much greater familiarity with her story than could be gleaned, for example, from being present at her execution. I have suggested that he may have known of the disinheritance through James Burbage, but further than that, there are strong grounds for supposing that he knew people who knew her, particularly through her documented connection to the Worcester household. And, of course, he may have met her in person, though we have no evidence that he did. Shakespeare certainly would have known, at least from 1603, the secretary to the Earl of Worcester, William Sterrell, through Sterrell's appointment during that year as keeper of the buildings which housed the Office of Revels. Sterrell was the Catholic double agent who seems to have been responsible for sending Garnet's secret correspondence to Rome and receiving material coming the other way from the Catholic exile Persons.[1]

---

[1] See 75.

Perhaps, before it was sent, Garnet allowed a select few to read the letter of 11 March that contained his glowing tribute to Anne Line. Connections with Jesuits and with William Sterrell may seem to cast Shakespeare in a light that is very much at odds with the impression given by some of his biographers, but it is absolutely consistent with the *only* contemporary comment on Shakespeare's religious sympathies (at least the only one that has wide recognition) – namely, the scathing reference by John Speed in 1611 to 'this papist [Fr Persons] and his poet [Shakespeare], the one ever feigning, the other ever falsifying the truth'.[2] This remark was prompted by Shakespeare's lampooning of the Protestant martyr hero John Oldcastle in the character Falstaff. With Imogen he does something perhaps even more infuriating to the likes of John Speed: he takes a Catholic recently executed as a felon, turns her into a heroine, and smuggles her portrait past the censor to be played in all its glory before the high and low of London. Happily for us, if Anne Line was a source for *Cymbeline*, then *Cymbeline* is at least a 'kind of' source for Anne Line.

Hazarding an Interpretation

The historical King Cymbeline (Cunobelin) was thought to have been the King of the Britons at the time of the birth of Christ, and it is generally accepted that Shakespeare has cribbed his history, rather loosely, from Holinshed. According to modern historians, Cymbeline reigned over a good part of southern Britain from about AD 10 to about AD 40, during which time there is evidence of good relations with the Romans and flourishing trade. After his death it appears that the Roman tribute was withheld, and in AD 43 Britain was invaded and nearly 400 years of direct Roman rule began. The Emperor Claudius himself arrived a little after the initial conquest and made his way, accompanied by war elephants, to the capital of the new province of 'Britannia' at Camulodunum.[3]

---

[2] Speed, *Historie of Great Britaine* (London: 1611), bk 9, 15. Noted by Munro, *Shakespeare Allusion Book* (224f) in 1909 and generally accepted as referring to Shakespeare, although he is not named in the text. However, Alison Shell (*Shakespeare's Religion*, 84) is reluctant to draw firm conclusions. She writes that, 'given that the imputation of popish sympathies was such a common and indiscriminate insult at the time, Speed need have meant no more than that Shakespeare's play [*Henry IV Pt 1*] and others gave ammunition to Catholics'. The other contemporary allusion is the famous description of Shakespeare as an 'upstart crow' at the beginning of his career in London around 1592. As Wilson suggests, the pejorative use of the word 'crow' may well have been intended to imply Catholicism (see Walsham, *The Reformation Landscape*, 88, 91; Wilson, *Secret Shakespeare*, 11–13).

[3] Londinium would soon surpass Camulodunum in importance, but initially the Romans chose to base themselves at the existing capital that had been the headquarters of King Cymbeline.

Various sources for Shakespeare's play have long been acknowledged. Apart from Holinshed's *Chronicles*, already mentioned, Boccaccio's *Decameron* and an obscure text called *Frederyke of Jennen* are thought to have supplied the story of Posthumus's wager on his wife's chastity. This is all well and good, but it is evident from the academic literature that big questions still remain, and the sources identified thus far have failed to unlock a really coherent meaning for the play as a whole. Thus, Alison Thorne, in the 2002 volume *Shakespeare's Romances*, writes of *Cymbeline* as a 'clever device to perplex and tease' with 'persistent absurdities and enigmas' (178, 189). This is by no means untypical of current scholarship which at best comes to rather vague conclusions such as that Shakespeare is experimenting with a new form – the romance play – or that *Cymbeline* is something to do with the formation of British identity in the years following the union of the crowns of Scotland and England. While there is something to be said for both these points, as explanations of the play as a whole they are unsatisfactory and incomplete and there remains a great deal to puzzle over – indeed, so much so that a reader of *Shakespeare's Romances* may well conclude that Shakespeare is deliberately toying with his audiences by presenting a tale signifying nothing:

> Instead of trying to solve the riddle of the play's 'meaning' by identifying the key to its multiplicity we might more profitably attend to the ways in which this, the most elusive of Shakespeare's so-called 'romances', reflects ironically on the question of its own illegibility.[4]

In other words, 'Don't ask me what it means – I haven't the foggiest idea.' In the absence of the key, an allegory becomes an impenetrable riddle, and so Shakespeare reduces scholarship to the following resort:

> I shall try to show how *Cymbeline* incorporates a reflexive, meta-critical commentary on the hazards of interpretation through reiterative use of the interlocking tropes of reading, writing, or narrating, and seeing.[5]

Oh the 'hazards of interpretation'. But the puzzlement over *Cymbeline* has a long history – witness the now more or less obligatory quote from Dr Johnson:

---

[4] Thorne, 177.
[5] Thorne, 178.

EPILOGUE: THE SYMBOL-LINE ALLEGORY

> This play has many just sentiments, some natural dialogues, and some pleasing scenes, but they are obtained at the expense of much incongruity. To remark the folly of the fiction, the absurdity of the conduct, the confusion of the names, and manners of different times, and the impossibility of the events in any system of life, were to waste criticism upon unresisting imbecility, upon faults too evident for detection, and too gross for aggravation.[6]

Later critics refused to believe that the whole play had been written by Shakespeare, and blamed the imbecility on a collaborator. However, reaction has not always been so negative, and during the nineteenth century *Cymbeline* was celebrated as never before. Interestingly, this enthusiasm centred very much on the character of Imogen, who, in this age of Romanticism, was rhapsodised as the 'woman above all Shakespeare's women' and as a symbol of the perfect, otherworldly form of her sex: 'in Imogen we find half-glorified already the immortal godhead of womanhood'.[7] Nosworthy, in the Arden critical edition, dismisses this comment as a wild specimen of 'the perverted ritual of an Imogen cult', but what may seem quite overblown to modern ears may be much closer to the sensibilities of Shakespeare's Neoplatonist contemporaries than Nosworthy realised. The mistake made by these nineteenth-century critics was in seeing Imogen as symbolising the perfection of womanhood, whereas Shakespeare is in fact doing more than this. His Imogen follows in the tradition of Petrarch's Laura and Dante's Beatrice, as an exemplary, idealised woman, used to reflect not so much on womanhood as on spiritual realities that are beyond manhood and womanhood. Behind the figures of Laura, Beatrice and Imogen is the sense that physical beauty can symbolise spiritual beauty, which in turn has its source in God. The unspoken assumption is that this will be understood in the light of Augustine's teaching that the spiritual path leads from the love of created things to the love of the Creator.

In general, when scholars have written about *Cymbeline*, the best they can do is explain certain aspects of the play. But there are two critics, Peter Milward and Clare Asquith, who have come closer to a satisfactory account of the play as a whole, and it is telling that in both cases they rely on a Catholic subtext to achieve this. Neither of these scholars arrived at their conclusions via an awareness of the symbolism of Anne and Roger Line; instead, they did so by tracing numerous more general indications in the text

---

[6] Samuel Johnson, *General Observations on the Plays of Shakespeare* (1756), quoted in Nosworthy, *Cymbeline*, xl.
[7] Nosworthy, xlii, quoting Swinburne.

and by seeing this particular play in terms of a broader dissident interpretation of Shakespeare's work.[8]

The Tribute Story

Of the several interwoven stories in *Cymbeline*, the simplest to explain concerns the payment of tribute to Rome. At the beginning of the play, Cymbeline, King of the Britons, is at peace with the Romans. Many years previously, Julius Caesar had come and seen and conquered, and had been persuaded to leave again by the promise of a regular payment of tribute. According to Holinshed's sources, good relations had ensued. He writes:

> [C]ymbeline, being brought up in Rome, and knighted in the court of Augustus, ever showed himself a friend to the Romans, and chiefly was loth to break with them, because the youth of the Britaine nation should not be deprived of the benefit to be trained and brought up to behave themselves like civill men, and to atteine to the knowledge of feats of warre.[9]

Had Shakespeare also consulted Camden's *Britannia,* as I have no doubt he did, he could have viewed a page of illustrations of ancient British coins, most of which date to the reign of Cymbeline. The first of these coins has an image that Camden interprets as the two-faced Janus: 'peradventure, because even at that time Britaine began to cast off and leave their barbarous rudeness'.[10] In other words, under Roman influence, Cymbeline changed a backward-looking country to one that looked forward to a more civilised future. The second coin has the inscription 'TASCIA', that Camden (wrongly, as it happens) suggests 'betokeneth a Tribute Penye'. Be that as it may, in Shakespeare's play, King Cymbeline receives a demand from the Romans for the payment of the tribute that had fallen into abeyance since the time of Julius Caesar. Egged on by the patriotic speeches of his wife and her son Cloten – 'we will nothing pay / For wearing our own noses' (III.i.13f) – he refuses the demand. The consequence of this defiance is that the Romans land an invading army at Milford Haven in Wales and a desperate battle ensues that, somewhat surprisingly, the Britons win. But if the

---

[8] See Milward, *Shakespeare the Papist*, 251–258; Asquith, *Shadowplay*, 253–257.
[9] Holinshed, quoted in Bullough, 44.
[10] Camden, *Britannia*, 'Conjectures as touching the British coines', para. 2.

audience has taken this to be a victory for patriotism and thumbing-the-nose-at-Rome, it is about to be disabused because in the final scene a magnanimous King Cymbeline proclaims his peace in surprising terms:

> My peace we will begin. And, Caius Lucius [Roman Commander],
> Although the victor, we submit to Caesar,
> And to the Roman empire; promising
> To pay our wonted tribute, from the which
> We were dissuaded by our wicked queen;
> Whom heavens, in justice, both on her and hers,
> Have laid most heavy hand. (V.v.459–465)

He continues in emollient form: 'A Roman and a British ensign wave / Friendly together' and 'Th' imperial Caesar, should again unite / His favour with the radiant Cymbeline, / Which shines here in the west' (V.v.480f, 474–476). The play ends with the words: 'Never was a war did cease, / Ere bloody hands were wash'd, with such a peace' (V.v.484f). The defiant little-Britain patriotism that had been thrown in the face of the Roman emissary earlier in the play seems to have died with the two characters, Cloten and the Queen, who had voiced it.

So, how might the sophisticated members of a London audience have received this voluntary submission to Rome around 1607–1610, when *Cymbeline* was first performed? They could hardly fail to be aware that this story could have a symbolic meaning. It is well recognised that the use of allegory, metaphor and subtext thrived in the culture of the time, in part due to the practice of censorship:

> It is frequently acknowledged that censorship gives birth to metaphors which thrive on ambiguity. Elizabethan and Jacobean dramatists were adept at giving themselves alibis by re-siting their political and satirical plays in the ancient world, or in imaginary courts of Arcadia, Genoa or Ferrara, or by dislocating the action altogether.[11]

Audiences could take their cue from lines such as 'you may then *revolve* what tales I have told you' (Belarius: III.iii.14) [my italics] to try and see behind the surface drama and catch the 'real meaning'. But in truth, little prompting is needed with regard to the tribute story, as it seems obvious that the question of Roman tribute was hinting at England's relationship with the papacy. The

---

[11] Clare, *'Art made tongue-tied by authority': Elizabethan and Jacobean dramatic censorship*, 214.

withholding of 'Peter's pence' by Henry VIII had been a symbolically important act of the English Reformation, and Henry VIII's 'stomach' was possessed of his daughter Elizabeth.[12] When Shakespeare's first audiences heard the nationalistic defiance of Cymbeline's queen with her invocation of Roman ships cracking like eggshells against British rocks and making Lud's town (London) bright 'with rejoicing fires' (III.i.33), they would surely recall the rhetoric of Queen Elizabeth and the celebrations over the failure of the Catholic Armada. This is an English Protestant voice, an appeal to the plucky island nation. Likewise, when Cymbeline refers to 'Caesar's ambition, / Which swell'd so much that it did almost stretch / The sides o' the world', it sounds very much like an English criticism of the papacy, and one that many English Catholics as well as Protestants could have some sympathy with. King Cymbeline's decision to pay the tribute is therefore exactly what it looks like – Shakespeare's English Catholic plea for the Crown to restore England's traditional recognition of the authority of the Pope.[13] It is pertinent to note that King James had once fancied himself as the convenor of an ecumenical council of the Church to achieve the great task of healing the split between Catholics and Protestants. Moreover, he had emphasised in his writings the importance of respect for legitimate authority in both Church and State, and the obvious Catholic response to this is precisely what we see barely concealed in *Cymbeline* – a plea for King James (or his son Henry) to be reconciled with the legitimate authority of Rome. To sweeten the pill, we are shown a humbled Rome recognised by a wise and beneficent British king acting from a position of strength.

Imogen and Posthumus

The tribute story, while very significant, is almost part of the backdrop in a play that revolves around the tale of Imogen and Posthumus. On the surface it goes like this: Posthumus is an orphan brought up at Court, where his

---

[12] This was the implication of Elizabeth's famous declaration that though she had the body of a woman she had the stomach of a man. According to a bizarre account given by a Catholic priest of his interrogation at the hands of Richard Topcliffe, the latter boasted of his intimacy with the Queen: 'That he hathe felt her belly, and said unto Her Majestie that she h[ad] the softest belly of any woman kynde... That she said unto him, 'be not thease the armes, legges and bo[dy] of King Henry?' to which he answered, 'yea'. See 'Letters & Despatches of Richard Verstegan, c. 1550–1640', *CRS* 52, 97.

[13] Willy Maley, has argued rather tentatively that Shakespeare 'could be seen to be ... championing a residual Catholicism' (*Postcolonial Shakespeare: British identity formation and Cymbeline*, 56). For a more forthright approach, see Milward (258), and also Asquith, who points out that 'Protestant writers [cf. *Mirror for Magistrates*] identified the imperial Roman attempts to invade Britain with the ambitions of papal Rome and associated Britain's refusal to pay tribute to Caesar with contemporary England's defiance of the Pope' (252–253).

childhood friend, the King's beautiful daughter Imogen, eventually becomes his sweetheart. They marry against the wishes of the King, who sends the lovestruck Posthumus into exile. When he arrives in Rome, Posthumus boasts to men he meets there of Imogen's virtues, including her fidelity, and this provokes a lascivious Iachimo to challenge Posthumus to a wager that he can conquer her chastity, a wager that Posthumus accepts. To cut a long story short, Iachimo fails, but on his return to Rome convinces Posthumus that he has succeeded, not least because he secretly observed a distinctive mole under Imogen's left breast. When Posthumus receives this information from Iachimo he is driven almost insane and orders his servant back in England to lure an unsuspecting Imogen to Milford Haven to kill her there. After much ado, anguish, repentance, etc., Posthumus is restored to the very much alive Imogen and they embrace as Posthumus sighs, 'Hang there like a fruit, my soul / until the tree dies' (V.v.263) – his best line by far. The wager story is one Shakespeare has culled from his literary sources, and it is obviously not the story of Anne and Roger Line, though it is related to it. This requires some unravelling.

First of all Shakespeare signals to his knowing audience through a whole gamut of clues that Posthumus and Imogen represent Roger and Anne Line. There is the obvious parallel that they marry for love, against the wishes of the father of the bride, and are separated when the groom is exiled, but Shakespeare wants to make the identity specific to this particular couple. Let us have a look at how that might work. Imagine that you are one of the coterie audience, seeing the play for the first time, perhaps in the Blackfriars Theatre. You are on the lookout for clues to hidden allegory early on, particularly with regard to the identities of the main characters. Almost immediately the play begins, you are presented with a scenario: the King is upset because his only daughter has referred herself to 'a poor but worthy gentleman', and 'She's wedded, Her husband banish'd'. A minor character enquires as to the identity of this poor banished husband and is told 'I cannot delve him to the root'. You prick up your ears. Surely that implies there is something to be dug out. Perhaps a clue is coming up. Then we learn, 'His father was Sicilius'. Okay, perhaps the allegorical identity has something to do with Sicily. What are the associations? Was there not a series of famous kings of Sicily called Roger – I, II and III?[14] Roger II had a particular claim to fame as he was the first to introduce the coin known as the ducat. By the time these thoughts have flashed across your mind, the dialogue has moved on and we have been told that Sicilius had 'gained the

---

[14] I am grateful to Clare Asquith for pointing this out.

sur-addition Leonatus'. Leon is 'lion' in Spanish, and 'leonatus' is born of a lion in Latin; lions figure in heraldry; there is a region of Spain called Leon. As you are pondering the kings of Leon you glance up at the walls of the Blackfriars Theatre. Of course! Katherine of Aragon (the divorce hearings took place at Blackfriars). The lions on her coat of arms (quartered with the castles of Castile) represent the region of Leon that was ruled by her mother, Queen Isabella of Castile and Leon. Her father, Ferdinand, King of Aragon, was also *King of Sicily*. You think you might be on to something. But you need to pay attention because you are being told that the 'poor but worthy' Leonatus is named *Posthumus* Leonatus, because his mother 'deceas'd / As he was born'. Katherine of Aragon could be seen as a kind of symbolic mother of the continuing English Catholic body that honours her memory. She was certainly 'deceas'd' at the time that many members of that body – such as Roger Line, for example – were born. Roger Line. Line, Leonatus – even the name is not dissimilar. And did the actor deliberately pronounce it 'Line-atus', or did you imagine that?[15]

Once you are on to the possibility that Posthumus is Roger Line – perhaps by halfway through the first scene – you are ready for the series of clues that confirm the identification as the play proceeds. Some of these are more subtle than others. For example, much is made of Posthumus's *ring* that he loses over the wager; Roger Line, of course, lost his Ringwood estate.[16] Moreover, he lost it because of his faith, and Fidele, meaning faithfully, is the name Imogen goes by for much of the play.[17] The dialogue in Act I scene v, when Posthumus arrives in exile in Rome, refers to 'the catalogue of his endowments' (I.v.5) (i.e. his inheritance) and other aspects of his life. For example, a Frenchman declares, 'I have seen him in France: we had very many there could behold the sun with as firm eyes as he' (I.v.11f). It is the eagle that beholds the sun with firm eyes, and Imogen has already described Posthumus as an eagle. This repetition emphasises the importance of a symbol that identifies Posthumus as a Catholic by analogy with the Roman

---

[15] If Leonatus is pronounced correctly with four syllables it breaks the meter in Shakespeare's text, suggesting that the actor may choose to compress the word. I am indebted to Asquith for this point.
[16] Rings and the loss of Catholic estates had already been linked in the minds of recusants by the case of Sir Francis Englefield, the most prominent of the Catholic exiles in Spain. He had tried to avoid his lands being seized by the Crown through the use of a legal conveyance that transferred ownership to his nephew until such time as Sir Francis chose to reclaim his estate by giving his nephew a gold ring. This legal device was so watertight that the Crown had to resort to an act of parliament in 1593 in order to enforce the confiscation (See Loomie, *The Spanish Elizabethans*, 23).
[17] The identification of Imogen with the figure of Faith (through her choice of 'Fidele' as an alias) is reminiscent of the association of Queen Elizabeth with the figure of Peace, a goddess who holds her hand in the 1582 painting known as the Allegory of the Tudor Succession.

eagle and, more specifically, with Catholic Spain.[18] This is because the 'full-winged eagle' featured prominently in the arms of the Catholic monarchs of Spain – Ferdinand and Isabella – and was incorporated into the arms of their daughter Katherine of Aragon when she became Queen of England. In fact, the black spread-eagle in these arms derives from Ferdinand's kingship of Sicily. Roger Line is linked to this symbolism both as an English Catholic honouring the memory of Katherine of Aragon, and more directly as an exile who received a pension from the Spanish crown.[19] We also know that Roger Line spent time in France, because he attended the college at Rheims, where there were many others, including the college itself, that were receiving financial support from Spain. All this is hinted at in the line 'we had very many there could behold the sun with as firm eyes as he'. The college represented a whole flock of eagles.

The eagle motif alerts the knowing audience to some more Roger Line material put into the mouth of the wise man Belarius, who is extolling the life of exile ('this life') despite its apparent disadvantages:

> ... And often, to our comfort, shall we find
> The sharded beetle in a safer hold
> Than is the full-winged eagle. O this life
> Is nobler than attending for a check:
> Richer than doing nothing for a robe
> Prouder than rustling in unpaid-for silk:
> Such gain the cap of him that makes him fine,
> Yet keeps his book uncross'd: no life to ours. (III.iii.19–26)

Roger Line had only one sibling, a brother called Richard, who inherited the Ringwood estate. Gerard recalls this man in a single, brief comment: 'I met him once in his elder brother's room. He was dressed in silk and finery, while his brother wore plain and cheap clothes.'[20] 'Check' means rebuke. '[A]ttending' could refer both to attendance at Court and, more subversively, to obligatory Protestant services with their anti-Catholic sermonising. 'Richer' appears to refer to Richard Line, who has gained his brother's cap. We now come to a rather striking clue, but in order to see it, we have to refer

---

[18] See also the riddle of the eagle and the tree, (IV.ii.346–352; V.v.436–477).
[19] There may be another specific reference to the arms of Ferdinand and Isabella in the words of the soothsayer in the final scene: 'the Roman eagle, / From south to west on wing soaring aloft, / Lessen'd herself, and in the beams o' the sun / So vanish'd' (V.v.471–474). Spain is south and west, and the eagle in the arms of Ferdinand and Isabella is depicted with the sun behind its head.
[20] Gerard, 83.

to the Folio text, because the crucial word is missing from modern critical editions such as the Arden version quoted above. We also need to be aware of recent research – namely, the discovery of the wills of Roger Line's parents. The Folio (1623), which contains the first published edition of *Cymbeline*, has 'Richer than doing nothing for a *babe*' [my italics]. Editors have altered 'babe' to 'robe' on the assumption that the Folio version was a typographical mistake.[21] But if *Rich*ard Line adopted his brother's baby son, as implied by the wills, what we are seeing is not a typo. Richard Line had, in effect, stolen away Roger Line's son and heir. This is not unconnected to the plot line that Belarius had stolen away the two sons of Cymbeline and brought them up as his own. What is happening here, very discreetly, is that Shakespeare is contrasting an accusation frequently made against the Catholic exiles – that they were stealing away the sons of England to their seminaries – with the reality of a young child being taken from its Catholic parents to be brought up by Protestants.

Shakespeare signals the allusion to Roger Line in the Belarius speech with the reference to the 'full-winged eagle', a good example of the use of code directed at a sensitised audience. But by this point in the play, we may imagine that a daughter of the Earl of Worcester, for example, picking up all these allusions to Roger and Anne Line, might be a little perplexed. The problem is that the wager story that is right at the centre of the play seems to have very little connection with Anne and Roger Line. The story is found in Boccaccio's *Decameron*, and there are one or two parallels, such as Anne Line's reputation for chastity and the declaration of Boccaccio's Bernardo that 'he had a wife so perfectly compleate in all graces and vertues, as any lady in the world', and 'he was verily persuaded, that if he stayed from her ten years space (yes all his life time) out of his house; yet never would shee falsifie her faith to him, or be lewdly allured by any other man'.[22] We can imagine Roger Line holding a similar faith in his wife. We can also imagine a similar cynicism greeting such sentiments as we find in the *Decameron*: 'what women may accomplish in secret, they will rarely faile to doe ... hold it for a certaine rule, that that woman is onely chaste, that never was solicited personally'.[23] Moreover, we read,

---

[21] Nosworthy, *Cymbeline* (Arden), 84f. *The Riverside Shakespeare* (1586) suggests 'bable' as an alternative to the original babe, with the note: 'bauble, trifle'.
[22] Bullough, 51.
[23] Bullough, 53.

EPILOGUE: THE SYMBOL-LINE ALLEGORY

> Thy wife is a Woman, made of flesh and blood, as other women are: if it be so, she cannot bee without the same desires, and the weaknesse or strength as other women have, to resist naturall appetites ... she must needs doe that which other Women doe.[24]

Perhaps this accounts for Imogen's anxiety about 'the she's of Italy' (I.iv.29) and their intentions towards her husband. While a modern reader may be inclined to assess the Boccaccio remarks in terms of gender issues, in Shakespeare's day, and indeed in Boccaccio's, the issue was the possibility of virtue in a world of human frailty. This was contentious in Shakespeare's time for two reasons. The first was that Luther's reformation had seemed to turn the striving for virtue – any virtue – into a vain and futile attempt to earn one's salvation. Celibacy in particular – practised as it was by Catholic priests, nuns, and individuals like Anne Line – was one of the prideful 'acts of supererogation' that were denounced in the thirty-nine articles of the Church of England. Second, there was no shortage of cynical voices ready to accuse women who harboured Catholic priests of sexual immorality. However, all that being said, the wager story in *Cymbeline* is still a far cry from the story of Anne and Roger Line, at least as far as we know it. Does Shakespeare's left hand not know what his right hand is doing? Posthumus is Roger, Imogen is Anne, but then a quite different story is being told.

The explanation is that a straightforward identification of these characters is not Shakespeare's intention, and to appreciate this we need to see another layer to his allegory. About seven years before he wrote *Cymbeline*, Shakespeare composed 'The Phoenix and the Turtle', a poem that was an almost unbreakable riddle. Only those who knew the inside story of Anne and Roger Line and the fact that Anne Line had three names, for example, could hope to understand it. But 'The Phoenix and the Turtle' is not just about Anne Line, because Anne Line is used in this poem as a symbol. Shakespeare returns to this in *Cymbeline* either because he has established a code that he wants to use again, or possibly to clarify what he had been attempting to achieve in 'The Phoenix and the Turtle'. For one reason or another, Shakespeare deployed the same metaphor he had used in the poem, in a play that is built on the *symbol of the Lines*. In other words *Cymbeline* is really Symbol-Line. This may appear too wince-inducing to be true, but where puns and Shakespeare are concerned there are no holds barred. In the poem, the phoenix and the turtle correspond to Anne and Roger Line, but these

---

[24] Quoted in Bullough, 53.

two-who-have-become-one-in-the-sacrament-of-marriage function as symbols of the spiritual and temporal aspects of the true Church. This is the allegorical key both to 'The Phoenix and the Turtle' and to *Cymbeline* and explains the numerous symbolic links between these two works. To take a quite uncontroversial example of such links, in both cases characters are seen 'simultaneously as human beings and as birds', an oddity that not only connects the two works but at the same time hints strongly at an allegorical layer of meaning, though this is certainly more obvious in the case of the poem.[25] It may be objected that in my comments on 'Sonnet 74' I have argued that Anne Line is a 'temporal' figure, as is implied by her alias 'Martha', yet here I am suggesting that in 'The Phoenix and Turtle' and in *Cymbeline*, Anne Line symbolises the 'spiritual' aspect of the Church. My response is that this is indeed what Shakespeare does, and furthermore, this is exactly what Henry Garnet also does. He often refers to Anne Line as Mrs Martha, but on one occasion he writes: 'Mrs Martha, or Mrs Magdelene, as we also wish to call her, *because she acts the part of both*' [my italics] – the two parts being those of Martha and Mary, traditionally symbolising temporal 'actives' and spiritual 'contemplatives'.[26]

The setting of 'The Phoenix and the Turtle' is the Requiem Mass for Anne Line. Roger Line is present in the poem, but as a disembodied spirit because he had died seven or eight years previously. This gives us another reason why Shakespeare carefully selected the curious name 'Posthumus' for Imogen's husband.[27] And what a subtle pun is 'senseless linen' to signify a disembodied Roger Line. What we are seeing is not just coded reference to a particular Catholic couple, but a very specific set of allusions to the riddle of 'The Phoenix and the Turtle'. In the poem, Shakespeare uses the tragedy of Anne Line's execution to symbolise the rejection of the truth and beauty of the old faith. In *Cymbeline*, the same symbols – Anne and Roger as the spiritual and temporal aspects of the Church – are re-deployed in a parable about deep divisions and turmoil among Catholics themselves, and specifically about the tension between those who looked to temporal power for

---

[25] See Nosworthy (lxxiii), who notes Imogen as the phoenix (Iachimo describes her as 'alone th' Arabian bird'); Cloten as the puttock (kite); the princes as the 'poor unfledg'd'; Belarius, 'like a crow'; the alleged seductress of Posthumus as 'some jay of Italy'; and Posthumus as the eagle. Nosworthy also includes in his list Iachimo as a raven, following Furnival, but this rests on a mistaken interpretation of II.ii.49 (the raven here is the one who reports evil deeds to his master, Apollo; see Ovid, *Metamorphosis* bk II, 'Story of Coronis').

[26] Garnet Letter, 11 March 1601.

[27] The name Posthumus occurs in Holinshed, but *not* as the husband of Innogen [*sic*]. Imogen.

deliverance (i.e. to Milford Haven) and those with a spiritual outlook.[28] Many Catholics felt deceived by some of the more militant among their number, and it is worth noting that the wager story is about the dire consequences of deception – Boccaccio introduces his version of it with the motto 'The deceiver is often trampled upon by such as he hath deceived.'[29]

Between the composition of the poem and that of the play a momentous event had occurred that had resulted in more rejoicing fires in London town – namely, the discovery of the Gunpowder Plot. English Catholics were acutely aware that however much the authorities had provoked and exploited this episode, it was nonetheless a terrible self-inflicted wound, and it is in this light that Shakespeare presents it. There are a number of allusions to the Plot in *Cymbeline*, but they are generally ignored by critics because of the difficulty of making sense of them. For example, it was put about that when the Jesuits Henry Garnet and Oswald Tesimond had been informed by Catesby of the arrest of Guido Fawkes, they had exclaimed 'we are all utterly undone', words that Shakespeare puts (almost verbatim) into the mouth of Belarius, a sympathetic character in *Cymbeline* (IV.ii.123).[30] The precise context of this exclamation is intriguing because Guido Fawkes had been intent on decapitating the regime, and Belarius's reaction in the play is his response to the news that Guiderius has succeeded in decapitating Cloten.[31] Suffice to say at this point that on the allegorical level, Belarius probably represents the older generation of Catholic priests, and Cloten an aspect of the new regime.[32]

---

[28] Clare Asquith arrives at essentially the same conclusion about Imogen and Posthumus but without the identification with the Lines. Thus she writes, 'The couple's complex story and the bitterness of their rift emphasises the seriousness with which Shakespeare viewed the rifts between English Catholics.' Asquith suggests that Imogen and Posthumus represent 'domestic and exiled Catholics'. See Asquith, *Shadowplay*, 253f.
[29] Bullough, 50.
[30] Catesby sent the news via Thomas Bates, but the response of the priests does not feature in Bates's own account of this episode. Nevertheless, the words 'we are all undone' soon became attributed to Garnet in popular accounts of the plot with the implication that the Jesuits were guilty of involvement. See Fraser, *The Gunpowder Plot: terror and faith in 1605*, 181; Tesimond, *The Gunpowder Plot*, 153. The details of the plot remain disputed by historians, and the intention may have been to target specifically the privy council rather than blow up the whole Parliament. Francis Edwards, in *Guy Fawkes: The Enigma of the Gunpowder Plot?*, has argued that the plot 'was largely the contrivance of Robert Cecil' and that the 36 barrels discovered in the undercroft of the House of Lords were filled with earth and concealed there on his orders. Edwards notes a report that Catesby was observed being let into Cecil's London house, suggesting that he may have been an agent provocateur, and John Whynniard, the man who allegedly leased the undercroft to the plotters, mysteriously died on the morning of 5 November. There are certainly oddities and inconsistencies in the official account of the affair, and it is clear that from very early on that it was treated with scepticism. Indeed, as Edwards points out, it was felt necessary in a history of the gunpowder treason published in 1679 to refute the idea 'that all this was a contrivance of Secretary Cecil'.
[31] The inference is not that Shakespeare is endorsing the Gunpowder Plot per se, but that a violent reaction to a violent regime is understandable.
[32] Milward (254) notes that Belarius was banished for being 'confederate with the Romans' (III.iii.68) and later hotly denied Cymbeline's accusation that he was 'a traitor' (V.v.321), as did many recusants.

There is another rather surprising reference to the plot in a pun on the famous 'Monteagle letter'. This anonymous missive received by Lord Monteagle was supposedly sent by his brother-in-law, Francis Tresham, to urge him away from attendance at the State Opening of Parliament; 'I have a care for your preservation,' it pleads, and warns darkly, 'they shall receive a terrible blow'. On receiving the letter, Monteagle took it without delay to Robert Cecil, thereby giving the authorities a crucial advance warning of the plot and prompting a thorough search of the undercroft of the House of Lords that discovered Fawkes with matches at the ready. This at least is the official account of events, but the official account has always appeared a little too neat. Francis Tresham always denied that he had sent the letter, and there have long been suspicions that the Machiavellian Robert Cecil was himself the originator of it. He may indeed have known of the plot by other means but used the device of an anonymous letter to protect his real source or to cover the tracks of an agent provocateur. Whatever its provenance, the arrival of the Monteagle letter became a crucial element in the popular narrative of the plot, and was portrayed as the point when, in the words of Robert Cecil,

> It has pleased Almighty God, out of his singular goodness, to bring to light the most cruel and detestable Conspiracy against the person of his Majesty and the whole State of this Realm that ever was conceived by the heart of man at any time or in any place wheresoever.[33]

God had intervened, that was the message. In the normal course of events, divine interventions – illustrated with no hesitation by the pamphleteers of the Gunpowder Plot – were handled rather differently in plays. On the stage, the device of a god appearing from on high and changing the course of a theatrical plot was frowned on as a *deus ex machina* contrivance and the lame resort of poor writers. This opinion derived from the *Ars Poetica* of the Latin poet Horace, the '*machina*' apparently referring to the crane used to lower a 'god' into the sight of the audience, a stunt that even in Roman times was becoming a little jaded. Is it conceivable that Shakespeare did not know about this and what the connotations were? Of course he did. When he staged a divine intervention in *Cymbeline* with the god Jupiter appearing to descend to the stage on the back of an eagle – presumably lowered on a pulley of some kind – this was a very deliberate *deus ex machina* moment. So what does it mean? Well, first of all, there is a rather strong hint that it relates

---

[33] Robert Cecil, 9 November 1605, quoted in Edwards, *Fawkes*, 4.

to the Gunpowder Plot, because at the end of his speech, Jupiter ascends again with the words, '*Mount eagle*, to my palace crystalline', deploying a pun on Lord Monteagle that was familiar from the pamphleteers.

There are two implications of this pun. The first is that Shakespeare is not impressed by the official propaganda about the plot. He sees through it. He may even be saying, 'You have not fooled us with that story about the Monteagle letter; you say God has intervened, but we can see the wires.' Certainly he is distancing himself from the popular propaganda depiction of the plot and suggesting that it is contrived. The second implication is more opaque in that it only becomes evident when the allegorical level of the play is revealed through the link with the symbolism of Anne and Roger Line. On this level, Posthumus represents the 'temporal' aspect of the Catholic Church, *including the radicals who had attempted to destroy King and Parliament*. Whether or not the powder had been ignited, the plot threatened to destroy Catholicism in England, as the reluctant plotter Francis Tresham would admit: 'It would not be a means to advance our religion but to overthrow it, for the odiousness of the fact would be such as that would make the whole Kingdom to turn their fury upon such as were taken for Catholics, and not to spare man or woman so affected.' This, to some extent, is what happened over the following 200 years. In Shakespeare's play, we find that Posthumus, symbol of the temporal Catholics, commits the terrible crime of threatening the life of the very one to whom he had pledged his love and undying allegiance – namely, Imogen, who symbolises the spiritual aspect of the Catholic Church. Appalled by his own behaviour, he descends into an abyss of despair over what he has done. Having killed, as he thinks he has, the beloved Imogen, he begins to seek his own death. At this dark juncture the souls of the departed enter the scene and intercede for Posthumus and it is in response to these prayers that God, in the form of Jupiter (the Christian God could not be depicted on stage), intervenes and begins the process of forgiveness and restoration that will culminate in the reunion of Posthumus and Imogen (this is the real divine intervention, as opposed to the manipulations of Robert Cecil). It is in this eventual reunion that we see the deepest meaning of the play as it symbolises the healing of a traumatised English Catholic body that been in conflict with itself on account of a mad conspiracy dreamed up at least in part by its own sons.

In terms of Anne Line's Jesuit friends, the aftermath of the Gunpowder Plot saw John Gerard flee abroad never to return and Henry Garnet finally tracked down after an intense search and executed (betrayed by a man called Humphrey Littleton). At the macro level, the Gunpowder Plot set the seal on a forty-year propaganda campaign to tar English Catholics with the brush of treachery. The Cecils, father and son, were handed their victory by the racked hand of Guido Fawkes. On the micro level, it is striking how close the plot came to Shakespeare himself, who appears to have been related to several of the plotters and may have known Robert Catesby since childhood, as his father John Shakespeare seems to have been a trusted acquaintance of Robert Catesby's father, Sir William. As Antonia Fraser has pointed out, the arc of the plotters houses spread through the English Midlands and centred on Stratford-upon-Avon. In London the plotters are known to have held a meeting at the Mermaid Tavern, where the landlord, William Johnson, was a friend and business associate of Shakespeare's, and another friend, Ben Jonson, was observed dining with Catesby and others just a few weeks before the plot came to light. If, as Finnis and Martin suggest, Shakespeare had some connection with the Earl of Worcester and his secretary William Sterrell, then he was also linked to at least one of those Catholic-leaning peers who would have become collateral damage had the plot succeeded.

While fundamental aspects of the Gunpowder Plot remain in doubt, it is certain that there was a Catholic plot led by Catesby, and that Garnet and others who got wind of it had tried to prevent any kind of violent act of rebellion by requesting a prohibition from the Pope against such action. We know enough, therefore, to see that the plot illustrates two sides of the English Catholic experience throughout this period. On the one hand there was the non-political and essentially spiritual mission of evangelising and ministering the sacraments, but on the other hand there were temporal plots and plans of invasion. The 'temporal' Catholic reality was inconsistent and unstable and we see it reflected in the character of Posthumus, who returns to England with the Roman invading army but then switches sides and fights fiercely on the side of the British defenders. Historically, we find that one minute English Catholics were offering their services to Spain to spearhead an invasion, while the next they were declaring stoutly that they were for crown and country and would fight an invading army more valiantly than any of their compatriots, though the Pope himself had sent it. Milford Haven, a key locus of the play and the landing point of the Roman army, had been discussed among Catholic exiles in the 1590s as the entry point for an invasion that would change the regime. It had great symbolic significance, as it had been through Milford Haven that the future Henry VII had returned from exile and begun his march to victory at Bosworth Field and the founding of the Tudor dynasty. This made it safe for Shakespeare to refer to it in the play, but at the same time it could carry a hidden and more startling significance – 'Hugely politic' is putting it mildly. The temporal Catholic Posthumus has the surname Leonatus. Even for those members of the audience who did not get the specific allusion to Spain discussed earlier, this name, particularly as voiced from a stage, could invoke 'the Lionheart' – King Richard I – who was above all a crusader, and thus an embodiment of precisely what is meant by the 'temporal Church', which is to say, Christian worldly power (as depicted on the ducat). This may not be a concept that modern Christians are either very familiar with or very comfortable with, but it was simply taken for granted at the time of Shakespeare. So, to be clear about what is being said here, Anne and Roger Line are used by Shakespeare as a symbol of the Catholic Church. Roger represents the temporal aspect of the Church (often equated with the laity), and Anne represents the spiritual Church (often the clergy). That is why Posthumus/Roger calls Imogen/Anne 'my soul'.[34]

Exiles in a Cave

The third story in *Cymbeline* is that of Belarius, mentioned above. He is an old soldier who many years before was banished by the King and lives in a cave in Wales with his two adopted sons, Guiderius and Arviragus, who are in fact the sons of King Cymbeline who were kidnapped in infancy. One of several confusing things about these three characters is that they all have two names: Belarius is Morgan; Guiderius is Polydore; and Arviragus is Cadwal. But this use of aliases is a pretty strong hint that these men could represent the Catholic priests and their co-workers for whom it was quite normal to work under an adopted name. It is possible that Belarius represents the older priests, such as the exile William Allen, founder of the Douay seminary, and that Guiderius and Arviragus stand for the young men who went abroad to study at the Catholic seminaries under the authority of such men. Belarius describes his location as 'a place which *lessens* and sets off' III.iii.13 [my italics], probably a pun on the 'lessons' of the seminary and the 'setting off' of newly ordained priests on their mission to England. If so, this is an excellent example of the way place is transposed in a play to conceal a subversive meaning – a device that has been noted as characteristic of Jacobean drama. Belarius's cave is ostensibly in Wales, but a series of clues seems to indicate that this may be a stand-in for Douay in the low countries, or, more likely, that both these locations are significant for the allegory. In

---

[34] The concept of the dual spiritual/temporal nature of the Church is linked to the theological notion of the two natures of Christ, who is both human and divine, and, on a popular level (theological sensitivities aside), to the notion of the soul animating the body.

addition to the 'lessens' example given above, Belarius notes that he is perceived 'like a crow', suggesting a Catholic identity; he dwells 'i' the rock', another Catholic reference, the rock being St Peter and his successors the popes; he refers to 'our mountain sport' – the mountain is a motif of the Catholic Church (see *Douay-Rheims Bible*); he treads 'these flats' and refers to his roof being 'low', hinting at the low countries; and he makes obvious reference to the Catholic devotion of the Divine Office, which was central to the daily routine at the seminaries, with his 'morning's holy office' and the repeated 'Hail, heaven' of his two adopted sons.[35] Moreover, there were two kinds of seminary students at Douay, to correspond to two sons – namely, those who were studying specifically for the priesthood. and those who were there to get a more general education in a Catholic institution because Catholics who declined to take the Oath of Supremacy were debarred from graduating at the universities in England. Last but by no means least, we come to Belarius's alias, 'Morgan', a clue that links Wales and the Douay seminary. As the Jesuit historian Robert Scully notes, 'Although the mastermind behind this institution was William Allen, *Morgan Phillips*, a Welsh Catholic exile under Elizabeth, gave considerable assistance to Allen, who had been his former pupil at Oxford', and left 'all his property' to the college on his death in 1577 [my italics].[36] If Shakespeare intends Belarius to evoke Morgan Phillips, he would not want to make this identity too obvious, and he may be deliberately throwing the censors off the scent by having Belarius refer to his banishment as occurring twenty years before. This would suggest to the more canny members of Shakespeare's first audience a date somewhere between 1586 and 1591 (assuming a first performance of *Cymbeline* between 1606 and 1611), and would apparently rule out Morgan Phillips, who died more than ten years earlier. However, a close reading suggests a rather different conclusion. Belarius declares:

> and this twenty years
> This rock and these demesnes have been my world;
> Where I have lived at honest freedom, paid
> More pious debts to heaven than in all
> The fore-end of my time. But up to the mountains! (III.iii.69–73)

Shakespeare is adept at synecdoche, meaning that he associates his fictional character with a particular historical individual – in this case, the fore-ended

---

[35] For more on Catholic motifs, see Asquith, *Shadowplay*, 289–300.
[36] Scully, *Into the Lion's Den: The Jesuit Mission in England and Wales, 1580–1603*, 156.

Morgan Phillips – in order to then make that character stand for some broader reality. I suggest that we are moving into this broader reality with the words of Belarius quoted above, as Morgan Phillips has become a metaphor for the mission of the Douay seminary.[37] Around twenty years before *Cymbeline* was written – in 1587 – a cave was discovered near the coast of North Wales that was 'the haunt of the recusants, Seminaries [seminary priests] and Jesuits in these parts'.[38] This was a place where Mass had been said and 'debts paid to heaven'. It was apparently used by William Davies, a renowned priest who had been trained at the Douay college endowed by Morgan Phillips and who became, in 1593, the only Catholic priest to be executed in Wales during the reign of Queen Elizabeth. More to the point, in the light of Shakespeare's Belarius, is that he had been a mentor to young men who went on to train in the continental seminaries. In March 1592 he was arrested at Holyhead in the company of four such would-be seminarians as he attempted to arrange for their passage to Ireland as the first leg of their journey to Spain and the college at Valladolid. For sixteen months he was held as a prisoner, for much of this time at Beaumaris Castle on Anglesea, and from there he conducted a popular priestly ministry, saying Mass, hearing confessions and giving spiritual counsel to visitors and correspondents. When it came to his execution, he was so respected in the town that none would perform the office of hangman and the two men eventually brought in from outside were pelted with stones by boys in the streets. According to Challoner, he formed, with his four young companions, 'a kind of religious community in the prison', rising at four in the morning, praying the divine office, hearing Mass, singing the anthem *O Sacrum Convivium* and having regular times for quiet meditation. The priest taught the young men 'to practise self-denial', and after meals, 'Mr Davies entertained them for a while with pious and edifying discourses'.[39] Given that the Earl of Worcester's seat was in Wales, there is no doubt whatsoever that members of the Worcester household would have been very familiar with the story of William Davies, including the discovery of the cave, his mentoring of young men, and his execution as a traitor even though he vigorously denied he was

---

[37] While Morgan Phillips supplies the most obvious connection to the Douay seminary, there are other Morgans associated with Catholic recusancy, including Lady Frances Morgan, daughter of the Earl of Worcester. She and her husband were significant Catholic benefactors who would provide in their will for the maintenance of four Jesuit priests to serve the Welsh mission (Scully, 166). For other recusant Morgans in Monmouthshire, including a priest, see Scully 184–185. Also, Thomas Morgan, agent and cipher-clerk of Mary Queen of Scots, had been a prominent member of the older generation of Catholic exiles in the 1580s and is thought to have hailed from Monmouthshire.

[38] Chancellor of Bangor, quoted in Scully, 171.

[39] Challoner, 194.

guilty of such a charge. How could they not recall all this when they encountered Shakespeare's Belarius?

The Wicked Queen and Cloten

The fourth story is that of the evil queen and her wretched son. If you are looking for an example of Shakespeare betraying his religious prejudices, hear the English Protestant defiance of Rome in the words of these two characters and then reflect on the depths of their villainy. Cloten is both ridiculous and vicious. He is the son of the Queen from a previous marriage and she schemes for him to obtain the throne – at first by engineering a marriage to Imogen, and when that fails, she plots to poison King Cymbeline, her unsuspecting husband. Together, the Queen and her son appear to represent the Elizabethan Settlement, possibly even in terms of the Queen as Queen Elizabeth and Cloten as the Anglican Church. If this is correct it would give us a temporal/spiritual symbol of the state religion to set against the Catholic symbol of Anne and Roger Line. Cloten's identity is suggested in three ways. First, he becomes obsessed with putting on the clothes of Posthumus – he wants to look a bit like him, just as the Anglican Church, with its bishops, liturgy and vestments, wanted to wear some of the clothes of Catholicism. Second, when he fails in his hopeless quest to woo Imogen, he determines to force himself on her, just as the Protestant establishment had been trying to force the state religion on the Catholics. Third, in the bizarre scene where Imogen wakes up to find Cloten's dead body and mistakes it for that of Posthumus, she is appalled that his head is missing. This was precisely the problem with the Anglican Church from the Catholic point of view: the head – the Pope – was missing. The human body as a metaphor for the Church of course goes back to the New Testament, but Shakespeare may be responding more directly to the writing of his contemporary, Edmund Spenser, as Ros King has pointed out:

> The trappings of his clothes cause [Imogen] to mistake Cloten's body for [Posthumus] – not unlike the way in which the Redcross Knight in Spenser's Protestant epic *The Faerie Queene* mistakes Duessa for Una, the false church for the true one.[40]

---

[40] King, *Cymbeline*, 151.

The bizarre headless-body scene is just the sort of thing that Dr Johnson was so scathing about, but it makes a great deal more sense once the allegorical layer is revealed.[41]

Jacobean courtiers familiar with the Roman histories may have found that Shakespeare's pair of anti-heroes, the Queen and Cloten, sparked a glimmer of recognition, for there was another mother-with-a-son-from-a-previous-marriage who seems to have provided Shakespeare with inspiration. It is time to recall the coin of Nero and Agrippina unearthed, quite possibly, on land that belonged to Anne Line's father. While it has proved impossible to identify exactly when that coin was found, I would hazard a guess that it was not long before *Cymbeline* was written.[42] I think Shakespeare knew of it and there had been some talk of it in London circles. Agrippina was ferociously ambitious for her son Nero, to the point of poisoning her husband to clear Nero's path to the throne. This, I contend, is the pattern for Cloten and the Queen who, we find out at the end of the play, has been plotting to poison her husband Cymbeline. What I am suggesting here is that Shakespeare is using awareness of this rare coin, via the story of Nero and Agrippina, to direct his knowing audience specifically to Maldon and to Anne Line. There is another highly significant fact that appears to confirm this, and about which I must admit I was completely unaware until late on in my study of the play – namely, that *Cymbeline's capital was at Maldon*. Or, to be more precise, it was believed to be so at the time Shakespeare was writing. This means that the opening scenes that so vividly evoke Anne and Roger Line's predicament vis-à-vis her father are set at Maldon, precisely where those events took place.

According to Holinshed's *Chronicles* (1587 edition), 'the towne of Camelodunum (which some count to be Colchester) [was] the chiefest citie appertaining unto Cynobelinus [Cymbeline]'. Modern historians identify Camelodunum with the town of Colchester, but William Camden had

---

[41] Asquith identified Cymbeline's queen with Elizabeth in *Shadowplay*, noting, 'It is she who alienates the country from Rome' and, 'Shakespeare has no qualms about sketching this venomous portrait of her' (254). According to Asquith, Cloten represents 'the coarse new order now threatening England', and she notes the association with the new religion: 'Shakespeare's last plays continue to address the growing threat to Catholicism from what was seen as a crafty facsimile religion – the Protestant "middle way", which adopted the appearance, vestments and ritual of the old religion while rejecting papal authority and the Mass.... The loss of Cloten's head, highlighted several times in Imogen's hysterical reaction to the discovery, would have reminded those with a knowledge of the theological disputes of the time that a body without a head symbolised a church without central authority' (255).

[42] It is of course possible that the Nero and Agrippina reference in the play is coincidental, but with all the other material pointing to Anne Line and Maldon this seems unlikely. Ben Jonson has Agrippina as a character in *Sejanus*, his 1603 play that was acted in by Shakespeare, demonstrating that there was a contemporary familiarity with her story.

asserted in his *Britannia*, published in 1586, that Camulodunum was at Maldon, and his view was widely accepted. He argued that the Anglo-Saxon name of the town – *Maeldune* – was a corruption of Ca-*mel*-o-*dunum*, and that both Roman coins and those of the British king Cymbeline had been found in the area. Camulodunum, as Camden recalls, is also associated with the greatest victory of the ancient Britons over the Romans when Boudica and her forces torched the Roman garrison and destroyed the ninth legion. This was long after Cymbeline's rule, but no doubt it was added to Shakespeare's brew as the play began to ferment in his mind. There is certainly no record of a great historical victory over the Romans at Milford Haven.

Coins

It is not a new idea that Shakespeare had coins on his mind when he wrote *Cymbeline*. Ros King suggests that Shakespeare used the coins described in Camden's *Britannia* 'for a great deal of local colour about ancient British culture' (e.g. the images of Janus and a boar).[43] But Shakespeare's knowledge covers more than just those coins depicted in Camden's book. It seems highly probable that he had seen collections gathered by members of the Society of Antiquaries at first hand as well as knowing about the Nero coin from Maldon that is not among Camden's illustrations. This is strongly suggested by the fact that another Roman coin found in Britain but not in Camden features a certain Postumus, a Roman who ruled over Britain, Gaul and Spain in the third century. Critics have long noted that the name Posthumus occurs in Holinshed (as the grandfather of Brute, the founder of Britain), but have failed to note this other 'Postumus' whose image on coins happens to be considered particularly noteworthy by numismatists because he sports a magnificent beard (unusual for a Roman). This is interesting, because when Shakespeare's Posthumus reaches a point where he pleads with God to take his life in exchange for that of his wife, he says the following:

> For Imogen's dear life take mine; and though
> 'Tis not so dear, yet 'tis a life; you *coin'd* it:
> 'Tween man and man they weigh not every stamp;
> Though light, take pieces *for the figure's sake* [my italics]. (V.iv.22–25)

---

[43] Ros King, *Cymbeline: constructions of Britain*, 65.

Shakespeare has surely seen a coin of Postumus held by some antiquarian collector who valued the unusual 'figure' more highly than the metal of which it was made.[44] Interestingly, the historical Postumus, a rebel against the emperor Gallienus, is a rather attractive character. He gained a reputation as an excellent soldier and a wise ruler whose life was cut short by assassins after he refused to allow his victorious troops to sack the city of Mainz. On his coins appear several images that appear to haunt the stage in *Cymbeline*: Postumus with the Roman emperor kneeling suppliant at his feet (*R.I.C.* 277); raising a kneeling figure (*R.I.C.* 157); leaning on a shield with captives at his feet (*R.I.C.* 235); with a lion's pelt over his shoulder (*R.I.C.* 292); with Jupiter on the reverse standing holding a thunderbolt and a sceptre (*R.I.C.* 309); and one with the image of faith (L. *fides*) on the reverse holding a patera and standard (*R.I.C.* 377).[45] *Cymbeline*, of course, contains the extremely unusual scene where a thunderbolt hurling Jupiter descends on the back of an eagle, and then rises up again at the end of his speech. A coin of Hadrian struck to commemorate his late wife Sabina 'depicts the deified Empress in the process of being borne to heaven on the wings of an eagle', and apparently 'this type became very popular on the posthumous coinages of both emperors and empresses, though in the case of the latter a peacock usually took the place of the eagle'.[46] A coin of Nero has Jupiter on the reverse standing on a thunderbolt.[47]

To all the above may be added the ducat, first coined by Roger II, King of Sicily. You may recall the suggestion that this Roger is alluded to in the first scene of the play as a hint at the identification of Posthumus with Roger Line. We have then said that Posthumus/Roger Line is a metaphor for the temporal Church, or the temporal aspect of Christianity. When we examine the ducat of Roger II, we find precisely this symbolism in play. On one side we have a bust of Christ holding the gospels, and on the other we have Roger II, with his son the duke, also called Roger, holding a cross between them ('ducat' is derived from 'duke'). Is this a coincidence? The theme, seen in the original Roger II ducat, of temporal power under Christ was continued in later, commonly used versions such as those minted in Venice

---

[44] The name Arviragus also occurs on Roman coins. See II.v.4–6 and II.i.59 for references to coining; *LLL*, V.ii.613, 'The face of an old Roman coin, scarce seen'; and Timon of Athens discovering gold coins and giving them away: *Timon*, III.iii.24ff. The 1605 play *Eastward Ho!* featuring the coiner 'Frank Quicksilver' was written by Jonson, Marston and Chapman, who had all been fellow contributors with Shakespeare to Robert Chester's *Loves Martyr* in 1601.

[45] For coins of Postumus see Sear, *Roman Coins*, 271–273. The *R.I.C.* references are quoted from Sear and relate to the standard *Roman Imperial Coinage* published by Spink.

[46] Sear, 37.

[47] Sear, 118.

which had an inscription that translates as: 'To you, Christ, this duchy, which you rule, be dedicated'. So far we have found coins to connect with Cymbeline, the Queen, Cloten, Posthumus Leonatus (Postumus with a lion), Roger of Sicily (supporting the Roger Line/Posthumus hypothesis), Imogen/Fidelia (Fides), Iachimo (as the captive of Posthumus), Lucius (as the Roman at the feet of Posthumus), and Jupiter, both with his thunderbolt and riding on an eagle. There could be two more: firstly, seventeenth-century antiquarians surmised (apparently wrongly) that a coin in the Cotton collection inscribed 'Arivog' referred to Arviragus; and secondly, Shakespeare invents the name 'Euriphile' for the mother of Arviragus and Guiderius, but I suspect this is a reference to a Greek Sybil by the name of Herophile subtly concealed from the eyes of the censor (she prophesied the fall of Troy among other things and London was seen as a new Troy)[48]. Herophile appears on Greek coins from the fourth century BC.

From ancient coins we move now to their close relatives the commemorative medals, and those struck during Shakespeare's lifetime, most notably to celebrate the failure of the Spanish Armada in 1588. It has been suggested before that the Queen appears to allude to the Armada in a speech urging resistance to the Romans (III.i.16-33 – considered in more detail later), but the link to the medals has gone unremarked. She refers to Cymbeline's kingdom as 'Neptune's park', a rather strained metaphor for the modest portion of a largely wild Britain ruled over by the historical Cymbeline. However, a gold medallion of 1589 depicts Britain as a carefully husbanded park surrounded by the sea.[49] The inscription translates as: 'No circle in the world more rich' and on the obverse is a bust of Queen Elizabeth. A silver Armada medal of 1588 depicts a Spanish ship being wrecked on an enormous rock and looking not unlike a broken egg, with men spilling out into the sea – Cymbeline's Queen compares the Roman shipping to eggshells that 'crack'd as easily 'gainst our rocks'.[50] The inscription on this medal – 'VENI, VIDI, VIVE' – also supplies a parallel, as the Queen alludes to Caesar's 'came and saw and overcame' in the same speech.

We know that Shakespeare was a creative magpie with an eye for shiny detail. Evidently, he had found the world of coins and medals. But he is not using this information simply to add colour, or flights of fancy, 'the very

---

[48] There appears to be more than one Sybil called Herophile but it serves Shakespeare's purpose to conflate them.
[49] British Museum, reg. no. 1866,1218.1.
[50] British Museum, reg. no. 1950,0805.3.

coinage of your brain' (*Hamlet*, III.iv), he is using it to lay a trail of clues to his subtext. Behind the Queen and Cloten we see Nero and Agrippina, and so we arrive, via the Maldon coin, at Maldon/Camulodunum, the capital of King Cymbeline. This loop joins up so neatly that some will stop at this point thinking they have understood Shakespeare's game, but not those who know that Anne Line came from Maldon – they can follow the trail all the way to the allegorical heart of the play.

Numbers

If you are trying to send coded messages to your audience, apparently innocuous numbers can be put to subtle use. There are two notable examples in *Cymbeline*, the first in a comment by the sardonic Second Lord in reference to the hapless Cloten, who has been pestering Imogen:

> That such a crafty devil as is his mother
> Should yield the world this ass! a woman that
> Bears all down with her brain; and this her son
> Cannot *take two from twenty, for his heart,*
> *And leave eighteen*. Alas, poor princess,
> Thou divine Imogen, what thou endurest [my italics]. (II.i.52–57)

I suggest that, for Shakespeare, eighteen is a code for Anne Line and one that he had used before in giving 'The Phoenix and the Turtle' eighteen stanzas. There are several possible reasons for this association, including the memorable coincidence of her arrest on 2 February 1601, which was the eve of the anniversary of her wedding eighteen years before. There was also her chronic suffering that recalled the story in St Luke's Gospel of the woman who had eighteen years of illness before being healed by Jesus (Luke 13.11–17), a story that had given rise to the idea that eighteen was a sacred number. Cloten does not realise that the woman he is vainly attempting to woo is in fact a complex allegorical figure who in the first instance represents a saint who died in 1601. Perhaps the Second Lord is being a little harsh. Audiences who were unaware of the Anne Line key might be able to discern the following, less specific device. Twenty is a score. If you drop the first and last letters you are left with *cor*, which is the Latin word for heart. Thus Cloten cannot do the favour for his heart of working out that Imogen is not available. He 'Cannot take two from twenty, for his heart, And leave eighteen.'

The other notable number device in *Cymbeline* occurs when Imogen appears to die and Aviragus laments as follows:

> The bird is dead
> That we have made so much on. I had rather
> Have skipp'd from sixteen years of age to sixty,
> To have turn'd my leaping-time into a crutch,
> Than have seen this. (IV.ii.97–201)

Sixteen from sixty leaves forty-four the number of years of the reign of Queen Elizabeth, during which the Catholic faith in England had been progressively asphyxiated.[51]

Shakespeare is a Renaissance poet. Multiple levels of meaning and diverse connotations are grist to his mill. But if he is skilful, all the different elements will fit neatly together once we have figured out how. The discussion of English Catholics coming to terms with the Gunpowder Plot may seem bizarre, but it fits the classical imagery of Jupiter with his thunderbolt. In book II of Ovid's *Metamorphoses* we find Jupiter compelled to use his thunderbolt to strike down Phaeton, a rash young man whose determination to take the bridle of the chariot of the sun from his father Apollo threatened the earth with fiery destruction. Shakespeare may allude to this myth because amongst the plotters were the sons of leading Catholic gentry, and so Catholics could not simply reduce the plotters to the cartoon spawn of Satan that they quickly became in the Protestant narrative of the Plot. Those leading Catholic gentry had been grieved as Apollo had been 'grievde to see his childe so mad' and had grieved the more when his heedless child had been struck dead.[52]

The eagle on which Jupiter descends can seem oddly disconnected from other eagle references in *Cymbeline*, but once the fundamental symbolism is understood, this is not so, as we see from Dante where the eagle first of all represents law and justice.[53] On this account the Romans adopted the eagle because it symbolised the rule of law. In Catholic Christendom the rule of law is law *under God* and in *Cymbeline*, Jupiter represents the Christian God (from whom all just law derives) who hears the supplications of Posthumus's departed relatives and bestows grace on Posthumus in response to

---

[51] Elizabeth acceded in 1558 and died in 1603, apparently making 45 years. However, by the old reckoning, the year began on 25 March and Elizabeth died on 24 March 1602/3, making the length of her reign 44 years.
[52] Ovid, *Metamorphoses*, Bk II, ln 200.
[53] Dante, *Paradise*, esp. canto 18 (sphere of Jupiter), also 6, 20; *Purgatory*, 32.

their prayers, thus saving his soul. We are in the Catholic thought-world of Dante.

Canto six of Dante's *Paradise* consists of a speech by the Emperor Justinian, the great codifier of Roman law both ecclesiastical and civil, a two-fold classification that Dante suggests derives from the doctrine of the two natures of Christ. Justinian, the last great Roman Emperor, ruled the eastern empire in the sixth century from his capital at Constantinople where he built the Hagia Sophia. His reign was marked by a dramatic reconquest of substantial parts of the former western empire, including North Africa and much of Italy and southern Spain. In Dante this is symbolised by a return of the Roman eagle to the west. Suddenly we are back to *Cymbeline* and the words of the soothsayer: 'I saw Jove's bird, the Roman eagle, wing'd / From the spongy south to this part of the west (IV.ii)' and again:

> the Roman eagle,
> From south to west on wing soaring aloft,
> Lessen'd herself, and in the beams o' the sun
> So vanish'd: which foreshow'd our princely eagle,
> The imperial Caesar, should again unite
> His favour with the radiant Cymbeline,
> Which shines here in the west. (V.v)

In *Cymbeline* the Roman armies come from Italy to Britain, a movement towards the north-west. Shakespeare could just as easily have the eagle soaring aloft from south to *north*, but he seems to be telling us that Britain is part of the *west*, repeating 'west' three times as the destination of the eagle, as it is in Dante. We may be approaching one of those clues that picks the lock of the entire play. If Shakespeare's eagle is Dante's eagle, is Justinian's reconquest of the west, this symbolic bird becomes acutely relevant to the faith-divided Europe of the time that *Cymbeline* was written (from a Catholic perspective) because Justinian's reconquest was a return of Catholic orthodoxy to the western empire that had been taken over by heretical Germanic tribes (read Protestants). Rome itself was seized back from the Arian Visigoths. Shakespeare is not suggesting a military reconquest of schismatic England by Catholic powers, he is saying that now such attempts have failed, King James should, like King Cymbeline, magnanimously accept the authority of Rome and so become the great peace-maker. With the benefit of hindsight this may appear somewhat unrealistic, but Shakespeare was a poet not a politician. But are we not hanging a great deal on an eagle flying west rather than north? Perhaps, were it not for another weighty clue: the priests from Douay and the other continental seminaries had attempted to reclaim England by conversion, and we have suggested that the priest-like Belarius symbolises such men. Justinian's great general who won back north Africa and Rome was called Belisarius. Note the formula: Belarius + is = Belisarius. There are several parallels; Belisarius was a eunuch, like those eunuchs for Christ, the celibate priests; he was famously exiled by a wicked heretical queen (Theodora, but read 'Elizabeth'); and according to legend he was reduced to such poverty that he begged for bread at the gates of the City of Rome that he himself had set free. Not only was the story of Belisarius well known in medieval times (he is mentioned in Canto six of Dante's *Paradise*) but there is an eponymous play about Belisarius by the German Jesuit poet Jakob Bidermann dated 1607 – intriguingly, within the five or six-year window when Shakespeare's *Cymbeline* could have been written. The Belisarius theme recurs in other seventeenth-century plays from France and Spain; suggesting a continuing appeal to Catholic audiences.[54]

If it is easy to miss the allusion hidden in the name of Belarius, the same is true of his late wife Europhile who is mentioned four times in the dialogue. I will not have been the first to have thought that her name has to have some significance, but then lacking an explanation moved on. The trail of coins made me return, this time to 'Herophile' the Sybil or prophetess, and then back again to Dante. In the *Divine Comedy*, Dante imagines the soul of the sainted Beatrice in heaven interceding for him. Beatrice finds the soul of the Roman poet Virgil and she sends him to guide a spiritually lost Dante down through the circles of Hell and then up the slopes of the mountain of Purgatory. She chooses Virgil for this task partly because she knew that Dante greatly admired him, but also because Virgil wrote the *Aeneid* (the great Latin epic of Aeneas, from whom the Romans descended) in which Aeneas goes on a journey into the underworld. Few details of this are needed to pick up Shakespeare's clue, except that it was the Sybil of Cumae, also known as Herophile,[55] who facilitated Aeneas's descent and guided him on his journey to find his father's spirit, just as Beatrice enabled Dante's descent and later was his guide through the spheres of paradise (Dante will meet the spirit of his ancestor, Cacciaguida, in Paradise). We could say that Herophile

---

[54] See Muir, *Love and Conflict in Medieval Drama*, 182. The Arden *Cymbeline* ignores Belisarius but notes that Shakespeare may have taken the name 'Belarius' from either the 'Bellario' of Fletcher and Beaumont's *Philaster*, or, more likely, from the earlier 'Bellaria' of Greene's *Pandosto* – despite the fact that both these characters are female and on the face of it appear to have little connection to Shakespeare's Belarius. However, it may be that Greene's Bellaria is also derived from Belisarius, because the latter was exiled due to the jealousy of the Emperor Justinian, and Greene's Bellaria provokes the intense jealousy of her husband leading to tragic consequences central to the play.

[55] According to Lactantius, *Divine Institutes* 1.6, in *Ante-Nicene Fathers*, 7.

is a 'type' of Beatrice – a kind of pre-figuring. Symbolically these two spiritually powerful women are linked. With this in mind we can return to *Cymbeline* and to the two most puzzling references to Euriphile which occur when Guiderius and Arviragus are preparing to lay to rest the apparently dead Fidele (Imogen). First they tell us that they will lay Fidele *next to Euriphile* their mother, then Arviragus proposes the following: 'Let us ... sing him to the ground, / As once to our mother: use like note and words, / Save that Euriphile must be Fidele'. They then proceed with a 'song' that contains neither name. This anachronism could be a deliberate signal to think carefully about what is happening on the allegorical level. If Herophile pre-figures Beatrice, and in the play Euriphile in a sense 'pre-figures' Imogen, is it not implied that Imogen is a kind of Beatrice?

It may appear that Shakespeare is expecting rather a lot of his audience, even a sophisticated coterie audience, in making the Euriphile/Herophile connection. However, for Catholics at least, there was another hint provided by the context – a 'kind of' funeral – because *the* funeral song, sung at every Catholic funeral since time immemorial, was the *Dies Irae*, and the Roman Sybil gets a mention in the very first stanza:

Dies Irae! Dies illa	[The day of wrath, that day
Solvet saeclum in favilla:	Will dissolve the world in ashes
Teste David cum Sibylla!	As foretold by David and the Sibyl!]

This brings us neatly to a fundamental assumption of medieval Catholics that it is crucial to recognise. Namely, they believed that God's providence was at work in the pre-Christian pagan world as well as among the Jewish people to prepare for the coming of the Christ child. They believed that God had inspired both Hebrew prophets and (albeit unknowingly) Pagan figures such as Virgil and the Sybil of Cumae to prophesy this (Virgil, *The Eclogues* IV). They also believed that God had raised up the Roman Empire in order to bring about the *Pax Romana* of Augustus, and thus the right conditions for Christianity to spread rapidly throughout the known world. King Cymbeline, according to legend, was contemporary with Augustus and with the birth of Christ, a time Dante refers to as 'near the hour when the whole heaven strove to lead the world to its serenity'.[56] King Cymbeline's desire for peace with the Romans is then a cooperation with the providential plan of God, and again we find evidence that Shakespeare's play is at root a religious one.

'What's Hecuba to him, or he to Hecuba?' Hamlet asks himself as he

---

[56] Dante, *Paradise* 6.55f.

ponders the performance of an actor whose eyes brim with tears as he evokes the legendary grief of the Trojan Queen; 'What would he do, / Had he the motive and the cue for passion / That I have? He would drown the stage with tears' (II.ii). There is one more name with classical associations to note before we move on, and that is Polydore. I suggest that, as with Euriphile and Belarius, a slight change has been effected in the spelling to divert the eye from the subtext, and in 'Polydore' we catch an echo of Polydorus, the youngest son of Hecuba and Priam. His own story is tragic enough – he was an innocent messenger who appealed to King Polymestor and was murdered by him – but I suspect the key to the significance of Polydorus is that his sister was the brave Polyxena, who was made a human sacrifice to appease the shade of Achilles. There are echoes of Anne Line in Polyxena's combination of defiance, fearlessness and modesty. She made clear that she regarded her death as unjust – 'No god will be appeased by such a rite as this!' – but accepted it, inviting the priest to sheath his sword in her throat or in her chest, and declaring that no man would make a slave of Polyxena.[57] We also see the attempt to preserve her feminine dignity even in her last moments, an element that we have seen in the accounts of the deaths of Anne Line and St Perpetua:

> She sinking softly to the ground with fainting legs, did bear
> Even to the very latter gasp a countenance void of fear.
> And when she fell, she had a care such parts of her to hide
> As womanhood and chastity forbiddeth to be spied.[58]

Hecuba had thought that of all her children, Polyxena, being a woman, would be spared a violent death, and no doubt friends of Anne Line had thought the same. Hecuba's grief reached its final extremity shortly after the sacrificing of Polyxena when she makes her way to the beach and discovers the slain body of her last child, Polydorus, washed up on the shore. What's Polyxena to him, and he to Polyxena? They are brother and sister, as Polydore and Imogen are brother and sister. Polyxena is a type of Anne Line.

---

[57] The quotations are from Ovid, *Metamorphoses*, XIII; the story is also found in Virgil and the tragedy *Hecuba* by Euripides, among other sources.
[58] Ovid, *Metamorphoses*, XIII.570-573 (spelling modernized).

EPILOGUE: THE SYMBOL-LINE ALLEGORY

More Textual Clues

We have already referred to the connection between King Cymbeline, Maldon, and Anne and Roger Line. There is another hint hidden in the detail of the well-known patriotic speech by the Queen that she made to put some backbone into her husband:

> Remember, sir, my liege,
> The kings your ancestors, together with
> The natural bravery of your isle, which stands
> As Neptune's park, ribbed and paled in
> With *rocks* unscalable and roaring waters,
> With *sands* that will not bear your enemies' boats,
> But *suck them up to the topmast*. A kind of conquest
> Caesar made here; *but made not here* his brag
> Of 'Came' and 'saw' and 'overcame': with shame
> (The first that ever touch'd him) he was carried
> From off our coast, twice beaten: and his shipping
> (poor ignorant baubles!) on our terrible seas,
> Like egg-shells mov'd upon their surges, crack'd
> As easily 'gainst our rocks.[59] For joy whereof
> The famed Cassibelan, who was once at point
> (O giglot fortune!) to master Caesar's sword,
> made Lud's town with rejoicing-fires bright,
> And Britons strut with courage [my emphasis]. (III.i.16–33)[60]

Instead of '*rocks* unscalable', the First Folio has '*oakes* unscalable'. The Arden edition changes this on the assumption that 'oakes' was a printer's error. Certain critics in the past had argued for oakes to be retained, but to no avail, and the text is almost universally rendered 'rocks'. However, if we consider the possibility that Shakespeare is signalling the importance of Maldon, the

---

[59] The phrase 'poor ignorant baubles' is reminiscent of anti-Catholic rhetoric. Many ships of the Spanish Armada were wrecked on the shores of the British Isles during ferocious gales as they made their long way home around Scotland and Ireland.
[60] According to Holinshed, it was not Cassibelan who found himself at a point to master Caesar's sword, but his brother Nenius. Moreover, again according to Holinshed, this situation arose not through heroism or skill but because Caesar had aimed a blow at Nenius and his sword had got stuck in Nenius's shield. In other words, it happened, as Shakespeare's Queen puts it, through 'giglot fortune'. Shakespeare is precise about this detail and yet clearly attributes the incident to the wrong man. This suggests that Shakespeare may be deliberately portraying the Queen as someone who distorts history to suit her own argument, an accusation that Catholics made of Protestants.

deprecated Folio version leaps from the page and shakes us by the collar. In Camden's description of the Dengie peninsula we read: 'along this shore much adoe have the inhabitants to defend their grounds with forced bankes or walles against the violence of the *Ocean*, ready to inrush upon them'.[61] Could this not have informed Shakespeare's image of the paling-in of the land ('Neptune's park, ribbed and paled-in')? I think it probably could, and a little investigation of the local archaeology reveals an abundance of evidence to confirm this. Palings suggest wooden posts used to construct a fence or defensive wall, and wooden posts have been discovered in abundance. Maldon is at the head of the Blackwater Estuary that lies to the north of the Dengie peninsula, and jutting above the black mud at more than a dozen sites around this coast have been found long lines of wooden posts made from ancient oak. In a few places remains have been found of hazel latticework that would once have been woven between the stout posts to form the walls noted by Camden. These were certainly substantial structures. Oak posts measuring nine inches in diameter have been placed in double and sometimes triple rows extending up to 390 metres. Much of the evidence is now below the waterline except on the lowest of tides, when the jagged timbers are revealed like the rotten teeth of a beached leviathan. If local sailors found themselves in conversation with a Camden or a Shakespeare, we can readily imagine them passing on their stories of the old oaks guarding their shore. Camden assumed that the structures were the remains of vain attempts to hold back the sea, but recent archaeology has suggested that the majority of them were built as fish traps by the Saxons. Some have been carbon-dated to AD 640–797, though other remains may be a thousand years older. If Shakespeare's Queen is referring to the oaks of the Blackwater Estuary, it is not the only reference she makes to the idea that local knowledge can help us to decode because in contrast to most of the British coastline, the deep sand and mudbanks skirting the estuary are exactly the sort of place where a ship could be 'sucked in to the topmast', and there is in fact an archaeological site of a sunken wreck off the Dengie village of Maylandsea. Lest these hints by the Queen of the specific topography of the Blackwater Estuary be thought too subtle, Shakespeare has her tell us straight out that this is *not the place* where Caesar made his brag – in other words, we are not in Kent, we are somewhere else, and we are being prompted to think about where that might be. The Queen has already given us yet another clue: 'A kind of conquest Caesar made here'. Is this not exactly what happened when Claudius made his ritual victory procession to

---

[61] Camden, *Britannia* (1607), 'Description of Essex', para. 10.

EPILOGUE: THE SYMBOL-LINE ALLEGORY

Camulodunum/Maldon to receive the ceremonial obeisance of the defeated British chieftains?

Janet Clare, in her study of the effect of censorship on Elizabethan and Jacobean plays, concludes: 'Readers were familiar with codes of reference which enabled the writer to comment on prohibited matters.'[62] We have already seen some of these codes in action, and they are scattered throughout the play. In the scene where Imogen questions the servant about her husband's departure on the ship, we have 'my needle' (Anne Line), 'senseless linen' (Roger Line) and 'crow' (Catholic marker); Belarius also uses the word 'crow'. However, we have not yet considered perhaps the most obvious place to look for such symbolism, and that is the mole on/under Imogen's breast that functions as her unique distinguishing mark. In Shakespeare's sources the mole is more or less nondescript, but he gives us the following:

> On her left breast
> A mole cinque-spotted, like the crimson drops
> I' the bottom of a cowslip: here's a voucher,
> Stronger than ever law could make: this secret
> Will force him think I have pick'd the lock and ta'en
> The treasure of her honour. No more. To what end?
> Why should I write this down, that's riveted,
> Screw'd to my memory? (II.ii.37–44)

And later, when Iachimo is making his boast to Posthumus:

> If you seek
> For further satisfying, under her breast—
> Worthy the [F. *her*][63] pressing—lies a mole, right proud
> Of that most delicate lodging: by my life,
> I kiss'd it; and it gave me present hunger
> To feed again, though full. You do remember
> This stain upon her? (II.iv.133–139)

---

[62] Clare, 21.
[63] This is another example where the Folio version has been 'corrected' by some editors but the original carries a subversive meaning. In this case the implied sense is that the badge of Catholicism makes Imogen worthy to be sentenced to death by pressing.

For a recusant Catholic audience, possible allusions abound in these two passages, including to redemption, the eucharist, the martyrs Thomas More and Margaret Clitheroe, and the tabernacle, with even the breast as the crudded mountain symbolising the Church. But let us focus specifically on the peculiarities of the mole itself. To begin with, a five-spotted mole is a very odd thing indeed. Surely a mole *is* a spot or mark. Moreover, it was pointed out more than a century ago that the five spots of the cowslip are *not* crimson. Steevens called this the 'solitary Shakespearean botanical slip' and a lapse 'so palpable as to be detected on the instant'.[64] In fact they are a dark yellowy-brown and look rather like moles on the skin. Shakespeare describes them as 'crimson drops', suggesting blood. So, what does this mean? The sole modern interpretation that recognises the blood analogy sees the 'bottom of the cowslip' as the vagina.[65] While this is possible, for Catholics in Shakespeare's original audience, drops of blood, plus the number five, add up to the five wounds of Christ. The 'five wounds' was not only a widely practised Catholic devotion in medieval England, but had been the image that had adorned the banners of the Pilgrimage of Grace in 1536, the most significant of the popular rebellions against the imposition of the Reformation in England.[66] The wounds of Christ are 'a voucher, / Stronger than ever law could make' because they plead a New Testament salvation more efficacious than the Old Testament law could ever be. When Iachimo asks 'Will you hear more?', Posthumus cuts him off with the words 'spare me your arithmetic', confirming that the number five is significant (II.iv.141–2). He has no need to hear the figure that he knows identifies Imogen.[67]

If the description of the cowslip is significant, what about the cowslip itself? Again we find a set of allusions that provide support for our interpretation. First, the cowslip had obvious Catholic associations as it was also known as 'St Peter's wort', and as 'keys of heaven', due to the resemblance of the fading flower heads to a bunch of keys. Second, the known medicinal uses of the flowers include the treatment of conditions known to have been suffered by Anne Line, including headaches, fevers and 'paralysis' (among the medicinal names are *herba paralisis* and palsywort). It could well be that Anne Line so often resorted to cowslip remedies that those who knew her would recognise this as an identifier, but we have no confirmation of this in

---

[64] Quoted in Furness, *Cymbeline*, 120.
[65] See Thorne, 184.
[66] The Catholic martyr Margaret Pole is associated with the badge of the five wounds of Christ – '*insigne, quinq. plagar Christi*' – in the 1584 text, *Ecclesiae Anglicanae Trophaea* (27). See facsimile in Scully, 238–239.
[67] The scathing 'your arithmetic' may be a sideways reference to the Protestant tract *God's Arithmeticke* (1597) by Francis Meres.

the sources. Another possibility is suggested by an entry in Gerard's *Herball* published in 1597. Here we read of 'An unguent made with the juice of Cowslips and oile of Linseed'. This preparation is also attested elsewhere and was used on the skin to treat burns, but more commonly to improve the complexion. Perhaps among the first audience of *Cymbeline* were faces beautified by it. Linseed is the seed of the flax plant, also called 'Lint', 'Lyne', and in Gerard's *Herball*, 'Line'.

To this very specific allusion may be added a more general one. Spring flowers, including the cowslip, the primrose and the field daisy, were known as 'primeroles', a word that was also used for attractive young women. A fairy in *A Midsummer Night's Dream* declares, 'I must go seek some dewdrops here / And hang a pearl in every cowslip's ear' (II.i). The cowslip is the *primula veris* (true primula), implying an apt symbol for a young woman who is both beautiful and true.

Cymbeline is packed with subtle allusions. When Imogen apparently dies she is laid on the ground and Guiderius says to his brother, 'Nay, Cadwal, we must lay his head to the east; / My father hath a reason for't' (IV.ii.255f). Critics have suggested that the mysterious reason is that the play is set in pagan times and pagans were laid to rest with their heads to the east rather than to the west, as became the Christian practice. The problem with this interpretation is that Shakespeare has played fast and loose with the historical facts throughout his play, so why then the sudden precision? The answer is that he remains quite unconcerned with such realism on the surface layer of the play because he is in the business of constructing an allegory, and it is on that allegorical layer that he is being precise. Imogen, in the 'symbol of the Lines', represents the Church, and churches, in practically every English village, are laid down with their head to the east.

I have said that the wager story is not about Anne and Roger Line, but there are numerous signs that throughout it, Shakespeare is retaining a link with their story. Imogen flees the palace of her angry father, an obvious parallel to Anne Line leaving her father's house at Maldon. Imogen then in a sense loses her husband (through his rejection of her), a parallel perhaps to Anne Line losing Roger. She wanders from 'East to Occident' (IV.ii.372) in pursuit of Posthumus, suggesting both Anne Line's origins in the eastern county of Essex and the journey from Newgate prison to Tyburn, which is from east to west. When Pisanio tells her that she can travel only twenty miles a day, she exclaims, 'Why, one that rode to's execution, man, could never go so slow' (III.ii.71f). The journey leads Imogen to the point at which she becomes dependent on others for her food and lodging, in the cave of Belarius – a wise man; Anne Line became dependent on others – probably in the Wisemans' household (note the Wiseman motto: '*Sapit qui deo sapit*' – he is wise who is wise through God). Imogen is notably sick and then *seems* to die, as Anne Line had many times *seemed* to die. Imogen enters the service of Caius Lucius; Anne Line served the Jesuits, whose mission was dedicated to St Luke, and it has been suggested by Asquith and others that names such as Lucius can symbolise the Jesuits. After the battle, Imogen became a prisoner; Anne Line was a prisoner before she was finally reunited with her husband in heaven. These are merely a selection of the more obvious parallels and allusions.

Of the other characters, I have a few words to say about Iachimo, the Italian would-be seducer, and Pisanio, the would-be faithful servant. The character of Iachimo (Jack, James) may well have as its target King James, but more immediately harks back to a certain 'Captain Jacque', an Italian contemporary of Shakespeare who was brought up in England. The point vis-à-vis King James would be that he tried to seduce the Catholics with a promise of toleration when he came to the throne but then provoked the 'temporals' to the murderous course of the Gunpowder Plot by re-imposing rapacious anti-Catholic laws.[68] This interpretation seems to fit in broad terms, but when we focus in a little it becomes clearer that the Iachimo character is a Catholic figure, albeit a shady and devious one. Iachimo in the play is rebuffed by Imogen when he makes his pass at her. Imogen, representing an innocent, idealised English Catholicism, is indignant – 'Away! I do condemn mine ears that have so long attended thee' – and she disdains him 'and the devil alike', threatening to denounce him to her father, the King. This rebuke could hardly be stronger, and yet within minutes he has managed to talk her round to pardoning him to the extent that she says 'take my power i' the court for yours'. This suggests the possibility that Iachimo represents the political, plotting Catholics, who were always ready to try and seduce their co-religionists into rebellion, and who used their Catholic connections to move throughout English society, including the Court. Certainly, if one were to imagine as a play the story of English Catholicism at this period there would have to be a character like Iachimo. Unlikely as it may seem, there was just such a man called Jacomo di Francisci (known as Captain Jacque) who, about twenty years prior to the writing of *Cymbeline*, had been in London and had some dubious involvement in that prequel to

---

[68] Catesby's extremism was fed both by King James's turn against the Catholics that became evident in February 1604 and by the peace treaty between England and Spain that was signed in August of that year and that had failed to provide for religious toleration. Catholics seemed to be facing the prospect of a return to the dark days of Elizabeth's reign, with no hope of assistance from the continental powers.

the Gunpowder Plot, the Babington conspiracy, an episode that Catholics believed had been a cynical exercise in entrapment by agents provocateurs.[69] Jacomo seems to have been both one of the chief instigators of the plot and a government spy supplying intelligence to the Lord Chancellor, Christopher Hatton. Fourteen men were hanged, drawn and quartered in the aftermath, but Jacomo di Francesci was let off with a stint in the Fleet prison. One might suppose that Catholics of all hues would forever after shun such a man, but life was more complicated than that. The role of the agent provocateur involved behaving exactly as one would if one was genuinely hoping that the plot would succeed while providing the authorities with enough titbits of information to reassure them otherwise. Jacomo could very easily have been playing a double game in the Babington affair. Either way, it would become clear that Jacomo, who was born in Antwerp of Italian parents, was a Catholic of the type inclined to plotting and swashbuckling exploits. He had served as lieutenant to Sir William Stanley in Ireland and, after returning to England in the late 1580s, he left again to join Stanley in the English Catholic regiment in Flanders.[70] As such, he would be intimately involved in various proposals for a Catholic invasion of England through the port of Milford Haven.

Such attempts require considerable funds, but despite being in the employ of the Spanish Crown, the English regiment of exiles had been extremely short of money. However, Captain Jacque had a friend called Richard Williams who, around 1591, led a gang of disaffected Catholic blades in the seizure of a considerable haul made up of gold and silver plate and coin in a raid on Winchester Cathedral, and it appears that the English regiment may have been the intended beneficiary.[71] If so, Jacomo di Francesci probably had a hand in this carefully planned heist, and he was reported to be 'very great' with Richard Williams when the latter turned up in the exile regiment.[72] An even more audacious raid by the same gang was attempted on

---

[69] For information on Jacomo di Francisci I have relied on St John Brooks, *Sir Christopher Hatton*, 264ff; Haynes, 22f; and Nicholl, *The Reckoning*, 234–249.
[70] Asquith has suggested that the banished Duke and his band of followers in *As You Like It* are based on William Stanley and his regiment of exiles, and notes that three different characters in this play are given the name Jacques, the name of Stanley's lieutenant (*Shadowplay*, 139–141).
[71] See Nicholl, 234–249 for the Winchester raid and later 'coining'. It is possible that the money and plate held at Winchester had been intended to finance an imminent military expedition either to Portugal or France. These plans had involved a muster that, for the county of Southampton alone, amounted to 9,979 men (*CSP* 227.40). In October 1589, reference is made by 'the Mayor and Justices of Winchester' to 'money advanced by the town for the service of the soldiers before the expedition to Portugal' (*CSP* 227.14). See also *CSP* 226.53. If the proceeds of the Winchester raid were used to fund the Catholic exile regiment, and if exiled Catholic soldiers are symbolised by Shakespeare's Guiderius, this may explain the other name of this character, which is Polydore, a possible pun on 'poly d'or', or many-gold.
[72] Nicholl, *The Reckoning*, 245.

Whitehall Palace in London to steal the royal valuables but was abandoned as the would-be burglars fled into the night fearing they were about to be captured. It was claimed later that the plate from Winchester had been melted down and turned into counterfeit coinage in the room at Gray's Inn of Sir Griffin Markham, a Catholic convert with access to the Court. Furthermore, it has been suggested that Christopher Marlowe, playwright and government agent, was sent to Flanders by Lord Burghley to try and trace the proceeds of the Winchester raid.[73] This mission may explain why Marlowe was returned to England after being accused of 'coining', though if such activities took place they were probably 'a stale to catch birds of his kind', and Marlowe was doing the bidding of his paymaster. These dubious goings-on took place around 1591–92, just at the time when Catholic exiles were eyeing Milford Haven as a possible entry point for invasion.[74] When we turn to the text of *Cymbeline* we find that the character Jacomo, immediately after he has placated the indignant Imogen, tells her that he has been involved in some enterprise involving 'Some dozen Romans of us and your lord … to buy a present for the emperor'. It sounds innocent enough. He continues:

> Which I, the factor for the rest, have done
> In France: 'tis plate of rare device, and jewels
> Of rich and exquisite form; their values great
> And I am something curious, being strange,[75]
> To have them in safe stowage: may it please you
> To take them in protection?

---

[73] See Haynes, 22–26; Nicholl, *The Reckoning*, 244–248.

[74] This is clear from various entries in the *Calendar of State Papers*. For example (from July 1589), 'Information against Sir Wm. Stanley [Catholic exile] for planning the invasion of Ireland by the King of Spain, and then, to making a sudden descent at Milford Haven' (*CSP* 225.51); 'Notes for Mr. Secretary for the fortifying the three forts at Milford Haven' (*CSP* 229.83); and from April 1590, 'News from Milford of the approach of the Spanish frigates' (*CSP* 229.88), an ominous indication of Spanish intentions.

[75] At least two of the participants in the raid had connections with Lord Strange, according to Charles Nicholl (*The Reckoning*, 244), and one of them, Sir Edward Bushell, can be linked to Shakespeare closely enough to suggest that he could have been the source of Shakespeare's inside knowledge of the raid; he came from Stratford and was related to Richard Quiney, whose son Thomas married Shakespeare's daughter Judith in 1616; a 'Mr Bushell', probably Edward Bushell's brother Thomas, is mentioned in the letter of Richard Quiney to Shakespeare dated 1598 in terms that indicate he was a trusted acquaintance of Shakespeare; Thomas Bushell's first wife, Elizabeth Winter, was related to Shakespeare through his mother, Mary Arden; Shakespeare was involved with Lord Strange's company of players in the early 1590s at the same time as Edward Bushell was one of Strange's gentlemen retainers; and in 1601 Edward Bushell took part in the Essex rebellion with Shakespeare's known patron the Earl of Southampton, after attending the notorious performance of *Richard II* that had taken place on the previous day.

Imogen replies, much as a naïve Markham may have done of the Winchester haul, 'Willingly; And pawn mine honour for their safety.' She then allows Iachimo's men to carry a heavy trunk into her bedchamber from which Iachimo himself will emerge in the dead of night. It has to be said that this specific plot device, including the detail of a chest supposedly filled with jewels and plate, can be found in Shakespeare's sources, so it could certainly be argued that no further explanation is required.[76] However, this does not preclude the possibility of the double meaning suggested by the names Iachimo and Jacomo, and the latter's connection to the Winchester haul. This suggestion does fit rather well, in terms of both the overall politico-religious schema and the minor theme of coins and coining. We may conclude from all this that Shakespeare is using Iachimo to say to his fellow Catholics: 'Beware of the devilish voices from among your own number that have tempted you to betray the essence of your Christian faith.' At the same time, Shakespeare is using his intimate knowledge of the Catholic dissident world to present King James with a wicked version of himself in Iachimo, and with a virtuous and wise version in the King Cymbeline of the final scene.

Pisanio is a portrait of the Catholic in service who finds himself stuck in the middle of powerful forces and tied in knots by conflicting loyalties. He wants to be a faithful servant to his master Posthumus, but his master commands him to kill Imogen, whom he knows to be innocent and whom he adores. He is forced by Cloten, who by this time is intent on raping Imogen, to disclose where she has gone. He is tricked by the Queen into giving poison to Imogen that he thinks has killed her, and that almost does. Many would-be faithful Catholics could identify with this character, and the play does not exaggerate the reality. Many were haunted by very real murderous threats, forced disclosures, the dilemma of how to be faithful and to whom, and the guilt when someone was raped, imprisoned, poisoned or executed, when the authorities had used a compromised Catholic to achieve their aims. Moreover, there is a striking realism in the fact that the murderous threats in *Cymbeline* do not all originate with the symbols of tyrannical Protestant authorities. Indeed, they come most shockingly from the Catholic figure of Posthumus. One wonders if Shakespeare is showing his sympathy for someone like Thomas Bates, the servant of Robert Catesby, who was manipulated by his master into taking a vow of secrecy and of support for the Gunpowder Plot before he realised quite what he was letting himself in for. It was he who was sent by Catesby to tell Garnet and Tesimond of the

---

[76] See Nosworthy, xx-xxiii.

discovery of the plot and who supposedly overheard the words 'we are all utterly undone' that could as well have been voiced by the entire English Catholic body. Francis Tresham was another who seems to have been inveigled by Catesby into the plot against his better judgement, and we should probably take at face value his claim that '[t]he act seemed unto me to be very damnable'. As Catesby was aware, if the attempt failed, anyone who knew of the plot in advance would be judged to have been part of it, and so, by revealing the plot under an oath of secrecy, he was placing his hearers in a dreadful dilemma. Should they disclose the plot to the authorities, they would be breaking their word, perjuring themselves before God, and betraying friends to death, and yet, agonisingly for Tresham, in keeping faith with Catesby he would be endangering the lives of other friends, such as his brother-in-law, Lord Monteagle. It is not difficult to see why Tresham was suspected of sending the warning letter, but he always denied it to the day he died mysteriously in prison in December 1605, either from natural causes, or by his own hand, or by poisoning.[77] In the fantasy of the play, Pisanio, all of whose dilemmas seem to revolve around Imogen, somehow manages to muddle through by trying his best to be faithful in all directions, and he is rewarded in the end by the sight of Imogen alive. In real life, Thomas Bates was hanged, drawn and quartered with the other remnants of his master's gang.

Audience

If *Cymbeline* is a complex allegory with highly specific codes of reference, we must ask ourselves, who was all this aimed at? Many, including King James, could be expected to get the relatively simple message of the tribute story, but the Anne Line material was surely beyond all but a select few who were very familiar with her life. Perhaps Alison Thorne and others are at least partly right about Shakespeare's ironic reflection on his play's unintelligibility. He no doubt took some bittersweet satisfaction in the obliviousness of a great many members of his audience to what was being played out before their eyes. No doubt, as has since become traditional, they allowed the incongruities to wash over them as they were beguiled by theatrics. At the same time, Shakespeare must have had an audience in mind for his complex subtext. Clare Asquith is among those who have suggested the

---

[77] Francis Tresham's end remains a mystery. The lack of a known burial led Francis Edwards to the conclusion that he had been spirited into exile by the authorities (see Edwards, *Tesimond*, 231–246).

impressionable young Prince Henry, who would die prematurely in 1612, but who, in the preceding years, inevitably became a focus for those seeking to influence the future direction of the country. There may be something in this, but the Anne Line material suggests a somewhat wider group, that is hinted at in Foley's description of the Court reaction to Anne Line's condemnation quoted earlier:

> The ladies of the Court had, either in jest or in earnest, stormed against the Lord Chief Justice [Popham] and loaded him with maledictions because he had condemned a lady to be hung for receiving a priest into her house.[78]

Among the ladies of the Court were numerous Catholics, including converts such as the Countess of Rutland, the daughter of Sir Philip Sidney who gathered a Catholic circle around her that was served by the Jesuit William Wright.[79] The Countess of Worcester was also linked to the Jesuits and would have known Anne Line from her attendance at Mass in her house. The dowager Countess of Arundel (who also had a house on the Strand) had sent her carriage to retrieve Anne Line's body after the execution. This particular countess was not the type of lady to spend her time attending plays, but the wife of King James, Queen Anne of Denmark, by all accounts most certainly was. The new queen both loved the theatre and was a Catholic convert. In her wake were other Catholic women, such as Jane Drummond, her first lady of the bedchamber, in whose retinue was a Scottish Catholic priest who passed as one of her servants. Anne of Denmark brought a Catholic influence to bear at Court that was reflected on many levels. For example, she commissioned Court masques from the Catholic Ben Jonson and the Catholic-leaning Inigo Jones and Samuel Daniel. On 20 December 1607, the French ambassador to England, Antoine Le Fevre De La Boderie, reported a more positive feeling towards Catholics, or at least a less bad one – *moins de mauvais volonte* – and cited as evidence the fact that while King James was away hunting at Royston, the Queen was calling on Catholics (*La Reine a appellees pour en etre sont Catholiques*) in her preparations for an extravagant Court entertainment. The date of the letter identifies this as Ben Jonson's *The Masque of Beauty*, and La Boderie's comment has been taken to

---

[78] Foley, I.427.
[79] The Countess of Rutland, née Elizabeth Sidney, was the wife of Roger Manners, fifth Earl of Rutland.

refer to the ladies who received the honour of being invited to perform,[80] Now, apart from Lady Knollys, 'frequently in trouble with the authorities on this question', the four cast members most readily identifiable as Catholics were the four daughters of the Earl of Worcester, who most likely knew Anne Line from her attendance at Mass at their father's house fourteen years before.[81] By 1607, their names were Lady Catherine Petre, Lady Anne Wintour, Lady Catherine Windsor, and Lady Elizabeth Guldeford. Behind the 'Masque of Beauty' we find friends of Anne Line, and it is therefore quite apparent that if *Cymbeline* was performed at Court around the time it is believed to have been written, there would most certainly have been an audience for the highly specific Symbol-Line allusions that we have noted. Just to reinforce this point, remember that these four daughters of the Earl of Worcester had another sister in Wales, who was that encourager of cave-haunting priests, Lady Frances *Morgan* of Llantarnam, and remember also that the secretary to the Earl of Worcester, William Sterrell, was in charge of the buildings used by the players such as William Shakespeare to prepare for court entertainments.

In terms of the broader context, it is significant that Queen Anne took an avid interest in the future marriages of her sons and therefore in the vital matter of succession. When the treaty between England and Spain was signed in 1604, she discreetly sounded out the prospect of a marriage between Prince Henry and the Spanish Infanta, and there were several other Catholic matches proposed in the years that followed. This context makes the interpretation of Shakespeare's tribute story as a plea for reconciliation with Rome all the more plausible. That critics have so often chosen to ignore it is more a testament to their determination to raise Shakespeare above the troubled waters of religious controversy, than to a clear-sighted assessment of the evidence.

Concluding with a Hope-filled Tragedy

The book you have in your hand is the most complete 'life' of Anne Line that has yet been compiled, but it can only be a shadow of the sources that Shakespeare was drawing on. I suspect they included a whole catalogue of

---

[80] *The Masque of Beauty* was performed on 10 January 1608 at the Banqueting House at Whitehall. La Boderie's letter is quoted from Herford and Simpson, *Ben Jonson*, Vol.X, 458.
[81] See Herford and Simpson, 440ff. The other participants were the Countesses of Arundel, Bedford, Derby and Montgomery, and Lady Chichester, Lady Anne Clifford, Lady Gerard, Lady Hatton, Lady Arabella Stuart and Lady Walsingham (*ibid*).

memories, whether his own or as related to him, the stuff of dreams from which the artist draws a fictional character from a real person; the sound of a particular voice, the quickness of certain eyes, the coldness of a bitter wind, the candles lit, the psalms sung, the ancient coins handled, the Dengy mud and the script of private letters.

We have noted no less than three examples where critical editions have 'corrected' the original text because their editors have convinced themselves that Shakespeare would not have written what they see on the page, but where the original reading makes complete sense in the light of the subtext. There is another correction to the Folio that is also worthy of comment. It has become conventional to describe *Cymbeline* as a romance play – a tradition that began in the nineteenth century – but in the First Folio it is titled *The Tragedie of Cymbeline*. Why might this be? The simplest answer is that *Cymbeline* has elements of all three of the conventional categories of tragedy, comedy and history – it is not so much a tragi-comedy as a historico-comedic-tragedy with additional elements reminiscent of the medieval romance tradition – and as Shakespeare's play did not fit neatly into any of the three normal categories, the editors of the Folio chose tragedy as the best fit. This is the *too* simple answer.

The truth is that *Cymbeline* may not *seem* to fit the category of tragedy because it does not end Hamlet-like in a welter of blood, but in every other respect it fits the definition of tragedy given in Aristotle's *Poetics* remarkably well.[82] Indeed, the parallels are so clear, it is as though he had Aristotle's text open on his desk as he wrote the play and took great care to follow the instructions contained therein. For Aristotle, the essence of tragedy is that it evokes the emotions of 'pity' and 'fear' in order to lead the audience to a catharsis – a purging – of these emotions. We experience pity, he says, when we see an innocent person suffering – Shakespeare gives us Imogen – and we experience fear when we see a flawed person like ourselves suffer – Shakespeare gives us Posthumus. He notes that we do not become emotionally engaged when obviously wicked characters suffer, and so it is with Shakespeare's Cloten and the Queen. According to the *Poetics*, a tragedy should have the six elements of *plot, character, diction, thought, spectacle* and *song*, all of which are found in verdant form in *Cymbeline* very much as described, including such details as the structure of two songs. For Aristotle, complexity of plot is a virtue that contributes to the richness of the play, and the two most effective plot elements are reversals of fortune and scenes of

---

[82] Parts VI-XXII. The phrase 'to be or not to be' occurs in Aristotle's *Poetics* in relation to the quality of thought (part VI), a pretty strong indication that Shakespeare is familiar with the detail of this text.

recognition. Again, we see these elements exemplified in *Cymbeline*. He asserts that the artist shows his skill both by touches of realism in the portrayal of characters and by addressing great themes: Shakespeare does both. The mark of genius, says Aristotle, is the making of good metaphors: enough said. These elements and more suggest strongly that Shakespeare is following the *Poetics*, but the happy ending tells us that he is doing something new. *Cymbeline* descends into raging despair and cruelty but resolves and transcends this darkness in the final scene. Nosworthy argued that Shakespeare had written an experimental romance, but perhaps 'experimental tragedy' would be a more accurate description. Shakespeare is taking the tragedy of Aristotle and giving it a Christian form in which the horror of Good Friday is redeemed by the glory of the resurrection. If he is to lead his fellow Catholics to catharsis he cannot leave them despairing of their current position, he must give them hope for the future, and this is what he does in *Cymbeline* and the other 'late romances'. In 1601 he had lamented the death of English Catholicism in 'The Phoenix and the Turtle', albeit with a glimmer of hope for a phoenix reborn, but in the death of Desdemona in *Othello* and then of Cordelia in *Lear* we see barely even a glimmer. Then hope returns in *Cymbeline*. All these works are addressing 'the same weed', the real-world tragedy of English Catholicism, so when the First Folio designates *Cymbeline* as a tragedy, that may be because Shakespeare believed he had made a 'kind of' tragedy here.

To conclude, *Cymbeline*, the final play in the Folio, is not really about Anne and Roger Line – they are merely metaphors in a play about the twin tragedies of the split between England and Rome, and the split within the English Catholics between those who fight and those who pray. Fundamentally, *Cymbeline* is also about the split between Britain and her true self, or between Britain and her redeemed soul. These interlocking divisions in Shakespeare's world are the great themes from which this play has emerged. There is romance in the happy ending, but this is an imagined idealised future, a hope and a prayer to encourage Shakespeare's fellow believers in difficult times. In Shakespeare's idealised future, the religious conflict that blighted his era is over and there is peace and unity both in the universal Church and in the newly united kingdom of Britain.

Alison Shell, in *Shakespeare's Religion*, has enunciated a principle that has remained central to the scholarly consensus on her subject – namely, that for Shakespeare, aesthetic concerns take precedence over matters of religion. *Cymbeline* shows that she is quite wrong about that. In his desire to tell the hidden story in the subtext he has created a work that on the surface has 'faults too evident for detection'. However, the determination to raise

EPILOGUE: THE SYMBOL-LINE ALLEGORY

Shakespeare above the level of religious conflict is so deeply ingrained that it may take more than clearly demonstrating the contrary view to shift the paradigm. History is written by the winners, it is often said, and Shakespeare was on the side of the losers. It therefore remains difficult to 'read what silent love hath writ' (Sonnet 23). The message of *Cymbeline* is that in the end purification and reconciliation will come through the working of Divine Providence, and true spirituality, represented by Imogen, will be restored to its rightful place in Britain.

And so it remains to repeat again, if you wish to see a portrait of Anne Line, look to Imogen in the play *Cymbeline*. For her husband, look to Posthumus, but with care, because he is being used as a symbol, and therefore the faults of Posthumus may not be the faults of Roger Line. All the same, I like to think that Shakespeare has taken some of the more personal details from real life, so that when Posthumus refers to Imogen as 'my queen' he is echoing the name Roger Line gave to his wife:

> My queen! my mistress!
> O lady, weep no more, lest I give cause
> To be suspected of more tenderness
> Than doth become a man. I will remain
> The loyal'st husband that did e'er plight troth:
> My residence in Rome at one Philario's,
> Who to my father was a friend, to me
> Known but by letter: thither write, my queen,
> And with mine eyes I'll drink the words you send,
> Though ink be made of gall. (I.i.92–101)

The hidden portrait of Anne Line is glimpsed perhaps most distinctly in Act IV scene ii (48–58) where Arviragus and Guiderius describe the sleeping Fidele (Imogen in disguise):

> *Arviragus:* How angel-like he sings!
> *Guiderius:* But his neat cookery! He cut our roots
>   In characters,
>   And sauced our broths, as Juno had been sick
>   And he her dieter.
> *Arviragus:* Nobly he yokes
>   A smiling with a sigh, as if the sigh

                Was that it was, for not being such a smile;
                The smile mocking the sigh, that it would fly
                From so divine a temple, to commix
                With winds that sailors rail at.
Guiderius: I do note
                That grief and patience, rooted in him both,
                Mingle their spurs together.

Shakespeare's poem 'The Phoenix and the Turtle' may be the most exquisitely crafted tribute to Anne Line, but the most beautiful monument in verse is the lyric known as 'Fear no more the heat o'the sun', voiced like a text of the Divine Office over the body of the phoenix Imogen. This is such a well-known text and one so hallowed by use in many a funeral service that one hesitates to comment on it. Of course, like all that Shakespeare wrote, it belongs to all people and all ages, but first of all it probably belonged to Anne Line.

Fear No More the Heat of the Sun

Guiderius: Fear no more the heat o' the sun,
                   Nor the furious winter's rages;[83]
                   Thou thy worldly task hast done,
                   Home art gone, and ta'en thy wages:[84]
                   Golden lads and girls all must,
                   As chimney-sweepers, come to dust.[85]
Arviragus: Fear no more the frown o' the great;
                   Thou art past the tyrant's stroke;
                   Care no more to clothe and eat;[86]

---

[83] Every winter Anne Line suffered malarial fevers that could be very extreme.

[84] In the Gospels Jesus reassures his disciples that they have a home in heaven – 'there are many rooms in my father's house' – and teaches that those who have given up houses and land for the sake of the Kingdom will receive their reward in heaven – that is, they will take their wages.

[85] 'Golden' may hint at Hesiod's virtuous golden age of pastoral innocence in the countryside where Anne and Roger probably first met. When they married and then became Catholics, the inheritance of this golden couple turned to dust and their name was blackened. The word 'chimney' may hint at the many priest-holes that were constructed behind chimney breasts. John Gerard once hid for three days in one during a search at the Wisemans' house, and it may be that Francis Page was concealed in the same way at Fetter Lane, where, as Gerard wrote, 'Mistress Line had prepared a hiding-place' (85).

[86] Anne Line cared for the priests.

EPILOGUE: THE SYMBOL-LINE ALLEGORY

	To thee the reed is as the oak:[87]
	The sceptre, learning, physic,[88] must
	All follow this, and come to dust.[89]
Guiderius:	Fear no more the lightning flash,
Arviragus:	Nor the all-dreaded thunder-stone;
Guiderius:	Fear not slander, censure rash;
Arviragus:	Thou hast finish'd joy and moan:
Guiderius:	All lovers young, all lovers must
with Arviragus:	Consign to thee, and come to dust.[90]
Guiderius:	No exorciser harm thee![91]
Guiderius:	Nor no witchcraft charm thee![92]
Guiderius:	Ghost unlaid forbear thee![93]
Arviragus:	Nothing ill come near thee!
Guiderius:	Quiet consummation have;[94]
with Arviragus:	And renowned be thy grave! (IV.ii.258–281)

---

[87] The lands of Anne Line's childhood and of her lost dowry had many reeds, with a few isolated oaks in the hedgerows. A brook still runs by the site of Jenkyn Maldons, into nearby marshes.

[88] 'This world can witnesse, that in Divinity, Lawe and Phisicke, and all other faculties and functions, either of Piety, or policy, all *Englande*, I may say all *Christendome*, scarce knoweth any men more renourned than our ENGLISHE Catholikes', Robert Southwell, *Humble Supplication* (1595), 51.

[89] The repeated refrain 'come to dust' may recall that Anne Line's trial took place on Ash Wednesday, the day when Catholics would hear the repeated injunction in the liturgy 'Remember man that thou art dust, and to dust thou shalt return', as the cross was signed by the priest on the forehead of each participant.

[90] The line 'all lovers must / Consign to thee' may refer to Anne Line as a symbol of the church to which all lovers must go to be married and be *co-signed* in the register.

[91] Echoes of the Puritan preachers of Maldon.

[92] Echoes of the Essex witch trials.

[93] This is probably a specific reference. Perhaps Anne Line's mother died in childbirth without the Catholic sacraments, and so was a 'ghost unlaid' to rest.

[94] Suggesting both an echo of Jesus's words from the cross, 'It is consummated' (Jn 19:30), and the reunion with her husband in heaven.

Acknowledgments

John Finnis and Patrick Martin inspired the quest that resulted in this book by their article 'Another Turn for the Turtle' in 2003. More recently, they have helped me to identify various references to Anne Line in State Papers that I might otherwise have missed or misinterpreted. The manuscript was initially proof-read by Fiona Jones, who tidied up the English, and then read by Dr Nicole Coonradt and Lady Clare Asquith, who suggested numerous further improvements to both style and content. My historical research was encouraged and sharpened by Dr Anne Dillon as I prepared an article on Anne Line for the journal *Recusant History* published by the Catholic Record Society. Much of my research was carried out at the British Library and I am grateful to the staff in the Manuscript Room for finding the crucial indenture that had been given the wrong reference in the only published source. Thanks are due also to the staff at the Bodlian Library, The National Archives, Westminster Diocesan Archive, Essex Record Office, Hampshire Record Office, Maldon Town Council, Dunmow Town Council, and to Fr Julian Shurgold for his recommendation, Joanna Bentley at Book Guild Publishing, Fr Stuart Foster at Brentwood Diocesan Archive, and Peter Bogan and John Thornhill, archivists at St Peter's Church, Winchester. I am grateful to the British Museum, Essex County Council, Classical Numismatic Group, Inc., Compagnie Générale de Bourse, The Frick Collection and Professor Mika Merviö for use of illustrations, to Janet Doe for allowing me to photograph Mortimer's Hall, and to Michael Andrews-Reading for informing me about the wills of Roger Line's parents. The front cover illustration makes use of a detail from a watercolour copy by my late grandmother, Margery K Hilditch, of Henry Holiday's famous painting 'Dante and Beatrice' in the collection of the Walker Art Gallery in Liverpool.

This book has been years in the making and the patient support of family and friends has been my waybread on the journey.

Bibliography

Abbreviations

BL – British Library
Cal. Hat. Mss. – Calendar of the Salisbury manuscripts at Hatfield House
CRS – Catholic Record Series, published by the Catholic Record Society
CSP – Calendar of State Papers
ERO – Essex Record Office
ODNB – *Oxford Dictionary of National Biography*, online edn, Oxford University Press
OED – *Oxford English Dictionary*
PCC – Prerogative Court of Canterbury
SP – State Papers
VCH – Victoria County History

Sources for Anne and Roger Line and immediate family

BL. *Additional Charter 5982*.
[Brudenell MS] see below, 'Jollet'.
Calendar of Assize Records: Essex Indictments, Elizabeth 1. Ed. J.S. Cockburn. London: Her Majesty's Stationery Office, 1978.
CSP *Addenda 1580–1624*, 32.64.
Champney, Anthony. *Annales Elizabethae Reginae*. MS (1618). Westminster Diocesan Archive.
A Detection of damnable driftes, practised by three Witches arraigned at Chelmisforde in Essex, at the laste Assises there holden, whiche were executed in Aprill, 1579 etc. London, 1579.
[Douay Diaries] *The First and Second Diaries of the English College, Douay, and an appendix of unpublished documents*. Edited by Fathers of the Congregation of the London Oratory, with an historical introduction by Thomas Francis Knox. London: David Nutt, 1878.

ERO T/A 418/10/6, ASS 35/8/4/6.
Fitzalan-Howard, Henry Granville. *The Lives of Philip Howard, Earl of Arundel, and of Anne Dacres, his wife*: Edited from the Original MSS by the Duke of Norfolk, E.M. London: Hurst and Blackett, 1857.
Foley, Henry, S.J., *Records of the English Province of the Society of Jesus*, 7 vols., first series, 1877-83.
Garnet, Henry. Letter to Claudio Aquaviva, 11 March 1601. ARSI [Jesuit Archives Rome] *Anglia* 31 II, fols. 172v.–183v.
Gerard, John. *The Autobiography of an Elizabethan*. Translated by Philip Caraman, S.J., 2nd edn., with introduction by Michael Hodgetts. Oxford: Family Publications, 2006.
Jollet, Thomas. *Authoritates*. (Brudenell MS), Bodleian Lib. MS Eng. th. b. 2.
McCoog, Thomas, M. *English and Welsh Jesuits, 1555–1650, Part 2* (Record Series 75). Catholic Record Society, 1994.
Morant, Philip. *The History and Antiquities of Essex*. London: 1768.
Parish Register, St Clement Danes. Westminster City Archive.
PCC Prob 11/87; sentence 18 May 1609 [*sic*], Prob 11/114. [will of John Lyne].
PCC., 27 January 1603, Prob 11/101. [will of Agnes Lyne nee Phettiplace].
Manuscripts of the Duke of Rutland at Belvoir Castle. Vol. 1, Report 12, App. 4. London: Historical Manuscripts Commission, 1888.
Seccion de Estado, 612/125-27, Archivo General de Simancas. [Quoted in Loomie, 253].
SP 53/18/185.
SP 77/6/258.
SP 12/183a/154.
SP 12/190/78.
SP 12/195/95.
SP 12/195/133.
SP 12/249/142.
Stow, John. [*Annales of England*] *A summarie of the chronicles of England, diligently collected, abridged, and continued unto this present yeare of Christ, 1604*. Edited and annotated by Barrett L. Beer with preface by Roger B. Manning. Lewiston, NY; Lampeter: Edwin Mellen Press, 2007.
Visitations of Essex (Harleian Soc., Volume 13). London: Harleian Society, 1878.
Visitation of Hampshire and the Isle of Wight, 1686. New Series, vol. 10. London: Harleian Society, 1991.
Visitation of Hampshire Pedigrees 1530, 1575, 1622–34. New Series, vol. 64. London: Harleian Society, 1991.

Other sources

Alford, Stephen. *Burghley: William Cecil at the Court of Elizabeth I*. New Haven, CT and London: Yale University Press, 2008.

Allen, William. (Cardinal Allen). *A brief historie of the glorious martyrdom of XII. reverend priests, executed within these twelvemonethes for confession and defence of the Catholike Faith. But under the false pretence of treason, etc*. Rheims: Jean Foigny, 1582.

Alleyne mural monument, Gresley Parish Church [see Brydges for transcription].

Anstruther, Godfrey. *The Seminary Priests: A Dictionary of the Secular Clergy of England and Wales 1558–1850*. Vol. I. Ware: St Edmund's College; Durham: Ushaw College, 1969.

Aristotle, *Poetics*. Translated by S.H. Butcher. Available online at http://classics.mit.edu/Aristotle/poetics.1.1.html, accessed 15/10/2012.

Asquith, Clare. *Shadowplay: The Hidden Beliefs and Coded Politics of William Shakespeare*. New York: Public Affairs, 2005.

Aubrey, John. *Aubrey's Brief Lives: edited from the original manuscripts and with an introduction by Oliver Lawson Dick*. Reprint of 3rd edn. London: Secker & Warburg, 1960.

Baldwin, T.W. *William Shakespeare Adapts a Hanging*. Princeton, NJ: Princeton University Press, 1931.

Bayley, John. *The History and Antiquities of the Tower of London*, 2nd edn. London: Jennings & Chapman, 1830.

Brooks, Eric St. John. *Sir Christopher Hatton, Queen Elizabeth's Favourite*. London: Jonathan Cape, 1946.

Brydges, Sir Egerton. *The Topographer, Vol. 1*. London: Robson and Clarke, 1789.

Bullough, Geoffrey [Ed.]. *Narrative and Dramatic Sources of Shakespeare*. London: Routledge & Kegan Paul; New York: Columbia University Press, 1957–75.

Burke, John. *Extinct and Dormant Baronetcies of England, Ireland, and Scotland*. London: John Russel Smith, 1844.

Burke, John. *A General and Heraldic Dictionary of the Peerages of England, Ireland and Scotland, Extinct, Dormant and in Abeyance*. London: Henry Colburn and Richard Bentley, 1831.

Calendar of State Papers Domestic, Elizabeth 1.

Calendar of State Papers Foreign, Elizabeth 1.

Camden, William. *Britannia*. Philemon Holland translation. London, 1610.

Available online: http://www.philological.bham.ac.uk/cambrit/, accessed 13/10/2012.

Camden, William. *Britannia*. Edmund Gibson translation. London, 1695.

Caraman, Philip. *Henry Garnet 1555–1606 and the Gunpowder Plot*. New York: Farrar, Strauss & Company, 1964.

CRS 2 [*Miscellanea II*]. London: Catholic Record Society, 1906.

CRS 5 [*Unpublished Documents Relating to the English Martyrs, vol. 1 (1584–1603)*]. London: Catholic Record Society, 1908.

CRS 22 [*Miscellanea XII*]. London: Catholic Record Society, 1921.

Challoner, Bishop Richard. *Memoirs of Missionary Priests ... 1577 to 1684* (first published in two volumes, 1741, 1742). Rev. edn. J.E. Pollen, London: Burns Oates & Washbourne Limited, 1924.

Chambers, E.K. *The Elizabethan Stage*, vol. II. Oxford: Clarendon Press, 1923.

Chester, Robert, *Robert Chester's 'Love's Martyr', 1601, with Shakespere's 'Phoenix and Turtle' etc., etc*. Edited, with introduction, notes and illustrations, by the Rev. Alexander B. Grosart. London: The New Shakspere Society, 1878.

The Chronicle of the English Augustinian Canonesses ... at St Monica's in Louvain ... 1548–1625. Edited by Dom A. Hamilton. Part I, Edinburgh, Part II, London: Sands & Co, 1904, 1906.

Clare, Janet. *'Art Made Tongue-tied by Authority': Elizabethan and Jacobean dramatic censorship*. Manchester and New York: Manchester University Press, 1990.

Collins, Dorothy (Ed.). *Chesterton on Shakespeare*. Henley-on-Thames: Darwen Finlayson, 1971.

Cook, A.S. and C.B.Tinker. *Select Translations from Old English Poetry*. Boston: Ginn & Co., 1902.

Cooper, John. *The Queen's Agent: Francis Walsingham at the Court of Elizabeth I*. London: Faber and Faber Limited, 2011.

Dante. *Paradise*. Translated, edited, and with an Introduction by Anthony Esolen. Modern Library Paperback Edition. New York: Random House, 2004.

Dillon, Anne. *The Construction of Martyrdom in the English Catholic Community, 1535–1603*. Burlington, VT: Ashgate, 2002.

Dodwell, Martin. 'Revisiting Anne Line: who was she and where did she come from?' *Recusant History*, Vol. 31, No 3 (May, 2013) 375–389. London: Catholic Record Society.

Donne, John. *Devotions Upon Emergent Occasions*. Edited, with commentary, by Anthony Raspa. Montreal and London: McGill-Queen's University Press, 1975.

Edwards, Francis. *The Enigma of the Gunpowder Plot, 1605: The Third Solution.* Dublin: Four Courts Press, 2008.

Edwards, Francis. *Guy Fawkes: The Real Story of the Gunpowder Plot?* London: Hart-Davies, 1969.

Enos, Carol Curt. Shakespeare and the Catholic Religion. Pittsburgh: Dorrance Publishing, 2000.

Enos, Carol Curt. *Shakespeare Settings.* Tuscon, AZ: Wheatmark, 2007.

Finnis, John and Patrick Martin. 'Another Turn for the Turtle: Shakespeare's intercession for Love's Martyr', *Times Literary Supplement,* 18 April 2003, 12–14.

Finnis, John and Patrick Martin. 'The Identity of "Anthony Rivers"', *Recusant History* 26 (2002), 39–74. Catholic Record Society.

Finnis, John and Patrick Martin. 'The Secret Sharers: "Anthony Rivers" and the Appellant Controversy, 1601–2', *Huntingdon Library Quarterly,* vol. 69, no. 2 (2006), pp. 195–237. Berkeley: University of California Press.

Finnis, John and Patrick Martin. 'Thomas Thorpe, "W.S.," and the Catholic Intelligencers', *English Literary Renaissance,* 33 (2003), 1–43.

Fraser, Antonia, *The Gunpowder Plot: Terror and Faith in 1605.* London: Weidenfeld & Nicolson, 1996.

Furdell, Elizabeth Lane. 'Allen, Sir John (*c.* 1470–1544)', *ODNB,* Oxford University Press, online edn, Jan 2008. http://www.oxforddnb.com/view/article/68011, accessed, 11/03/2013.

Furness, Horace Howard (Ed.). *Cymbeline,* Variorum edn. Philadelphia and London: J.B. Lippincott Company, 1913.

Hammerschmidt-Hummel, Hildegard. *The Life and Times of William Shakespeare, 1564–1616.* Originally published in German in 2003. English edition translated by Alan Bunce. London: Chaucer Press, 2007.

Harley, John. *William Byrd: Gentleman of the Chapel Royal,* amended edn. Aldershot: Ashgate Publishing Ltd., 1999.

Hasler, P.W. (Ed.). *The Commons 1558–1603.* London: Secker and Warburg, 1982.

Haynes, Alan. *The Gunpowder Plot: Faith in Rebellion.* Stroud: A Sutton, 1994.

Herford, C.H., Percy and Evelyn Simpson (Eds) *Ben Jonson* (vols VI-XI). Oxford: Clarendon Press, 1925–52.

Hodgetts, Michael. *Secret Hiding Places.* Dublin: Veritas, 1989.

Hogge, Alice. *God's Secret Agents: Queen Elizabeth's Forbidden Priests and the Hatching of the Gunpowder Plot.* London: Harper Collins Publishers, 2005.

Houlbrooke, Ralph. 'Lewin, William (*d.* 1598)', *ODNB,* Oxford University Press, 2004; online edn., May 2012, http://www.oxforddnb.com/view/article/16568, accessed, 11/03/2013.

Johnson, Mark and Bernadette Fallon. *The History of the Clockhouse, Great Dunmow, Essex*. Great Dunmow: All About Your House, 2008. Available for consultation at Dunmow Town Council.

Keen, Alan and Roger Lubbock. *The Annotator*. London: Putnam, 1954.

Kelly, Christine J. 'Line, Anne [St Anne Line] (d. 1601)', *ODNB*; online edn, January 2009, http://www.oxforddnb.com/view/article/69035, accessed 11/03/2013.

Kilroy, Gerard. *Edmund Campion: Memory and Transcription*. Aldershot: Ashgate, 2005.

King, Ros. *Cymbeline: Constructions of Britain*. Aldershot: Ashgate Publishing, 2005.

Klause, John. 'Politics, Heresy, and Martyrdom in Sonnet 124 and Titus Andronicus', in James Schiffer (Ed.), *Shakespeare's Sonnets: Critical Essays*, pp. 219–240. New York: Garland, 1999.

Lactantius. *The Divine Institutes*, in *Ante-Nicene Fathers*, Vol. 7. Available online at [http://www.newadvent.org/fathers/0701.htm] accessed, 9/03/2013.

Lansdowne MSS, British Library.

Lewis, Samuel. *A Topographical Dictionary of England*, Vol. III. London: S. Lewis and Co., 1831.

Loseley MSS., Surrey History Centre.

Lloyd, David. *State Worthies*, Volume 1. [First published, London, 1670.] Second edition. London: J. Robson, 1766.

Loomie, Albert, J. *The Spanish Elizabethans*. London: Burns & Oates, 1963.

Longworth, Clara, Contesse de Chambrun. *Shakespeare Rediscovered by Means of Public Records: Secret Reports & Private Correspondence Newly Set Forth as Evidence on His Life & Work*. New York: Charles Scribner's Sons, 1938.

Longworth, Clara, Contesse de Chambrun. *Shakespeare: a portrait restored*. London: Hollis and Carter Limited, 1957.

Maley, Willy. 'Postcolonial Shakespeare: British identity formation and Cymbeline', in *Shakespeare's Late Plays: New Readings*, edited by Jennifer Richards and James Knowles. Edinburgh: Edinburgh University Press, 1999.

Marlowe, Christopher. *The Complete Works of Christopher Marlowe*. Edited by Roma Gill. Oxford: Oxford University Press, 1987.

McCoog (Ed.). *The Reckoned Expense: Edmund Campion and the early English Jesuits*. Woodbridge: Boydell Press, 1996.

McCoog, 'Wright, William (1563–1639)', *ODNB*, http://www.oxforddnb.com/view/article/30066, accessed 11/03/2013.

Meres, Francis. *Gods Arithmeticke*. London: 1597.

Mikalachki, Jodi. *The Legacy of Boadicea: Gender and Nation in Early Modern England*. London: Routledge, 1998.

Milward, Fr. Peter S.J. *Shakespeare's Religious Background*. London: Sidgwick and Jackson, 1973.

Milward, Fr. Peter S.J. *Shakespeare the Papist*. Naples Florida: Sapientia Press, 2005.

Miola, Robert S. (Ed.). *Early Modern Catholicism: An Anthology of Primary Sources*. Oxford: Oxford University Press, 2007.

Morris, John (Ed.) *The Troubles of Our Catholic Forefathers: Related by Themselves*, first series. London: Burns and Oates, 1872.

Muir, Lynette. *Love and Conflict in Renaissance Drama: The Plays and Their Legacy*. Cambridge University Press, 2007.

Munro, John (Ed.). *The Shakespeare Allusion Book*. London: Oxford University Press, 1932.

Nicholl, Charles. *The Reckoning: The Murder of Christopher Marlowe*. London: Pan Books Limited, 1993.

Nosworthy, J.M. (Ed.). *Cymbeline*. The Arden Shakespeare. London and New York: Methuen, 1969.

Ovid. *Ovid's Metamorphoses: The Arthur Golding Translation, 1567*. Edited, with an introduction and notes, by John Frederick Nims. New York: Macmillan and Co., 1965.

The Oxford Dictionary of English Proverbs. 3rd edn. Revised by F.P. Wilson. Oxford: Clarendon Press, 1970.

Oxford Latin Dictionary. Oxford: Clarendon Press, 1982.

The Passion of the Holy Martyrs Perpetua and Felicity. Translated by R.E. Wallis. From *Ante-Nicene Fathers*, Vol. 3. Edited by Alexander Roberts, James Donaldson and A. Cleveland Coxe. Buffalo, NY: Christian Literature Publishing Co., 1885. Revised and edited for New Advent by Kevin Knight. [http://www.newadvent.org/fathers/0324.htm] accessed 04/03/2013.

Peckham, Sir George. *True Reporte of the Late Discoveries and Possession of the New-Found Landes*. London, 1583.

Questier, Michael C. *Catholicism and Community in Early Modern England*. Cambridge: Cambridge University Press, 2006.

Reiter, Paul. 'From Shakespeare to Defoe: malaria in England in the Little Ice Age', *Emerging Infectious Diseases*, vol. 6, no. 1 (January–February 2000). Atlanta, GA: Centers for Disease Control and Prevention, 2000.

[Rheims Bible] *The New Testament of Jesus Christ*. (English Recusant Literature, 1558–1640, vol. 267). Facsimile reprint of 1st edn., Rhemes,1582. Ilkley: Scolar Press, 1975.

Roberts, Enid. 'Salisbury, Thomas (1561x4–1586)', ODNB; online edn. Oct 2006, http://www.oxforddnb.com/view/article/24543, accessed, 11/03/2013.

Roman Imperial Coinage, vol. 1. Sutherland and Carson, eds. Revised edition. London: Spink, 1984.

Rosen, Barbara. (Ed). *Witchcraft in England, 1558–1618*. Paperback edition with new introduction. Amherst: University of Massachusetts Press, 1991.

Salmon, Nathaniel. *A New Survey of England*. London: J. Roberts and J. Leake, 1728.

Scully, Robert, E. *Into the Lion's Den: The Jesuit Mission in Elizabethan England and Wales, 1580–1603*. St. Louis: Institute of Jesuit Sources, 2011.

Sear, David, R. *Roman Coins and Their Values*. 4th revised edition. London: Spink & Son, Ltd, 1988.

Shakespeare, William. *The Riverside Shakespeare*. 2nd edition. Boston: Houghton, Mifflin Company, 1997.

Shanahan, Daniel. 'Anne Line, nee Heigham: where was she born?' *Essex Recusant*, vol. 5, no. 1 (1963), 22–26. Brentwood: Essex Recusant Society.

Shanahan, Daniel. 'Petticoats on the Gallows', *Essex Recusant*, vol. 10, no. 3 (1968). Brentwood: Essex Recusant Society.

Shapiro, James. *1599, A Year in the Life of William Shakespeare*. London: Faber and Faber Limited, 2005.

Shell, Alison. *Shakespeare and Religion*. London: Arden Shakespeare, 2010.

Simpson, Richard. *Edmund Campion: A Biography*. Catholic Standard Library edn. London: John Hodges, 1896.

Smith-Bannister, Scott. *Names and Naming Patterns in England 1538–1700*. Oxford: Clarendon Press, 1997.

Southwell, Robert. *An Epistle of Comfort* (English Recusant Literature, vol. 211). Edited by D.M. Rogers. Ilkley: Scolar Press, 1974.

Speed, John. *The history of Great Britaine ... from Julius Caesar to our most gracious soveraigne King James*. London: H. Hall and J. Beale, for J. Sudbury and G. Humble, 1611.

State Papers, *Letters & Papers Hen VIII*, vol. 13 [Books of the Court of Augmentations].

Statutes of the Realm, edited by A. Luders, T.E. Tomlins, J. Raithby et al., 11 vols (London, 1810–1828).

Tanner, J.R. *Tudor Constitutional Documents A.D. 1485–1603: with an historical commentary*. First published 1922. London: Library Association, 1971.

Tesimond, Oswald. *The Gunpowder Plot. The Narrative of Oswald Tesimond, alias Greenway*. Edited and annotated by Francis Edwards S.J. London: Folio Society, 1973.

Thorne, Alison, ' "To Write and Read / Be henceforth treacherous": *Cymbeline* and the problem of interpretation', in *Shakespeare's Late Plays: New*

Readings, edited by Jennifer Richards and James Knowles. Edinburgh: Edinburgh University Press, 1999.

Victoria County History, Essex, vol. II, 1907.

Victoria County History, Essex, vol. VI, 1973.

Verstegan, Richard. *The Letters and Despatches of Richard Verstegan, c.1550–1640*. (CRS 52), edited by Anthony G. Petti. London: Catholic Record Society, 1959.

Walsham, Alexandra. *The Reformation Landscape: Religion, Identity, & Memory in Early Modern Britain & England*. Oxford: Oxford University Press, 2011.

Wilson, Ian. *Shakespeare: The Evidence*. London: Headline Book Publishing Limited, 1993.

Wilson, Richard. *Secret Shakespeare: Studies in Theatre, Religion and Resistance*. Manchester and New York: Manchester University Press, 2004.

Index

A Detection of Damnable Driftes, 21
A Dialogue concerning Witches, 22
A Discourse of the subtill Practises of Devilles, 22
Achilles, 160
Act against Bulls from Rome, 29n.
Act Against Fugitives over the Seas, 35n.
Act Against Jesuites and Seminarists (27 Eliz. c.2.), 77, 78, 98, 107, 113
Act Against Popish Recusants (1593) 87, 88
Act to retain the Queen's Majesty's Subjects in their due Obedience, 44n., 58
Additional Charter 5982, see sources
Admiral, Lord, 81, 97, 98
Aeneas, 158
Aeneid, 158
Agrippina, 12, 151, *see also* coins and medals
ague, 16–19
Alford, Stephen, 28, 29
All's Well That Ends Well, 118, 119
Allegory of the Tudor Succession, 138n.
allegory, 122, 123, 132, 135, 137, 138n. 141, 165, 170, *see also Cymbeline*
Allen, William, 26–29, 75, 77, 147–8
Alleyne, Agnes, xvii, xviii, 5, 7
Alleyne, Christopher, xvii
Alleyne, Giles, (of Hatfield Peverell) xvii, 7n.
Alleyne, Giles, (of Hazeleigh) xii, xvii, 7–9, 49, 53, 82, 83
Alleyne, John, xvii, 19n.
Alleyne, Richard, xvii, 7n.
Alleyne, Sir Christopher, 'of the Mote', xvii, 36n.
Alleyne, Sir John, xii, xvii, 7n., 52
Anne of Denmark, Queen, 37, 119n, 129, 171
Antwerp, 49, 65, 68, 69, 74, 167
Apollo, 142n., 156
Arden, John, 94
Arden, Mary, 168n.
Aristotle, 173, 174

Arundel, Anne, Countess of, 94, 115, 116, 171, 172n.
Arundel, Philip Howard, Earl of, 23, 41
As You Like It, 48n., 167n.
Asquith, Clare, vii–ix, 9n., 25n., 26n., 71, 92, 93, 122, 123, 166, 167n.;
  and *Cymbeline*, 133, 136n., 143n, 148n., 151n.,170
Aubrey, John, 11, 17
Auger, William, 20
Augustine, 133

Babington, Anthony, 63, 64, 71n.
Babington Plot, 61–66, 71, 76, 167
Ballard, John (Captain Fortescue) 64
Banister, Mary (née Southwell), 92
Barkworth, Mark,
  Benedictine, 109, 121, 122
  conversion, 78, 121
  prison and execution, 102, 110, 111, 114, 119–122
  relics, 117
  Spain, 52, 121
Bates, Thomas, 143n., 169, 170
Beatrice, ix, xvi, 133, 158, 159
Beaumaris Castle, 149
Bedlam, 73
Belisarius, 158
Bellamy family, 65
Bellamy, Robert, 57n.
Belvoir Castle, 119n.
Bennett, Elizabeth, 22
Berden, Nicholas, 61, 63, 64, 70–73
Bidermann, Jakob, 158
Black Chapel, 88
Blackfriars, 8, 60, 96, *see also* theatre
Blackwater Estuary, 6, 162
Blunt, Sir Christopher, 116
Boccaccio, 132, 140, 141, 143
Bosworth Field, 31, 146

INDEX

Boudica, 11, 152
Bridewell (prison) 60, 61, 70, 73n.
Bristow, Dr, 26, 27
Britannia, see Camden
Browne family, (Viscounts Montague) 71, 92, 93
Browne, Mary, 71
Brudenell MS; 18, 49, 73, 98n., 102n., 103–4, 107–8, 112–14, 119, 122
Brute, 152
Bryhtnoth, 6
Burbage, James, Cuthbert and Richard,
  Rutland impresa, 119
  theatre, xii, 3, 7–8, 82–3, 130
Burghley, Lord, (William Cecil) 24, 28–30, 33, 56, 64, 168
Bushell, Edward, 168n.
Bushell, Thomas, 168n.
Byckley, Ralphe, 72
Byrd, William
  at Hurleyford with Garnet, 66, 93
  legal dispute, 56
  links to Petre, Worcester, 24, 25, 36, 92n.
  son, 22

Calvinist, 6, 42, 49
Camden, William, xiii, *Britannia*, 6, 12n., 134, 152, 162
Campion, Edmund, ix, 23, 25, 27, 43n., 46, 116n.
  Shakespeare, 79
Camulodunum,
  history, 131, 163
  Maldon, 12, 151, 152, 155
Candlemas, (Feast of the Purification),
  Anne Line, 52–3, 97
  cross-quarter day, 59, 101, 106
  feast, 100, 101
Carr, Robert, 46n.
Cassibelan, 78n., 161
Catesby, Robert, 143, 146, 169, 170
Catholicism,
  actives and contemplatives, 91, 103, 104, 109n.
  Catholic divisions, viii, 142–147, 174
  discernment, 108
  English Catholic exiles, viii, 9, 76, 92
  English Mission, 76, 79n41, 92–94
  equivocation, 109
  Justinian reconquest, 156, 157
  limbo, 109, 110
  liturgy and prayer, 9, 14, 21, 29n24, 25, 34, 68n6
  persecution, 28, 65, 88
  predicament in England, viii, ix, xi, 35, 174
  rebels and plotters, 26, 27
  spiritual and temporal, 104
  theatre, 8
Cecil, Robert, 50, 63
  Gunpowder Plot, 143n., 144, 145
censorship, 131, 135, 148, 154, 163
Challoner, 16, 57–59, 98, 111, 121, 149
Chamberlen, Peter, 31
Champney, Anthony, 16
Chapman, 153n.
Chaucer, 5
Chelmsford Assizes, 20–22, 26
Chelmsford, 6, 19, 55
Chester, Robert, 17, 153
Chesterton, G.K., xi
Chronicles (Holinshed), 151
Church papist, viii
Clare, Janet, 135, 163
Claudius, 12, 131, 162, 163
Clink prison, 66, 71n, 98
Clitheroe, Margaret, 164
Clock House, 3, 31, 55n., 56
coins and medals,
  angel, 70n.
  Armada medals, 154
  Avirog, 154
  ducat, 137, 153
  Hadrian and Sabina, 153
  Herophile, 154
  julio, 115
  Jupiter, 153
  Nero and Agrippina, 11, 12, 151, 155
  noble, 70
  Postumus, 152, 153
  Winchester raid, 167–169
Coleridge, ix
colonisation of the Americas, 84n.
Comedy of Errors, 8, 9, 49, 78
Compton, Lady, (Anne Spencer) 73
Compton, Lord, 73n.
Cooke, Mildred, 33, 50
Copley family, 92
Copley, John, 103n.
Copley, Margaret (Mrs Gage), 63, 92, 103n
Copley, Robert, 63
Cordale, Francis, 75
Coriolanus, 16n.
Cotton Collection, 154

INDEX

Cotton of Warblington, 92, 117
Council of Trent, 23, 24
Counter in Wood Street, 57, 59–64, 68, 72, 83
Court of Wards, 56
cowslip, *see Cymbeline*, cowslip
Cross-quarter day, *see* Candlemas
Cunobelin, 131, *see also* Cymbeline, King
Curry, John, 118n.
Cymbeline, King, (in history/Cunobelin)
    providential peacemaker, 159
    Rome, 133–135
Cymbeline, vii, xii, xv, xvi, 43, 67, 128
    aliases, 147
    Allegory, 135, 147, 174
    Arden edition (Nosworthy) 133, 140, 158n., 161
    Armada, 136, 154, 161n.
    as tragedy, 172–174
    Belarius, 108n., 135, 139, 140, 142n., 143, 158n, 163, 165
        exiles in a cave, 147–150
        Morgan, 147, 148
        priest symbol, 143, 147–150
        wise man, 165
        see also Belisarius
    birds, 124, 142, 168
    British identity, 129, 174
    Cadwal (Arviragus) 147, 165
    Caesar, 135, 136n., 157, 161, 162
    Caius Lucius 135, 154, 166
    Catholic divisions, 142, 174
    cinque-spotted mole, 163, 164
    coins, 134, 152–155, *see also* coins and medals
    contemporary audience, 135, 144, 165
    coterie audience, 128, 140, 170–172
    cowslip (*primula veris*, primerole, St Peter's wort, keys of heaven, *herba paralysis*, palsywort) 163–165
    criticism, 132–134
    Cymbeline, King, 45, 67, 129–131, 134, 135, 147, 150, 155, 157, 159, 169
    dating, 128
    Dr Johnson, 133
    eagle, 138–140, 144, 145, 153, 156, 157
    Elizabeth I, 138n., 149, 150, 154
    Elizabethan Settlement, 150, 151
    Europhile, 154, 158
    exiles in a cave story, 147–150
    Fear no More the Heat of the Sun, 176, 177
    First Folio edits, 140, 161–163n., 173, 174
    fish-traps, 162
    France, 138
    friendship with Rome, 133–135, 174
    Gunpowder Plot, 129, 143–6
    Hark, hark, the lark, 45, 46
    Herophile, 154, 158, 159
    historical background, 131, 134
    Iachimo, 137, 142n., 154, 163, 164, 166, 169
    Imogen and Posthumus story, 132, 136–147
    Imogen, 42, 43, 45, 46, 55n5, 130, 131, 133
        knife, 113
        music, 108n3
        revival 107n2
        Sonnet 74, 105
        virtue, 140
    James I, 136, 157, 166, 169–171
    Jupiter, 144, 145, 153, 154, 156
    Leon, 138
    Milford Haven, 134, 137, 143, 146, 152, 167, 168
    Morgan (Belarius) 147–9
    Neptune's park, 154, 161, 162
    nineteenth-century criticism, 133
    numbers, 155, 156
    Pisanio, 67, 68, 165, 166, 169, 170
    Polydore (Guiderius) 147, 160, 167n.
    Protestant voice, 134–136, 161
    Queen and Cloten story, 150–152
    Queen, 134, 150, 151, 154, 155, 158, 161, 169, 173
    Rome, Romans, 131, 134–138, 150, 151n., 157, 158, 172, 174, 175
        friendly relations, 135
        papacy, 136
    Second Lord, 155
    Sicilius Leonatus, Sicily, 137, 138
    sources, (literary) 131, 132;
    spiritual/temporal symbolism 147n., 150, 153, 154
    Symbol-Line allegory, 128–177, *esp.*, 141, 142
    symbols, 147n., 148, 163–5, 150, 153, 154
    'The Phoenix and Turtle', 130, 147
    themes, 129, 174
    tribute story, 134–136
    Troy, 154
    Wales, 128, 129, 134, 147–149, 172
    'west', 135, 139n., 157, 165

Dante, ix, xi, 133, 156–59, 178
Darcy, 22
Davies, William, 149
de Pympe, Anne, xviii

INDEX

Decameron (Boccaccio), 132
Defoe, Daniel, 18, 19
Dengie, 6, 18, 36, 162
Derrick, Francis, 75n., 80n.
deus ex machina, 144
Dickenson, 35n.
Digby, Sir Everard, 54
disinheritance, vii, 42, 44n., 55, 56, 57, 87, 138n.
dissident, 93, 123, 134, 169
Dodwell, Martin, vii–ix, xivn.
Dodwell, Thomas, 34
Donne, John, 24, 51
Dormer, Jane (Duchess of Feria), 92
Douay Diaries, 76, 77
Douay Rheims Bible, 77, 148
Douay, (Douai) viii, 24, 26, 27, 62
   Cymbeline, 147
   English College, 76, 77, 79
   relocation to Rheims, 77
   and Shakespeare, 79, 80
Drummond, Jane, 171
Dunmow, 3, 4
   and Anne Line, 3–6, 55–6, 88
   Dunmow Flitch, 5

Eastward Ho!, 153n.
Edwards, Francis, 143n., 144, 170n.
Eliot, George, 24–7, 46
Elizabeth I, 13, 24, 26–28, 35, 136n., 49, 64, 65, 99, 115, 116, 136, 138n., 149–151n., 154, 156, 158
England divided over Catholicism, viii, 8, 13, 28, 29, 174
Englefield, Sir Francis, 138n.
English regiment, 76, 167
equivocation, 109
Essex Rebellion, 26n., 116, 135, 127n., 168n.
Essex, Earl of, 26n., 41, 75, 80
Essex, xi, xii, xvii, 6, 16, 17, 24–6, 32, 36, 56, 62n., 88, 127, 165
   ague, 16–19
   witch trials, xi, 19, 21, 22, 177
exile, viii, ix, 35, 36, 46, 48n., 64, 67, 70, 75–79, 91, 92, 103n., 130, 137–140, 143n., 146–149n., 158n.
exorcism, 49, 177

Fambridge Ferry, 55
Fawkes, Guido, 143, 144, 146
Fenner, George, 75
Ferdinand and Isabella, 95, 138, 139

Fetter Lane, 51, 63, 92, 97, 103, 112, 176n.
Filcock, Roger, 52, 98n., 102, 107, 108, 127
   execution, 110, 111, 119, 120
   studies, 78, 122
Finnis, John, viii, 75, 118n., 98n.
   'Phoenix and Turtle', xi, 75n, 91n.
   Sterrell, 37, 116, 146
First Folio, 42, 78n., 123, 174
   emendations, 140, 161–3, 173, 174
fish traps, 162
Fitzwalter, Reginald, 4
Fitzwilliam, Mary, *see* Guldeford, Lady Mary
Flanders, 26, 75, 91, 103n., 110, 167, 168
Flanderswick, 55, 56n.
Fleet prison, 167
Fordingbridge, xviii, 41n.
Fox (*Acts and Monuments*), 13
Francisci, Jacomo di, (Captain Jacque) 166–9
Fraunces, Christopher, 20
Fraunces, Elizabeth, 20, 21
Frederyke of Jennen, 132
French Embassy, 74
Fulwood, Richard, 80n., 94, 95
Fynee, William, 20

Gage, John, 103n.
Gage, Mrs (née Copley), 63, 76, 92, 97, 103, 109
Gage, Richard, 76
Gage, Robert, 63, 64
Garnet, Henry
   and Anne Line, ix, xii, 11, 14, 75n., 94, 105, 107, 125 biography, 10, 11, 29n., 37, 54, 66, 78, 93, 96n. 98, 116, 117, 122, 127
   description, 10
   and Gunpowder Plot, 143–6, 169
   letter of 11th March 1601, *see* sources
   and William Byrd, 24, 66, 93
Gennings, Edmund, 71n.
Geoffrey of Monmouth, 78n.
Gerard, John
   biography, xii, 54, 63, 66, 80n., 83, 88, 89, 94–6, 116n., 118, 127, 145
   description, 54
   see also sources, *Autobiography of an Elizabethan*
Gerard, Lady, 172n.
Gerard, Sir Thomas, (father of John) 63, 84n.
Gerard, Thomas, (brother of John), 73
Gerard's *Herball,* 165
Gibson's additions, 12n.
Gifford, George, 22, 49

INDEX

Gifford, Gilbert, 62
Globe *see* theatre
God's Arithemeticke, 118n., 164n.
Gooch, Thomas, 56n.
Great Dunmow *see* Dunmow
Gregory XVI, Pope, 27n.
Griffin crest, xviii
Griggs, Edyth, 45
Guildford *see* Guldeford
Guise, Duke of, 27n.
Guldeford family and Anne Line connection, 31–37, 91–93
Guldeford, Anne, (Anne Line snr) xviii, 31–5, 41, 42
Guldeford, Benedicta (née Horne), 35, 36
Guldeford, George, xviii, 31
Guldeford, Lady Elizabeth (née Shelley), 35
Guldeford, Lady Elizabeth (née Somerset), xviii, 128, 172
Guldeford, Lady Mary (née Fitzwilliam), xviii, 31–6, 50, 92
Guldeford, Mary, *see* West, Lady Mary
Guldeford, Richard, xviii, 35, 36
Guldeford, Sir Henry, (fl. Hen.VIII) xviii, 31, 95
Guldeford, Sir Henry, xviii, 36, 37, 92, 128
Guldeford, Sir John, xviii, 31, 32
Guldeford, Sir Richard (fl. Hen. VII), xviii, 95, 36
Guldeford, Sir Thomas, xviii, 35
Gunn, Gregory, 35n.
Gunpowder Plot, 52, 129, 143–6

Haec est Dies, 114, 120, 121
Hallins, 75
Hamlet, 108, 154, 159
Hartley, William, 9
Hatfield Peverell, xiii, xvii, 7, 19, 20
Hatton, Christopher, 167
Hatton, Lady, 172n.
Hazeleigh, xvii, 3, 7, 31, 55, 82
Hecuba, 159, 160
Henry IV Part I, 26n., 131
Henry IV, Part II, 70
Henry VIII, 123
Henry VIII, xviii, 5, 7, 19n., 31, 52, 95, 136
Herophile, 154, 158, 159
Higham family, xvii, 36, 44n.
Higham, 'Old Higham', 21
Higham, Alice (Anne Line) xvii, xviii, 10, 31–3, 41, 50, 55, 89, 90

Higham, Anne (Anne Line's sister), xvii, 10n., 32
Higham, John, xvii
Higham, Robart, xvii
Higham, Roger, xvii, 7
Higham, William (jnr) xvii, 10, 28, 41, 48, 54, 55, 58, 60–64, 66–70, 72, 74, 76, 80n., 83, 122
  abroad, 62, 122
  arrest and imprisonment, 57, 58, 60, 61, 74
  Jesuit, 76
  music, 75, 76
  release on surety, 75
Higham, William (snr)
  of Dunmow, 5
  family tree, xvii, 10n.
  of Hatfield Peverell, 19
  of Jenkyn Maldons, 7, 11, 32, 33, 44n.
  and indenture, 55–7
  and possible second marriage, 45
  and rejection of Anne Line, 42, 48, 49, 55, 66, 82
  and witchcraft, 19–22
Hoghton, Katherine (née Gerard), 79n.
Hoghton, Thomas, 79n.
Holiday, Henry, ix, 178
Holinshed, 131, 134, 142n., 152, 161n.
Holmes, Robert, 35n.
Holywell, Priory, 8
  Holywell Lane, 9, 83
  theatre site, 8, 83, 84
Horace, *Ars Poetica*, 144
Horne, Benedicta, (Benedicta Guldeford) xviii, 35, 36
Hospital of St Giles, 7, 11, 55
Howard, John, Duke of Norfolk, 31
Howard, Philip, 23, 115, 116, 127
Huggenson, Michael, 70
Humble Supplication to her Majesty, 36, 64, 78n., 177n.
Hurleyford, 66, 93
Hyrache (Santa Maria la Real de Irache) 121

indenture, *see* BL. *Additional Charter 5982*
Ingatestone, 24
Ingleby, 120

James I, 37, 46n., 136, 157, 166, 169–71
Janus, 134
Jay, Elizabeth, xvii
Jenkinson, 70

INDEX

Jenkyn Maldons, xvii, xviii, 5–7, 11, 18, 19n., 32, 45, 55, 125n., 177n., *see also* Additional Charter 5982
Jesuits,
  abroad, 27, 37, 158
  and Anne Line, 87–89, 91, 93, 94, 105, 109, 111, 130, 131
  anti-Jesuit attitudes and legislation, xi, xiii, 34, 77
  drama, 79, 158;
  English Mission, xii, 13, 23, 25, 27, 37, 74, 78, 88, 93, 94, 99, 103n., 110, 111, 116, 119, 127, 166, 171
  Gunpowder Plot, 143, 145
  Jesuit Order, 24, 80, 93, 104, 106
  Jesuit's Powder, 17
  St Luke, 78
  Wales, 149
  (*see also* Ballard, Campion, Garnet, Gerard, William Higham (jnr), Lillie, Owen, Page, Persons, Southwell, Walpole, Weston)
John of the Cross, 108
Johnson, William, 146
Jollet, *Authoritates*, *see* Brudenell MS
Jollet, Thomas, 74
Jones, Edward, 63
Jones, Inigo, 171
Jonson, Ben, 43n., 153, 171
  and Gunpowder Plot, 146
Julius Caesar, 134
Julius Caesar, 17n.
Jupiter, 145
Justinian, 157, 158n.

Katherine of Aragon, xvi, 96, 138
  Arms, 139
Kempe, Ursula, 22
Kilroy, Gerard, 74, 102, 103, 122
King of Spain, 37, 76, 92, 103n., 168n.
King, Ros, 150, 152
Knollys, Lady, 172

Laura, ix, 133
Laybrook, xviii
Lear, 174
Leicester, Earl of, 25, 26, 49, 64, 82
Leigh, Agnes, xvii
Leigh, Margaret, xvii, 19n.
Lewyn, William, 55, 56
Lillie, John, 94–6

Line, Agnes (née Pettiface/Phettiplace); xviii, 89
Line, Anne, (Anna Lina, Mistris Lyne, Mrs Martha, née Alice Higham)
  arrest and imprisonment, 63, 92, 97–99, 107–112
  birth and baptism, 3
  burial, 115, 117, 118n., 119n.
  Catholic networks, viii, 31–37, 91–93
  conversion, 23, 28, 33, 34, 42
  death, 14, 52, 114
  desire for martyrdom, 58, 107, 111
  family tree, xvii
  her son John, 14, 89, 90
  illness, 16–19, 107, 164
  letter to Garnet, 109
  letter to Page, 99
  marriage, 4, 41, 80
  memorialised in literature and song, vii, ix, xiii, 103, 174, *see also Cymbeline*, 'Oranges and Lemons', *All's Well That Ends Well*, *The Tempest*, 'The Phoenix and the Turtle'
  Mrs Martha, 91, 103, 109
  Polyxena, 160
  Protestant family, xii, *see* Higham, William (snr)
  reputation for sanctity, vii, 13, 14, 93, 98
  requiem, 117
  spirituality, 58, 59, 91
  supernatural phenomena, 107, 108
  teacher of children, 87
  trial, 102n., 110, 111
  underground mission, viii, 93, 94, 97
  upbringing, 31–33
  witchcraft, 21, 22
  see also Higham, Alice
  see also sources
Line, Anne, (snr) (née Guldeford), 31–35, 41, 42
Line, John (father of Roger) xviii, 87, 89
  will, 89
Line, John (son of Anne and Roger), 87
Line, Richard, (of Chichester) xviii, 33, 34, 42, 57n
Line, Richard, (brother of Roger) xviii, 42, 57, 139, 140
Line, Roger, viii, xiii, 33, 36, 55, 67n1
  arrest and imprisonment, viii, 57–61, 72, 74
  death, viii, 80, 81, 88
  exile, viii, 48, 49, 62, 66, 68
  family tree, xviii

INDEX

marriage, 41
pension, 76, 139
student at Rheims, 76, 77, 81, 139
literary archaeology, xiv
Littleton, Humphrey, 145
Longworth, Clara, 59n.
Love's Labour's Lost, 153n.
Lovell, Lady (née Roper), 92, 95
Loves Martyr, 17, 63, 173n.
Loyola, Ignatius, 108
Lucius, King, 78n.
Lumley, Lord, 73n.
Luther, Anthony, 56
Luther, Martin, 123
Lyford Grange, 25, 46

Macbeth, 51n, 104n., 108
malaria, 16–19
Maldon, 6, 7, 11, 12, 19, 36, 125
    Camulodunum, 12, 151, 152, 155
    and *Cymbeline*, 151, 161–3, 165
    and Nero coin, 11, 12, 151
    and witchcraft, 19, 21, 22, 49, 177n.
Maley, Willy, 136n.
Markham, Sir Griffin, 168
Marlowe, Christopher, 78, 168
Marquis of St Germain, 96
Marriot (pursuivant), 98, 111
Marshalsea, prison, 16n., 66, 88, 89
Marston, 153n.
Martin, Patrick, viii, 75, 118n., 98n.
    and Sterrell, 37, 116, 146
    and 'The Phoenix and the Turtle', ix, 75n, 91n.
Mary Queen of Scots, 26, 27n., 36n., 62–6, 70, 71n., 129, 149n.
Maylandsea, 162
Mayne, Cuthbert, 23
Merchant of Venice, 48
    interest, 105n.
Meres, Francis, 118n., 164n.
Metamorphoses, 142n., 156, 160
Michelgrove, xviii, 32, 35
Midsummer Night's Dream, 42, 165
Milford Haven, xviii, 134, 137, 143, 146, 152, 167, 168
Milles, Francis, 63, 64
Milward, Peter S.J., 27n., 106n., 133, 134n., 136n., 143n.
Montague, *see* Browne
Monteagle Letter, 144, 145, 170
Monteagle, Lord, 144, 145, 170

moon-calf, 123
More family, 92
More, Thomas, 24, 123, 164
Morgan, Lady Frances (née Somerset), 128, 172
Morgan, William, (of Llantarnam), 128
Mortimer, Elizabeth, xviii, 31, 32
Mortimer, Isabella, 31
Mortimer, Sir Robert, 31
Mortimer's Hall, xviii, 31–4, 44n., 178
Muggins, 111

Neevell, Thomas, 75
Nenius, 161n.
Nero, 12, 151, *see also* coins
Newdigate, Fr. (historian) 59n.
Newgate, prison, 29, 51, 121
    and Anne Line, 52, 99, 107–112, 165
Norfolk, Dukes of, 31, 92
Nosworthy, 133
Nunc Dimittis, 100, 101
Nutter, Robert, 35n.

Oath of Supremacy, 77
Office of Revels, 37, 130
Oldcastle, Sir John, 131
Oranges and Lemons, xiii, 50–52, 108n
Orwell, Vincent, 75
O Sacrum Convivium, 149
Othello, 174
Ovid, 142n., 156, 160
Owen, Nicholas, 74, 127
Oxford University, 76, 77, 79, 148
Oxford, Earl of, 56

Page, Francis, 98, 99, 102, 111, 117, 176n.
Paget, Charles, xvii, 36n.
Paget, Margaret (Audrey) xvii, 36n.
Paget, Sir William, (Lord) xvii, 36n.
Paget, Thomas, xvii, 36n.
Palace of St John of Jerusalem, 37, 130, 172
Paradise (*Paradiso,* Dante), 156, 157, 159
Parish Register, St Clement Danes, 41, 50
Parrat, 120
Pax Romana, 159
Payne family, 92, 95
Payne, John, 22–30
Peckham, Sir George, 83, 84n.
penal laws (Anti-Catholic legislation) 29n., 35n., 44n., 58, 77, 78, 87, 88, 107, 113
Perpetua and Felicity, Saints, 13–15, 87, 160
Persons, Fr (Parsons), 27, 37, 130, 131

195

INDEX

Peter's Pence, 136
Petrarch, xv, 133
Petre, Catherine (née Somerset) 92n., 172
Petre, Lady Ann, 24, 25, 27
Petre, Sir John, 24, 25, 36, 56, 92n.
Petre, Sir William, (1) 27
Petre, Sir William, (2) 37, 92n.
Pettiface (Phettiplace), Agnes (mother of Roger Line) xviii, 10
Phaeton, 156
Phelippes, Thomas, 37, 62, 69–72, 75
Phillips, Augustine, 83n.
Phillips, Morgan, 148, 149
phoenix, ix, 17, 18, 106
   and *Cymbeline*, 113, 130, 141, 142, 155, 174, 176
   'The Phoenix and the Turtle', vii, ix, xi, xv, 4, 7, 63, 74
Piers Plowman, 5
Pilchard, Thomas, 35n.
Pilgrimage of Grace, 9n., 164
Poetics, 173, 174
Pole, Alice, 21
Pole, Margaret, 164n.
Polydorus, 160
Polyxena, 160
Pooley, 63, 64
Popham, John, 11, 97–99, 101, 102, 110, 111
Postumus, 152–154
Presentation, feast of, *see* Candlemas
Priam, 160
prisons, *see* Beaumaris Castle; Bridewell; Clink; Counter in Wood Street; Fleet; Marshalsea; Newgate; Tower of London
Privy Council, 26, 34, 37, 62, 79n., 94
Protestantism in England, 129, 136, 139, 141, 150 *see also* Puritanism
Purification of Our Lady, *see* Candlemas
Puritanism, xi, 6–9, 28, 44n., 48, 49, 82, 88, 116, 177n.
Purleigh, 55
pyretology, 18

Quiney, Judith (née Shakespeare), 168n.
Quiney, Richard, 168n.

Raglan Castle, 128
Rebellion of the Northern Earls, 26
recusant, 43n, 47n, 87
   Act against Popish Recusants, 87, 88
   prison lists, 57, 59, 61, 62, 71, 72

readings/subtext, 47n., 53, 103, 125, 126, 164
records, viii
recusants
   Alleyne, Christopher, 36n
   Byrd, William, 56
   Englefield, Sir Francis, 138n.
   Guldeford, Richard and Benedicta, 35
   Tresham, Thomas, 73
   Wells, Swithun, 71
   West, Lady Mary, 34
   Wales, 149
Renaissance humanism, 159, 160
Renzo, Ortelio, 75
residence of St Anne, 119n.
Rheims, (English seminary) viii, 16n., 76–79, 139
Rich, Lord, 28
Richard I, 147
Richard II, 29, 30, 168n.
Ringwood Grammar School, xviii, 42, 57n.
Rivers, Anthony, 75
Robinson, Robert, 75
Roger II, King of Sicily, 137, 153
Rogers, Thomas, *see* Nicholas Berden
Roman Matrons, 13, 14, 87, 105
Romans in Britain, 11
Rome, 13, 24, 62, 76, 78n., 96, 105, 122, 130, 152, *see also Cymbeline*
Roper family, 24, 25, 92, 95
Rosen, Barbara, 19–21, 26n.
Rufford Hall, 79
Rutland Papers, 83, 98, 102, 119–121
Rutland, Countess Elizabeth (née Sidney) 171
Rutland, Earls of, 83
   Francis (sixth earl), 83, 119, 171
   Roger (fifth earl), 83

Saintmain, Henri, 75
Salusbury, John, 63
Salusbury, Thomas, 63
Savage, John, 63, 64
Scot, Reginald, 22
seminary priests, 23, 24, 29, 72, 75, 78
   safe house, 93
   Wales, 149
   see also Douay, Valladolid
Septimius Severus, 14
Sessions House, 51, 98, 102, 107, 108, 111
Seville, 24
Seymour, Jane, 7
Shakespeare, John, 27n.

INDEX

Shakespeare, William
  and Anne Line, 118
  Catholic sympathies, viii, xi, xiv, 71, 122, 123, 131, 136n., 151n., 159
  contemporary of Gerard, 54
  and Gunpowder Plot, 146
  and Lancashire, 79
  personal connections
    Alleyne, 82
    Burbage, 82
    Bushell, 168n.
    Campion, 79
    Catesby, 146
    Fulwood, 80n.
    Gerard, 80
    Johnson, 146
    Jonson, 146
    Rutland/Manners, 83, 119
    Southampton/Wriothesley, 35n, 84n., 71, 92
    Sterrell, 130, 131, 146, 172
    Strange/Stanley, 74, 79, 80, 82, 127n.
    Webbe, 83n.
  retirement, 123
  student, 79, 80
  theatre, 8, 37
  see entries for specific works
Shakespeare's Religion, 174
Shakespeare's Romances, 132
Shell, Alison, 174
Shelley family, 92
Shelley, Edward, 64
Shelley, Elizabeth (Lady Guldeford), xviii, 35, 36
Shelley, Mr ('Shelly'), 24, 81, 92
Shelley, Richard, 35, 36n.
Shelley, Sir John, xviii, 32
Shelley, William, 35
Sherwood, Richard, 64, 68–75, 78, 124n.
Shoreditch
  and bells, 50, 53
  and *Comedy of Errors*, 8, 9
  and Giles Alleyne, 7–9, 82, 83
  and Rutland, Burbage, Peckham, 83
  and William Higham (jnr) 58
Sidney, Elizabeth, 171
Sidney, Sir Philip, 33n3, 171
Singleton, 120
Slyvell, Ralph, 98
Smerwick, 49, 50
Smith, Richard, 76
Society of Antiquaries, 152

Socrates, 44n.
Somerset, Thomas (son of earl of Worcester) 37
Sonnet 110, 15
Sonnet 23, 175
Sonnet 73, 7
Sonnet 74, xi, 102–106, 116, 142
sources for Anne and Roger Line and immediate family
  BL. *Additional Charter 5982*, 54–56, 82
  Calendar of Assize Records: Essex Indictments, Elizabeth 1, 21n.
  CSP Addenda 1580–1624, 24, 81
  Champney, *Annales Elizabethae Reginae*, 16
  A Detection of damnable driftes, 21, 22
  Douay Diaries, 76, 77
  ERO T/A 418/10/6, ASS 35/8/4/6, 20
  Fitzalan-Howard, *The Lives of Philip Howard and of Anne Dacres his wife*, 115, 116
  Foley, *Records of the English Province of the Society of Jesus*, 33, 87, 99, 107–114
  Garnet, *Letter, 11 March 1601*, 13, 16, 36, 101, 111, 115, 142
  Gerard, *The Autobiography of an Elizabethan*, xii, xv, 54, 55, 57–60, 71n., 75, 76, 80, 88, 89, 91–95, 97–99, 101, 107, 118n., 139, 176n.
  Jollet, *Authoritates* [Brudenell MS] 18, 49, 73, 98n., 102n., 103–4, 107–8, 112–14, 119, 122
  McCoog, *English and Welsh Jesuits, 1555–1650, Part 2* (Record Series 75) 62n., 76
  Morant, *History and Antiquities of Essex*; 7n.
  Parish Register, St Clement Danes, 41, 50
  PCC Prob 11/87; sentence 18 May 1609 [sic], Prob 11/114 [will of John Lyne], 87, 89, 90
  PCC Prob 11/101 [will of Agnes Lyne], 89, 90
  Manuscripts of the Duke of Rutland, 83, 98, 102, 119
  Seccion de Estado, 612/125–27 [quoted in Loomie], 76
  SP 53/18/185, 64
  SP 77/6/258, 116, 117
  SP 12/183a/154, 80
  SP 12/190/78, 72
  SP 12/195/95, 59, 61
  SP 12/195/133, 61
  SP 12/249/142, 68–70
  John Stow, *Annales of England*, 113
  Visitations of Essex 3, 5

INDEX

Visitation of Hampshire & the Isle of Wight, (1686), 90
Visitation of Hampshire Pedigrees, 90
Southampton, Second Earl, 71
Southampton, Third Earl *see* Henry Wriothesley
Southwell, Robert, 60, 64–66, 78, 92, 93, 106n., 116n., 127, 177n.
Spanish Infanta, 172
Speed, John, xiv, 131
Spenser, Edmund, 150
spiritual and temporal distinction, 29n., 50, 73, 104, 142, 145–7, 150, 153, 166
St Clement Dane, 41, 50, 52
St Osyth, 22, 26n.
Stanley, Ferdinando (Lord Strange) 73n., 74, 75, 168n.
   Shakespeare patron, 79, 80, 127n.
Stanley, Sir William (soldier) 76, 167, 168n.
Steevens, 164
Sterrell, William, 37, 73n., 74
   and Anne Line, 75
   and Phelippes, 75
   and Roger Line, 75, 80, 81
   and Shakespeare, 130, 131, 146, 172
   and William Higham, 75
   Thomas in Liege letter, 116
Stondon Massey, 25
Stow, John, xiii, 52, 63, 113
Strange, Lady Alice, (née Spencer) 73, 74
Strange, Lord, *see* Ferdinando Stanley
Stratford, 3, 5
Stuart, Arbella, 75
Stuart, Prince Henry, 129, 136, 171, 172
Sybil of Cumae, *see Cymbeline*, Herophile
symbolism
   campion flower, 46
   church orientation, 165
   cowslip, 163–165
   crow, 148, 163
   eagle, 44n6, 138, 139, 156, 157
   kite/puttock, 44n6
   Luke/Lucius, 78, 166
   Milford Haven, 143, 146
   mountain, 163
   number eighteen, 155
   number five, 9, 46, 53, 164
   'rare', 'O rare', 43
   raven, 142n25

Talbor, Robert, 18
Taming of the Shrew, 77, 78

Tesimond, Oswald, 143, 169
Thaxted, xvi, 5–7, 19, 88
The Battle of Maldon, 6
The Discovery of Witchcraft, 22
The Eclogues, 159
The examination ... of certaine Wytches at Chensforde, 20
The Faerie Queene, 150
The Forty Martyrs of England and Wales, vii, 127
The Masque of Beauty, 171, 172
'The Phoenix and the Turtle', vii, ix, xi, xv, 4, 7, 63, 74
The Rape of Lucrece, 17n., 71
'The Secret Sharers', 75
The Succession, viii, 172
The Tempest, vii, 16, 122–127
theatre
   The Blackfriars Theatre, 82, 137, 138
   The Globe Theatre, x, 8, 37, 71n, 79, 82, 126
   The King's Men, 37
   Leicester's Men, 82
   The Lord Chamberlain's Men, 82
   Lord Strange's Men, 82
   The Theatre, Shoreditch, 82–84
   lease, 7, 8, 82
   neighbours, 83
Theodora, 158
Thomson, Richard, 57, 58, 77
Thornborough, 63
Thorne, Alison, 132, 164, 170
Throckmorton Plot, 27n., 35
Throckmorton, (exile) 75
Throckmorton, Lord, 70
Times Literary Supplement, xi
Timon of Athens, 153n.
Titus Andronicus, 36, 65, 78n.
toleration, viii, 35, 47n., 126, 127, 129, 166
Topcliffe, Richard, 60, 70, 136n.
Topographical Dictionary of Essex, 11
Tottel's printers, 10
Tower of London, xii, 23, 25
   and Francis Page, 99
   and Gerard, 54, 94, 116
Tresham family, 95
Tresham, Francis, 73, 74, 144, 145, 170
Tresham, Mary, 74
Tresham, Thomas, 73, 74
Triangular Lodge, 74
Tudor, Henry (Henry VII), xviii, 31, 146
Tudor, Mary, 13

198

INDEX

Two Gentlemen of Verona, 29n., 123
Tyburn Tree, 114
Tyburn, xiii, 13, 22, 51, 52, 57, 99, 110, 112, 114, 116, 118, 119, 121, 125, 165

Valladolid, 24, 52, 62n.
   and Barkworth and Filcock, 52, 78, 121, 122, 149
   and William Higham (jnr) 76, 122
Vaux, Jane (of Harrowden), xviii, 95
Vaux, Lord, 49
Vaux, Mrs (née Roper), 92, 95
Venus and Adonis, 71
Verstegan, 64, 65
Virgil, 158–160
Virtue, viii, ix, xv, 13, 69, 80, 91, 118, 119, 126
   and the Reformation, 141

Wade, 120
Walpole, Calibut, 42
Walpole, Edward, 42
Walpole, Henry, 23
Walpole, Robert, 42
Walsingham, Francis, 26, 59, 61–66, 71, 72
   and Babington Plot, 61–66
   and Roger Line, 59
Walsingham, Lady, 172n.
Waterhouse, Agnes, 20, 21
Webbe family, 83n.
Wells, Swithun, 71
West, Barbara, xviii
West, Lady Mary, xviii, 34–36
West, Owen, xviii, 33

West, Thomas, second Baron de la Warre, 33n.
Westmoreland, Earl of, 26
Whittington, Dick, 52
Wickham, Henry, 75
Williams, Richard, 167
Winchester Cathedral raid, 167–169
Windsor, Lady Catherine, (née Somerset) 172
Winter, Elizabeth, 168n.
Wintour, Lady Anne, (née Somerset) 172
Wiseman family, 88, 166
Wiseman, Jane, 88
Wiseman motto, 166
witchcraft, xiii, 7, 19–26, 48, 49, 177
Woodham Ferrers, 45
Woodham Mortimer, 31–34, 55
Worcester, Countess of, 171
Worcester, Earl of, viii, xviii, 24, 25, 36, 37, 41, 74, 146
   and Anne Line, 24, 81, 130, 171, 172
   and court of King James I, viii, 37, 128, 129
   and Guldefords, 36, 92, 128
   household, 24, 81, 92, 128, 140, 149
Wright, William, 119n., 171
Wriothesley, Henry, (third earl of Southampton) 35n., 71, 83, 84n., 92, 168
Wriothesley, Mary, 35n.
Wriothesley, Thomas, 84n.
Wynchester, Lora, 20, 21

Young, Richard (Justys Yonge) 57, 60

ST. ALBERT PUBLIC LIBRARY
5 ST. ANNE STREET
ST. ALBERT, ALBERTA T8N 3Z9